The Chester Plays

Part II

Elibron Classics
www.elibron.com

Elibron Classics series.

ISBN 0-543-84800-0 (paperback)
ISBN 0-543-84799-3 (hardcover)

This Elibron Classics Replica Edition is an unabridged facsimile of the edition published in 1916 by the Oxford University Press, London.

The Chester Plays

RE-EDITED FROM THE MSS. BY

DR. MATTHEWS.

PART II.

Published for
THE EARLY ENGLISH TEXT SOCIETY
by the
OXFORD UNIVERSITY PRESS
LONDON NEW YORK TORONTO

PREFATORY NOTE

This final section of the Chester Plays has long been printed off. It is now issued, without the usual apparatus, in response to requests which have been made that it should be at the service of scholars.

I. G.

Feb. 10th, 1916.

(*Collation continued.*)

Line.	MS. of 1607.	Dev. MS.
43.	House	Houshould
44.	Now I	I nowe
46.	and	now
47.	hast	hath
48.	among	amonges
50.	helpe for ought that may befall	hye you leste this water fall
51.	worke	worthe
53.	already	allreadye
,,	Ham	Cam
57.	a	an
58.	byte	bytte
59.	grownden	grownde
	Iaphet	Iafett
63.	and	wee
,,	w*i*thout	bowte
	Uxor Noe	Noes wife
67.	be	bynne
68.	travayle	travell
	vxor Sem	Sem*m*es wyfe
*72.	fayle	fable
	vxor ham	Cam*m*es wife
73.	to gather	*om.* to
,,	sliche	slytche
*74.	cleane	clam
75.	anoynted	annoynt
,,	every stich	w*i*th stitche
	vxór Iaphet	Iafetes wife
80.	against	agayne
	Stage Direction.	
,,	Tunc faciunt, &c.	Then Noe beginneth to buyld the arke
*81.	I will begin	*om.* will
83.	we be ready	wee may be ready
85.	ioyne	pynne
86.	kepe	beare
*86.	wedder	weather
*87.	thider	thither
*89.	the	a
*91.	sayle	seale
* ,,	blast	baste
93.	bewsprytt	bowe spreete
94.	w*i*th	bothe
	Stage Direction.	*om.*
*97.	Castle	vessell
98.	childer	Children
,,	in leaped	in yee lepte
	vxor Noe	Noes wife
99.	sleppit	slepte
100.	frankish	frenyshe
101.	red	reade
*102.	doe now	so doe now
	vxor Noe	Noes wiffe
104.	all the day	*om.* the
105.	be	bine
106.	never	non

Line.	MS. of 1607.	Dev. MS.
106.	that dare I saye	I dare well saye
107.	this	That
110.	makes	makest
*111.	they wene thou	the weene that thou
112.	St. John	sayncte Iohn
	After 112 *Stage Direction.*	Then Noe w*i*th all his familye shall make a signe as though the wrought vpon the shippe w*i*th diuers instruements, and after that god shall speake to Noe as followeth
114.	That yow	*that* yee
116.	earth	yearth
117.	thou	thoe
118.	seaven and seaven	vij and vij
,,	or thou	or then thou
121.	two and two	ij and ij
*122.	w*i*thout	bowt
125.	two	twayne
127.	shalbe	man be
*128.	the	this
*129.	Of all meates	*om.* all
,,	must	mon
*130.	there	the
131.	no way may be foryeten	maye bee noe waye forgotten
*132.	all this	this all
137.	be	bynne
139.	that is	*that* it is
140.	nye	anoye
141.	40 (twice)	ffortye . . . fortye
*143.	my	*om.*
146.	sith non	sythen noe
149.	A 100 wynters and 20	An hundreth winters and twentye
151.	any	thy
*152.	vnto	to
*153.	you	yee
155.	in his stall	*om.* his
158.	this	thus
159.	this	the
,,	well may we see	you may well see
	Stage Direction.	
	Tunc Noe, &c.	Then Noe shall goe into the Arke w*i*th all his familye, his wyffe excepte, and the arke muste bee borded rownde

Line.	MS. of 1607.	Dev. MS.
		aboute, and one the bordes all the beastes and fowles hereafter rehersed muste bee paynted that ther wordes may agree with the pictures.
161.	libardes	leopardes
,,	Ham	Cam
165.	men	man
166.	bucke, doe	bucke and doe
*167.	and	all
,,	manner kinde	manere of kynde
168.	thinkes	thinketh
169.	and	*om.*
170.	Otter, fox, fulmart	otters and foxes, fullimartes
172.	have cowle here	here have colle
,,	vxor Noe	Noes wife
174.	marmoset	maremussett
176.	they	the
,,	vxor Sem	Semmes wiffe
177.	Yet more beastes are in	Heare are beastes in
178.	full crowse	*om.* full
180.	they	that
,,	nye	nere
,,	vxor ham	Camms wyffe
,,	vxor Iaphet	Iafettes wyffe
190.	*the*	*om.*
191.	ledden	leadenn
192.	men	man
*193.	here	there
*195.	come, on gods half! tyme, &c.	come, in godes name! halfe tyme, &c.
,,	vxor Noe	Noes wyffe
197.	sayle	seale
198.	heale	hayle
199.	without	withowten
206.	in	into
207.	whether thou	when thy
209.	wraw	wraowe
210.	for sooth	by god
*211.	fett	fetch
212.	without	withowten
*214.	yonder ship	*om.* ship
,,	vxor Noe	Noes wyffe
220.	stand without	stand there withowte
,,	Ham	Cam
*221.	fet	fetch
*222.	sonnes	sonne
223.	yow	yee
*224.	am	stande

Line.	MS. of 1607.	Dev. MS.
224.	gossopes	gossips
225.	comes in, full fleetinge fast	comes fleetinge in full faste
226.	it	that
231.	a draught	one draught
,,	drinkes	drinke
After 232.		Here is a pottell full of maluesaye good and stronge, yt will reioyse both harte and tonge, though Noe thinke vs never so longe yett wee wyll drinke atyte.
*236.	that you boughte	*om.* you
,,	vxor Noe	Noes wyffe
*239.	you	thow
240.	you	thou
,,	not	nought
,,	tunc ibit	*om.*
,,	vxor Noe	Noes wyffe
242.	And haue	*om.* And
,,	mote	note
,,	Et dat alapam vita	*om.*
244.	good to be	good for to be
245.	thinkes	thinke
246.	hugelie me greves	mee highly greeves
248.	doe as	doe hee as
**After* 248.		*Stage Direction.*—Then the singe, and Noe shall speake agayne.
254.	will I	I will.
	Stage Direction. Tunc Noe, &c.	Then shall Noe shutt the windowe of the arke, and for a little space with in the bordes hee shalbe scylent, and afterwarde openinge the windowe and lookinge rownde about sayinge:
257—304		*om.*
*307.	save	salfe
309.	my Childer, my meanye	my Children and my menye
311.	with	of
* ,,	may	mayest
312		and full devotyon
,,	Deus	God

Line.	MS. of 1607.	Dev. MS.
315.	trew	treeue
*317.	will I no more	I will not more
318.	synne	sinnes
321.	you	yee
322.	you	to
324.	afrayd	feared
*325.	sea *that*	saye all that
,,	flytte	fleete
326.	yow (second)	thee
327.	yow	yee
*328.	may	mon
330.	grasse	trees
,,	sith you	since yee.
*334.	wrong	wravge
335.	eates not	eate yee not
336.	you shall let	yee shall leave
*337.	you	aye yee
338.	to	vnto

Line.	MS. of 1607.	Dev. MS.
339.	that shedes	they that sheden
342.	that	*om.*
343.	now	*om.*
344.	in	into
345.	a forwarde now	And forwarde Noe
*349.	a heaste	an heeste
351.	the	this
*355.	token	tokeninge
*357.	That	The
358.	is	hath
*364.	this	thus
365.	toward	towardes
366.	toward	towarde*s*
*371.	no	not
	Finis paginae Tertiae.	Finis.

IV. The Barbers Playe, p. 63.

Line.	MS. of 1607.	Dev. MS.
	First heading— Pagina Quarta, &c.	*om.*
	The Barbers	The Barbers Playe
	Qualiter	Incipit quarta Pagina qualiter
	Abraham	*om.*
	de Caede	a cede
	4 regum	quatuor Regum
	et	*om.*
	occurret	Occurrit
	ei	*om.*
	Melchisadech	Rex Salim et c
	erit	*om.*
	cum Abrahamo	*om.*
	preco	Abraham.
	Nuntius	Preco dicat
*2.	now	mee
*3.	Now	howe
,,	is	hee
7.	yow] him]	yee] vs]
8.	*om.*	to tell you thys storye
14.	no longer I maye	I may no longer
15.	Lordinges	my lordinges
*16.	*your*	you
17.	Thou] and graunt]	ah thou] graunter]
	Et exit.	Abraham, havinge restored his brother Loth into his owne place, doth firste of all begine the play, and sayth;
19.	to me hase	thou hast
*20.	geven victorye	give mee the victorye

Line.	MS. of 1607.	Dev. MS.
22.	restored	restored him
23.	into] and they]	in] *om.* they]
*25.	wond	worne
26.	4] land]	iiij] land*es*]
27.	hast	hath
28.	and of ryches	and ryches w*i*th
29.	can wyn	have wone
*30.	tyth	teath
32.	to	and
37.	victorye	the vyctorye
*39.	my	I
	After 40	*Stage Direction.* here Lothe torninge him to his brother Abraham, doth saye.
41.	it	*om.*
45.	tithinge	teathinge
48.	tythe	the teath
	Stage Direction; Tunc venit armiger, &c.	Tunc venit armiger Melchysedech ad ipsu*m* et gratulando dicit armiger. *After* Tunc venit, &c.; here the messenger doth come to Melchysedech kinge of Salem, and reioysinge greatly doth saye.
	After Stage Direction: Armiger	*om.*
49.	kings] arighte]	kinge] on right]
50.	for to] and lighte]	*om.* for] and to light]

Line.	MS. of 1607.	Dev. MS.
52.	sith	since
54.	with hym enough	enough with him
Stage Direction in Latin.		Here Melchysedech lookinge vp to heaven doth thanke god for Abrahams victorye, and doth prepare himselfe to goo present Abraham.
	Melchis*edech*	Melchysedech rex Salem
58.	I will	will I
63.	spedes] fast	spede] *om.*
,,	Cuppa	pocula *Stage Direction:* Here the messenger offeringe to Melchysedech a standinge cuppe and bread alsoe dothe saye.
*66.	both	*om.*
*67.	in good manere	with good chere
	Melchisadech	Here Melchysedech answeringe sayth
70.	his	in his
71.	without	withowten
72.	great	his
Melchisadech *followed by Latin Stage Direction.*		Melchysedech comminge vnto Abraham doth offer to him a cuppe full of wynne and bred and sayth vnto him.
73.	must	moste
75.	euermore be he	ever muste thou bee
77 *and* 78		*inverted.*
*77.	you	thou
78.	bread	Here is bred
80.	beseke	beeseche
	Abraham	*om. instead is* here Abraham receyvinge the offeringe of Melchysedeck dothe saye.
83.	hase	hath
85.	He	Ye
86.	sith	sinse
87.	thou	that
88.	Tenth	teathe

Line.	MS. of 1607.	Dev. MS.
	Latin Stage Direction	here Abraham offereth to Melchysedeck an horse that is laden (*in margin*) *followed by* Melchysedeck receiuinge the horse of Abraham verey gladly doth saye.
	Melchisa*dech*	*om.*
*93.	perye	petrye
95.	at	of
*96.	receave	receyue here
	Latin Stage Direction.	Here Loth doeth offer to Melchysedeck a goodly cuppe, and sayth.
*98.	good] sent]	goodes as] lente]
	Stage Direction.	*om.*
108.	is done	is nowe doone
	After 108.	*In margin.* here Melchysedeck receaveth the cuppe of Loth.
110.	now God	god nowe
111.	to helpe	that helps
	After 112.	*In margin* here they doe goe together & Abraham dothe take *the* bred and wyne & Melc: the laden horse
	Expositor	Expositor equitando
114.	expound	expound yt
115.	that lewed	the vnlearned
117.	offring	present
123.	was all their	were there
124.	and	and eke
125.	sith] the]	synce] *om.*]
126.	with] him worship we	in] his death remember wee]
127.	on Sherthursday	at his laste supper
* ,,	in his maundye	our mandee
*133.	tythes-makinge	teathinges makinge
*135.	he was to God	to god hee was
136.	they both	*om.* they
141.	on Shere thursday	the fore sayde daye
[143]		this signifyeth the sooth to saye
144.	Melchisadechs	Melchysedeck his

Line.	MS. of 1607.	Dev. MS.
	After 144.	*Stage Direction.* Here god appeareth to Abraham and saythe
146.	and succour] I will]	and thy succour] will I]
	After 148.	*In margin* here Abraham tourninge to god saythe
149.	in] thou wilt see	on] wouldest see
*150.	free	full free
*157.	My frend Abraham	Naye Abraham frend
158.	heyre shall	hayre hee shall
160.	gotten	begotten
162.	looke vp and tell me	looke and tell
163.	shaye	straye
165.	thy meede	noe neede
167.	for thy good deede	withowten dreede
169.	Wherfore	Therfore
171.	forward here	here a forwarde
[173]		Soe myche folke forther shalt thou bee
[174]		kinges of this seede men shall see
177.	that from] henceforth	*om.*] hethen forward
178.	knaveschild] the	man Chylde] one the
179.	you saye	I thee saye
181.	and who] ne	Whoe soe] not
182.	forsaken with [me] shalbe	forsaken shalbe with me
183.	Inobedyent	vnobedyent
184.	therfore	*om.*
*187.	that men verey knowe maye	therby knowe thou maye
*193.	takes good intent	takys Intent
197.	is now	*om.* is
200.	Baptisme then began	then beganne Baptysme
201.	God*is* behetes here	god a promise behett vs here
*204.	might not	yt may
*205.	and seede] to forby	And one seede] for to bye
206.	Ihesus Christ	Christe Iesus
210.	here (*first*)	lord
212.	most	the best
214.	besyde	there besydes
215.	will yt	will that yt
224.	byddinge done	biddinge lorde done

Line.	MS. of 1607.	Dev. MS.
227.	Isaak] shall with me	Isaack my sonne] with mee shall
	After 228.	*Stage Direction.* here Abraham tourninge him to his sonne Isaack sayth
229.	my Derling	my dere darlinge
*231.	vpon thy back it bring	doe thou on thy backe bringe
*232.	must not long abyde	may noe lenger byde
	After 232	*Stage Direction in margin.* Abraham taketh a sworde and fyer
233.	I will	that I will
234.	I must	mee behoues to
235.	his	god*es*
236.	aye	ever
	After 236	*Stage Direction in margin.* here Isaack speakes to his father, taketh the bundell of stickes & beareth after his father
*237.	I am	*om.* am
238.	mekelie	moste meekely
239.	to beare] bowne	and to beare] full beane
*240.	you	ye
241.	Isaak (*second*)	*om.*
242.	I geve	nowe I giue
245.	me	vs
	Stage Direction Tunc Isaak, *&c.*	here they goe both to the place to doe sacrafice.
250.	mountayne	mou*n*te
	After 252	*Stage Direction in margin.* Abraham beinge minded to slea his sonne lifte vp (MS. vs) his hand*es* to heaven and sayth.
257.	deere	*om.*
258.	yt is	*om.* is
*259.	you	yee
*260.	you	ye
*263.	this	the
*264.	in	vpon
	After 264	*Stage Direction in margin.* Isaack fearinge leste his father will slea him sayth
266.	this	that

Line.	MS. of 1607.	Dev. MS.
267.	middle-yorde	myddy larde
	After 268	*Stage Direction in margin.* Abraham comfortinge his sonne sayth
*270.	godhead	good heade
271.	maner] stydd	manner of] fyelde
*274.	shall have	*om.* have
276.	burstes	breakeste
*279.	beare	beares
282.	breakes] even	breakest] anon
285.	O	Ah
*287.	here to spill	for to spyll
288.	hill	hilles
290.	might	may
293.	my	my deare
294.	doe this	doe to thee this
298.	knele	kneele downe
306.	this daye	to daye
308.	bloode	bodye
309.	shold	shal
310.	to	for to
312.	his	him
319.	out once	once out
321.	But	But yet
	After 322	*Stage Direction in margin.* here Abraham wringinge his hand*es* sayth
*325.	mot	most
327.	free	soe free
328.	me think	I am
329.	sith	synce
*331.	on	vpon
334.	free	soe free
*338.	yo*ur*	the
*344.	syth	sythenn
[346].		sythen I must dye the death to daye
347.	as you maye	as yee well maye
348.	you	yee
351.	doe awaye	doe away, doe away
352.	so mickle	of myche
*355.	come	come of
356.	hence gone !	hence bee gone
*357.	that	thow
	Stage Direction Tunc colliget, *&c.*	here Isaack ryseth and cometh to his father & hee taketh him and byndeth him and layeth him one the Alter for to sacrifyce him.
359.	A !	*om.*
361.	right	then
364.	and let me hence gone	for needes soe must It bee
*365.	that have	that you have
*367.	vnto you bowe	to doe your vowe
*368.	that I	that ever yee
*374.	of that I	for all that ever I
375.	forgeven that	forgiven father *that*
376.	vnto	vntill
378.	greaved] but]	greeves] euery]
381.	Loe] shalt	Nowe] shall
*385.	you	yee
*386.	kercher	carchaffe
	After 389	*Stage Direction in margin.* here kisse him & binde *the* carchaffe about his head & lett him kneele downe & speake.
*395.	on	of
*398.	lyes	lieth
399.	were hym	were mee him
401.	you	thee
*406.	shalt	shall
409.	you	yee
411.	praie god	praye you
*413.	Ah	My
*416.	in	of
	Stage Direction Tunc accipiet, *&c.*	Here lett Abraham take and bynde his sonne Isaack vpon the aulter, and leett him make a signe as though hee would cutt of his head with the sword; then lett the angell come and take the sworde by the end and staye yt, sayinge
425.	Naie !] thou] no]	And] to] none]
426.	se	wott
427.	hast]	hasse]
,,	II	secund*us*
*430.	spares] fraie]	sparest] faye
433.	hase send	hath sent
435.		*om.*
436.	it is	have him
438.	I shall doe	shall be donne
439.	here to me send	here mee sent
439.	Abraham	*om.*
441.	An	A
*442.	the	these
443.	it shall	now shall hee

Line.	MS. of 1607.	Dev. MS.
	Stage Direction. Tunc Abraham, *&c.*	Then lett Abraham take the lambe & kyll him & lett god saye
446.	ever	ayere
447.	so deare	to teare
449.	shalt] thou art worthy	shall] that pleased mee
*450.	I shall	shall I soe
451.	het	hight
455.	for	*om.*
456.	as	a
457.	And all	And of all
459.	the	through
	After 460	*Stage Direction in margin.* here the docter sayth
463.	you	yee
465.	deed that] you se] done in]	*om.* that] yee seene] done here in
468.	tree	roode
471.	his	his sonnes
472.	the	that the
476.	his] to vnderfonge	and] for to confounde
	Finis paginae Quartae	*om. Instead is Stage Direction* here lett *the* docter kneele downe & saye Such obedyence grante vs, o lord, ever to thy moste holye word, that in the same we may accorde as this Abraham was beyne. And then altogether shall wee that worthye kinge in heaven see, and dwell w*i*th him in great glorye for ever and ever. Amen. *Stage Direction* here the messenger maketh an ende. Make rowme lordinges and giue vs waye, and lett Balack come in and playe, and Balaham that well can saye, to tell you of prophecye. That lord that dyed one good frydaye the same you all both night and daye. farewell, my lording*es*, I goe my waye, I may not lenger abyde. Finis.

V. The Cappers Playe, p. 84.

Line	MS. of 1607	Dev. MS.
		Heading: The Cappers Playe
	Pagina Mose et Rege Balaak et Balaam Propheta	Incipit pagina Moyses & de lege sibi data
	The Cappers	*om.*
	Deus	Deus ad Moysen
*1.	life	leeffe
*2.	the] be	my] bine
*3.	you wott	yee wotten
5.	honour] saue	have] but
6.	ne Mawmentrye	noe false god*es*
7.	myn	name
8.	me lykes	liketh mee
10.	also by all waye	yt eke alwaye
13.	you	yee
15.	ne] abyde	nor] lenge
*17.	wyves] covettes	wyefe] desyre you
19.	ne (*twice*)	nor (*twice*)
20.	any thinge	nothinge
21.	Ne	Nor
22.	agayne] will	agaynst] love
23.	doe	keepe
24.	you	yee
	Stage Direction. Tunc princeps, *&c.*	*om.*
25—33.		*Heading* Moyses Good lorde, that art ever soe good, I will fulfill w*i*th mylde moode thy commandement*es*, for I stood

Line.	MS. of 1607.	Dev. MS.
		to here thee nowe full styll. ffortye dayes now fasted have I, that I might bee the more worthye to lerne this to-kenn trulye; nowe wyll I worke thy will.
	Stage Direction. Moses] mont]	Moyses] monte
	Heading Moyses	*om.*
33.	you	yee
35 *and* 36.		take theese wordes in your thought, nowe knowne yee what ys sinne.
37.	you may now	nowe yee may
*39.	his teachinge] done	this token] doe
40.	you not	yee ne
41—48.		*om.*
49—64.		*These lines come after the* 16 *lines, which the Dev. MS. inserts between* 88 *and* 89.
49.	You	*om.*
50.	to me that loven heale	you all to my spell
51.	doe everye deale	keepe well
52.	as	this
*53.	boldelye worches	bodely worke
57.	That] deede] deade shall be	Whoe] *om.*] dye shall hee
58.	fire	for ever
*60.	bade	beede
61.		*om.*
62.	purple, bisse, and other moe	purpur and kyse both too
	Expositor	Doctor
66.	of the old Testamente	the firste lawe *that* ever god sent
67.	and yet is used *with* good	x poynctes there bine, takes
68.	*with* all that good bene	that moste effecte ys in
69.	This storye all if we shold fong	But all *that* storye for to fonge
71.	wherfore]there	therfore] ever
*72.		shortly wee shall myn
73.	Also] read in	After] reden of
*74.	God in the	that in this
75.		god gaue the lawe witterlye
76.	his owne	*om.* owne
77.	tables of ston	stonye tables
78.	but when	before
79.	he] in anger	Moyses] *om.*
81.		But after, played as yee shall see
82.	of stone made	owt carved
83.	In *which*	*om.* In
84.	his] that were	the] hee sayde
*87.	them	him

Then comes in Dev. MS. Stage Direction in margin: here god appereth agayne to Moyses, *followed by heading* Deus, *and* 16 *lines as in MSS.* B W h.

Moyses, my servant, goe anon
and kerve owt of the rocke of stone
tables, to wryte my byddinge vpon,
such as thou had before;
And in the morninge looke thou hye
into the monte of Synaye;
lett noe man wott but thow only,
of companye noe more.

Heading: Moyses.

Lord, thy byddinge shalbe donne,
and tables kerved owt full soonne;
but tell mee, I praye thee, this boone,
what wordes I shall wryte.

Heading: Deus.

Thou shalt wryte the same lore
that in the tables was before;
hyt shalbe kepte for evermore
for that is my delyte.

Stage Direction: Tunc Moyses faciet signum quasi effoderet tabulas de monte, et super ipsas scribens, dicat populo:

Line.	MS. of 1607.	Dev. MS.
After 88	*Stage Direction* Tunc Moyses ex altera parte montis dice equitando	Tunc veniet equitando iuxta montem et dicat
	Heading: Balaack rex	*om.* rex
*90.	I had it in my	and I had in
92.	ech	everye
93.	stiflye	so stowtly
97.	soever] dose] noye	*om.*] doth] anoy]
*98.	prayes	prayeth
99.	therefore] they sone	then] the ever
100.	other men they haue	there enemyes
101.	will I	I will
102.	haue unthought me	am bethought

Line.	MS. of 1607.	Dev. MS.
103.	I will	*om.*
	After 104	*In margin* florish
105.	For sworde ne knife	Noe knife nor sworde
106.	these] shroes	that] people
108.	is hym	yt is
	After 108	*In margin* caste vp
110.	selfe they can	folke commen for to
*111.	as] gnawes	and] graweth
113.	so] blesses	soever] blesseth
114.	sickerlie that man	that man sothlye
115.	so	soever
116.	loos] hase	name] hath

Between 116 *and* 117 *the following* 40 *lines, in* Dev. MS., *as in MSS.* B W h.

But yett I truste venged to bee,
with dynte of sword or pollicye,
on these false losells, leaves mee,
leeve this withowten dowte.
ffor to bee wroken is my desyre,
my heart brennys as whott as fyre,
for vervent anger and for Ire,
till this bee brought abowte.

Surgite dei patriae et opitulamini nobis et in necessitate nos defendite.

Therfore my god, and god*es* all,
o! mightye Mars, one thee I call,
with all the powers infernall,
ryse now, and helpe at neede.
I am enformed by trewe reporte,
how the Mediators doeth resorte
to wynne my land to there comforte,
desended of Iacobs seede.

Now shewe your power, you god*es* mighty,
soe *that* these caytiffes I may destroye,
havinge of them full victorye,
and them brought to mischance.

In the margin sworde.

Beate them downe in playne battell,
those false losells so cruell,
that all the world may here tell
wee take on vengeance.

Owt of Egipte fled the bee,
and passed through the red sea;
the Egiptians that them pursued trewlye,
were drowned in that same fludd.
*The have on god mickell of might
which them doeth ayde in wronge and right;
whosoever with them foundeth to fight,
hee wynneth little good.

They have slayne—this wott I well—
through helpe of god of Israell,
both Seon and Ogge, kinges so fell,
and playnly them distroye.
Thearefore ryse vp, ye good*es* eiche one;
ye be a hundrethe god*es* for one;
I would be wroken them vpon,
for all there pompe and pryde.

Line.	MS. of 1607.	Dev. MS.
117.	Bachler	batchelere
118.	the	these
120.	mon	may
		**Stage Direction in margin.* Miles rex Balack loquitur.
	Heading, Miles	*om.*
122.	yt] well] and that	yt] *om.*] *om.*
123.	for Balaack	and Rex Balack
125.	wone	one
126.	riches	land*es*
*127.	if	as
128.	the	these
	Heading; Miles	*om.*
	Stage Direction. reges	regis
130.	prayes] right sone	prayeth] *om.* right
132.	do	done
133.	Forsooth I tell the	Abyde awhyle there
134.	that	for
135.	if	yf that
136.	that	and that
		Stage Direction: Tunc ibit Balaham ad consulendum dominum in oratione.
	Heading. Deus (in supremo loco).	Sedens dicat Deus
138.	Balaak his] that thou	Balackes] for to
139.	is blessed	blessed is
140.	not	*om.*
142.	be to me	to mee be
143.	truly	therby
145.	Thoughe the folke	Yett though Balack
152.	now leave I haue	leaue nowe have I
	Tunc equitabunt	Tunc Balaham et *miles equitabunt simul
	versus regem	*om.*
	eteundo dicat	*om.* eundo
153.	Now] the] I] upon]	Knight] my] *that* I] one

Line.	MS. of 1607.	Dev. MS.
154.	sith] I haue	nowe] have I
155.	they shalbe cursed] euery	cursed they shalbe] every eych
157.	If Balaak hold] has heighte	hould the kinge] beheight
158.	hest	hoste
160.	wend	wynd
	Stage Direction. Tunc Angelus, *&c.*	*om.*
	Between 160 *and* 161	*Heading.* Miles, *and following* 8 *lines, as in MSS.* B W h. Balaham, doe my lordes will, and of gould thou shalt have thy fill. spare thou nought that folke to spill, and spurne ther godes speach. *Heading.* Balaham ffrend, I have godes wonderfell, both Ruffyn and Reynell, will worke right as I them tell, ther ys noe wyle to seeke. *Stage Direction.* Tunc Balaham ascendit super asinam, et cum milite equitabit, et in obuiam venit angelus domini cum gladio extricto, et asina videt ipsum et non Balaham, ad terra prostrata iacebit et dicat: *Heading:* Balaham
*163.	me she	shee mee
164.	so her dose nye	so ever yt is
165.		What the divell! now she is fallen downe,
166.		but thou ryse and make thee bowne,
167.		and beare mee soone owt of this towne,
168.	full sore abye	abye I wys.

Line.	MS. of 1607.	Dev. MS.
	percutiet Asinam loquetur	percutiet Balaham asinam suam hic oportet
	in asina	transformiari in speciam asinae, et quando Balaham percutit, dicat asina
	Heading: Asina	*om.*
*169.	evell witterly	ill secerly
171.	me	me here
173.	begiles	begylest
175.	I before me	before mee I
176.	makes	maketh
177.	I not	not I
178 and 179.		*Inverted.*
178.	that ever before	and many winter
179.	woldest	will
180.	now	*om.*
182.	thou] Ass	that thow] non
183.	thus	soe
184.	I am	am I
	Balaam videns	videns Balaham
	adorans dicat	adoramus ipsum dicat Balaham *Also in margin.* Balaham on his knees shall fall sodenly downe and speaketh to the angell.
*186.	erre	or
187.	it	that yt
189.	thry	why
190.	I am	am I
191.	changes] falcelye	changed] soe falsly
192.	and	and nowe
193.	And the	If this
197.	is] goe	Lorde ys] gonne
198.	this	that
199.	otherwise] tho]	other waye] doe
	ibunt	equitabunt simul
	Balaack venit in obuiam	et in obuiam veniet rex Balaack et dicat rex
202.	anguish	anger
*204.	of	one
205.	so haue I	as I have
206.	puttes] in	putteth] within
207.	and	the ende of
208.	sure	syr
211.	thou shalt	shall thou
213.		Gould and siluer and eke pearle
214.		thou shalt have great plentee

Line.	MS. of 1607.	Dev. MS.
215.	men] cursed they	them] that yt sonne
216.	that] shalt see	all that] sayst
Stage Direction.	Tunc adducens, &c.	Tunc Balaack descendit de equo et Balaham de asina, et ascendent in montem et dicat Balaack rex.
Between 216 *and* 217.		*Heading:* Balaack *and following* 8 *lines as in MSS.* B W h. Lo Balaham now thow seest here godes people all in feare, Cittye, Castle and ryvere; looke now, how lykes thee? Curse them now at my prayer, as thow will bee to mee full deare, and in my realme moste of powere, and greatest vnder mee. *Stage Direction.* Tunc Balaham versus austrem dicat.
*217.	them	here
*218.	the	that
220.	alwayes	euerwell
221.	I may	may I
222.	this	them
225.	these folkes	this folke
230.	no] may I not haue	and] shall they none wave
232.	send me	send to mee
233.	Devilles] the poplart	dyuell] thee thow populart
235.	wot well	hope that
236.	woodlie	madly
*237.	euery one	euerycheone
*238.	blest	blessest
239.	shalt anon	shall gone
241—264.		*om.*
266.	of	*om.*
267.	springing	growinge
268.	rivers	ryuere
269.	God	that god
271.	warryeth warried is	cursys] cursed hee is
272.	that blessest	whoe blesseth
273.	Popelard thou preachest	Thow preachest populard
276.	came	come
278.	nones] nye	meanes] anoye
279.		Syr kinge, I told thee ere soe thrye
281—288.		*om.* *Stage Direction.* Tunc Balaham vertit se ad orientalem in plagam montis, et respiciens coelum spiritu prophetico dicit: Orietur stella ex Iacobb et exurget homo de Israell et consurget omnes duces alienigenarum, et erit omnis terra possessio eius.
293.	He	That
294.	dukes] strang	and dukes] strange
295.	the	this
297—432.		*om.*
433.	forth	hence
435.	of Iewes is	is both
438.	gaynes with] shryue?	agaynst] stryve
After 440.		*Stage Direction.* here Balaham speaketh to Balaack 'abyde a while.'
	MSS. B W h (104 *lines not in MS. of* 1607).	*Heading:* Balaham *followed by* 104 *lines as in MSS.* B W h.
9.	cure	care
20.	stalles	stales
21.	and	men
25.	they	the
32.	which] use	with] to vse
34.	distres	disease
37.	shall	will
42.	take] no] nor]	looke] ne] nay
43.	these] my	those] may
44.	foes	enimyes
46.	eke	ylke
49.	me	*om.*
52.	foes] you	enimyes] yee
55.	what	that
63.	themselves	them selfe
67.	these	those
70.	they	the
75.	would	would have
77.	so	*om.*

Line.	MS. of 1607.	Dev. MS.
81.	spake] me	*om.*] now
87.	haue him	him have
92.	an	and
93.	and one	Anon
95.	all	*om.*
96.	he	the
	Latin sentence:	
	est	est ei
	ec	&c
102.	againe] he (MS. of 1607)	*om.*] the
	Before 441	
	Expositor	*om.*
*442.	you see	yee have hard
443.	w*i*thout	w*i*thowten
*444.	is	was

Line.	MS. of 1607.	Dev. MS.
445.	these prophesies] you	this prophecye] yee
447.	presented	honoured
	Finis paginae Quintae	*om.*

Devon MS. continued.

Now worthye syrs, both great and smale,
here have we shewed this storye before,
and yf hit bee pleasinge to you all,
to morrowe nexte yee shall have more.
Prayenge you all, both east and west,
where that yee goe to speake the best;
the byrth of Christe, feare and honest,
here shall yee see, and fare yee well.
finis.

VI. The Wrightes Playe, p. 104.

Line	MS. of 1607	Dev. MS.
	The wrightes	The wrightes playe (*before the Latin*)
*1.	maiden	mother
3.	among	amongst
	Latin quotation:	
	In mense, *&c.*	*om.*
6.	wonderly	wondrouslye
	Latin quotation:	
	Illa vero, *&c.*	*om.*
10.	amonge	amongst
14.	his name Ihesu	Iesus his name
15.	be none	non be
*19.	raigne	rayninge
	Latin quotation:	
	Et dabit, *&c.*	*om.*
	Latin quotation:	
	Et regni, *&c.*	*om.*
26.	knewe	knowe
	Latin quotation:	
	quomodo erit, *&c.*	*om.*
*30.	holy	holye one
*32.	his	hee
	Latin quotation:	
	Sp*iri*tus sanctus, *&c.*	*om.*
36.	Bedill	Redyll
	Latin quotation:	
	A*t*que Elizabeth, *&c.*	*om.*
37.	gaine	agayne
	Latin quotation:	
	Et hic mensis, *&c.*	*om.*
*42.	send	sent
	Latin quotation:	
	Ecce ancilla, *&c.*	*om.*
	Stage Direction:	
	ibit angelus et	Angelus ibit et Maria
	Heading. Maria	*om.*
*51.	fruit	fruites
	Latin quotation:	
	Benedicta tu, *&c.*	*om.*
55.	gree	degree
	Latin quotation:	
	Et unde, *&c.*	*om.*
57.	greetest me	mee greetest
	Latin quotation:	
	Ecce enim, *&c.*	*om.*
	Stage direction: gaudentes] Magnificat anima	gaudiens] magnificat, etc.
*71.	now	is
	saluatori meo	etc.
	Latin quotation:	
	Et respexit, *&c.*	*om.*
	Latin quotation:	
	Et sanctum, *&c.*	*om.*
	79 *and* 80	*after* 88.
83.	in	of
	Latin quotation:	
	Ecce enim, *&c.*	*om.*
89.	bowne	bound
93.	them	*om.*
94.	dispereles	disparcles
	Latin quotation:	
	prestitit robor, *&c.*	*om.*
*98.	and	&
*100.	good	god
	Latin quotation:	
	Detrascit potentes, *&c.*	*om.*
*102.	betaken	he hath betakene
*103.	waken	wakinge
104.	and	&
	Latin quotation:	
	Et divites, *&c.*	*om.*
106.	and	&
108.	and	&

Line.	MS. of 1607.	Dev. MS.
	Latin quotation: Sicut locutus, *&c.*	*om.*
112.	mightes	might
	Latin quotation: Sicut erat, *&c.*	*om.*
115.	makes	make
	Latin quotation: Mansit autem, *&c.*	*om.*
	Stage Direction: tunc ibunt ad Ioseph	*om.*
121.	haue	*om.*
	Quotation.	*om.* *Heading* Ioseph.
*124.	hath	hasse
	Latin quotation: Ihesu vero, *&c.*	*om.*
130.	here	her
	Latin porro Ioseph, *&c.*	*om.*
135.	this XXX wynter	these xxx^{tle} winters
136.	that	noe
	Latin.	*om.*
	Quotation.	*om.*
*141.	her	*om.*
145.	an	and
*146.	him	to wife
150.	nor they	ney the
	Latin quotation: Hec autem, *&c.*	*om.*
154.	thus can me	mee can thus
155.	I] for	for I] *om.*
158.	now sleepe	sleepe nowe
	Stage Direction.	*om.*
	Latin quotation: Ioseph fili, *&c.*	*om.*
*166.	gotten is	begotten yt is
	Latin: a spiritu, *&c.*	*om.*
	Latin: Excitatus, *&c.*	*om.*
*174.	yore beheight	before hight
	Latin: somno, fecit, *&c.*	*om.*
	Octavian	Octavianus
	Latin quotation: Lucae Cap. 2, *&c.*	*om.*
194.	at my aboue	all me about
*199.	ne	nay
203.	me	*om.*
207.	nowe	*om.*
210.	proles	probes
*211.	Icy] larment	Ieo] lerment
*212.	metten	mette
*217.	Iay	Ieo
218.	Iey] beable	Ieo] leable
219.	tresarois] tresagait	treasoroce] treasagyle

Line.	MS. of 1607.	Dev. MS.
221.	Destret] su	Descret?] sa?
223.	declare, sake] et mater	declare et sauke] *om.* et
224.	mame	viua?
225.	Carsell] and	Coysell] or
227.	preistes	pryest
*232.	of	on
*237.	is all thinge	must all bee
239.	did	bydd
244.	is	yt
*247.	deis	dayes
*259.	mydds	middest
*273.	this	thus
*278.	the] this	they] thus
281.	bow	bowne
283.	talls	tayles
*287.	highe	highest
300.	in shyre] and	*om.* in] and eke
	After 300.	*Heading* Octavianus
306.	full	good
*309.	sent	assent
318.	nought	ought
319.	now	soe
320.	in] neede	this] meede
322.	penyble	baynable
*329.	of	of all
333.	nor	ne
*336.	I see	in mee
*340.	these	this
342.	I	I be
344.	unkindlie	vnkynde
346.	at] for to	of] *om.* for
354.	hast	hase
*358.	barne shall borne be	bab borne shalbe
* ,,	Sibble	*In margin.* Sybyll speaketh.
*373—376		*om.*
*378.	not	non
379.	will I	I will
388.	stiffe	stronge
394.	each	eke
*398.	pence	pences
402.	waile	weale
403.	bostles	bosters
*410.	percer	perces
*411.	axe	and
412.	wonne	wonnen
416.	that	what
417.	store now	*om.* now
	Latin quotation: Ascendit autem, *&c.*	*om.*
438.	this	that
	Stage Direction.	*om.*
446.	come	commen
451.	that	as
453.	blood seede	*om.* bloode

Line.	MS. of 1607.	Dev. MS.
455.	they ioye	the ioyen
*459.	it passes] their	they passed] *om.*
*466.	nay	ne
*473.	then] life in fere	*om.*] leeffe fere
474.	is	bee
	After 476.	*Stage Direction:* Tunc Ioseph accipiet Marian in brachia sua.
	After 479 *Stage Direction.*	*om.*
*482.	II	too
*484.	a-comen	and commen
*486.	as (*first*)	and
*491.	is to	ys commen into
501.	the	a
502.	with	by
505.	I haue brought	brought I have
506.	II	too
511.	life	lefe
,,	acquiescant	acquiescunt
*515.	much	full
	Latin quotation: Et peperit, &c.	*om.*
517.	penance non I felt	Payne felte I non
*519.	is he] my	he is] this
520.	you	thow
523.	wordes	worde is
526.	saw	law
548.	had	*om.*
550.	a	*om.*
* ,,	arenent	arentur
,,	dicat	dicit
554.	a sorye	an evyll
557.	is	ys nowe
	Stage Direction: dicens	*om.*
*	*Heading:* Angelus	Tebell
573.	A!	Ah!
575.	come	commen

Line.	MS. of 1607.	Dev. MS.
577.	lordinges	lordinges all
579.	without	withowten
590.	perye	perlye
594.	was	there was
598.	both twoo	*om.* both
599.	als] myddes] altho	alsoe] middest] of tho
600.	renowne	Rome righte
*601.	was	alsoe
609.	when	when that
*611.	Image	I may
*615.	they	there
617.	about	aboue
621.	saw	see
*625.	in	on
629.	that	in that
*631.	this	his
*632.	the world	the world the worlde
633.	that	to
647.	goe well	well goe
650.	3	three
651.	wonderly	wonderslye
* ,,	ostendant	ostendit
658.	vp an	vp on
661.	sees] so	seest] that
662.		*om.*
	Octavianus	Octavyan
*670.	through	throughowt all
681.	thou not	not thow
689.	you shall	thow shalt
*690.	in	one
695.	otherwayes	otherwise
698.	euery one	everychone
*701.	man	maye
702.	can	*om.*
	Heading.	*om.*
706.	wonders	wondrous
*712.	none	*om.*
717.	built	buyld
719.	unto	vntyll
727.	know	knowe nowe
*730.	right	*om.*

VII. The Paynters Playe, p. 132.

Line.	MS. of 1607.	Dev. MS.
		Heading: The Paynters Playe.
	Pagina	Incipit pagina
	Greges pascentibus	*om.*
	The paynters and glasiers	*om.*
1.	full wylde	*om.* full
5.	glide	Clyde
6.	on the	vnder
10.	ssuch	Suche
*11.	tytefull	taytfull
*22.	Ribbie	tybbe
27.	fetterfoe	and fetterfowe
31.	thraw	rowe
32.	of	from
34.	for to] of	*om.* for] from
36.	talch] to take	talgh] *om.* to
	After 40, *Stage Direction.*	*om.*
	Tunc potet	hic potat primus pastor
*45.	Haroye] *last* howe	harvye] *om.*

Line. MS. of 1607.	Dev. MS.
46. the	thy
47. but if	excepte
48. feale	heale
Stage Direction: Tunc flat, *&c.*	hic flabit primus pastor
*49. not	no
50. loe	soure
**After* 52	*Stage Direction in margin:* sitt downe
53. we be	be we
54. one thing	and though
Heading	*in margin.*
Stage Direction.	*om.*
Secundus (*heading*)	Secund*us* pastor vocat submissa voce
*61. father	fathers
63. knowest	knowys
Stage Direction.	*om.*
71. half	all
72. doe	done
76. an	and
78. bene to me all good	must bene all tamed
80. of	for
82. longes	longeth
*87. to his wife bowne	bowe to his wife
90. dame] kin	our dame] keynn
91. will I	*om.* I
primus	*primus* pastor
95. Secundus	Secund*us* pastor
Tertius	Tertius pastor
ban	be by
101. Yeg	*om.*
104. man	deede
Primus	Prim*us* pastor
*105. alyche	I lych
107. first	*om.*
Secundus	Secund*us* pastor
111. for to	*om.* for
113. baken	bacon
114. lyke	leekes
*116. grease	greese well
Tertius	Tertius pastor
119. and a	*om.* and
*120. Lancashyre	Lancaster shyre
122. groyne	grayne
123. on sale	ordayned
125—132.	*om.*
134. pull	put
135. pull	put
136. pudding	puddinges
,, Tertius	Tertius pastor
*138. whot] shall it hend	hott] serven yt here
139. good	good meate
Primus	Prim*us* pastor

Line. MS. of 1607.	Dev. MS.
141. And that is in	*om.*
143. This oxe	And this
*144. for *your* tooth	*with* my teeth
Tunc comedent	Tunc commedent et dicat prim*us* pastor
146. surelie	by god
148. and	but
Secundus	Secundus pastor
149. while	while that
151. it	*om.*
152. flaggen	flackett
After 152 Tertius	Terti*us* pastor
153. Nowe will]	And nowe will]
*fele	bibbe
*154. but	bowles
156. way] lost	where] leste
Primus	Prim*us* pastor
158. sheepe	flockes
Secundus	Secund*us* pastor
162. seeke us	vs seekes
*163. tilt	litte
Tertius	Tertius pastor
165. to *your*	*om.*
166. in land nowhere	no where in land
168. in	nowe in
Primus	Primus pastor
172. lowt] he	lowd] *om.*
* ,, venit	dicat
Heading.	*om.*
174. as] they foode	here as] the fed
175. would	wold
*176. me wald haue	noe waye
177. plaine (*second*)	*om.*
178. mon we good haue	we mon goe
179. then these	may
*180. beastes	beast
*181. nor	or
*182. needen	beelongen
183 *and* 184.	*om.*
185. Tarboist] and nettle	Tarboyste and] *om.*
After 185.	yee shall here
186. hemlockes	Nettle hemlock
188. choise	cheesse
*191. where	wheras
192. by east	*om.* by
*193. when	where
194. were] best	*om.*] lost
195. nor	ne
196. nay	Ryse
197. me	here
201—202.	*om.*
203. here drink mon	drinke here shall
205. thy lathes] a	this lott*es*] *om.*

Line.	MS. of 1607.	Dev. MS.
*206.	to lye thee	by yee
	Primus	prim*us* pastor
*210.	teeth] dugging	tooth] tugging
214.	lyveras	liveraste*s*
*215.	sawce] Iawce] and	sose] sowse] *om.*
218.	you what	your hot
	Secundus	Secundus pastor
221.	For that	*om.* that
222.	and	*om.*
225.	therin	*om.*
*226.	stamped	stopped
227.	creepe	do creepe
228.	home	whom
231.	not	nought
232.	wage	wages
*233.	or this	*om.*
*234.	se	but see
*235.	pynckes	pinches
*236.	euery	any
	Tertius	Tertius pastor
*237.	pitty	tree
239.	and	and then
	Heading.	Garcius
241.	will	shall
242.	were] you	bee] *om.*
*244.	wager	*om.*
	magistros	magistros suos et dicat *Heading.* Garcius
248.	is most	moste is
	Primus	prim*us* pastor
249.	never thou kever	thow never knewe
251.	I will	*om.*
	Secundus	Secund*us* pastor
	Tertius	Tertius pastor
255.	list	luste*s*
258.	Golians	golyons
259.	your	our
*260.	Dee	the daye
	Primus	Primus pastor
262.	shalt	shall
264.	if thou haue all	yf thow happe
*265.	here] to doe you	this] here to
*268.	walt	walter
	prim*us* proiicit*ur*	proiiciat primu*m* pastorem et dicat Secu*ndus* pastor
	Heading. Secundus.	Secu*ndus* pastor
269.	there	*om.*
270.	aske	axe
273.	that so grennes and grones	thee to groyns and grownes
276.	like] are done	tyke] *om.* are
	Stage Direction.	*om.*
	Tertius	Tertius pastor
*278.	let now goe	lett mee goe now
281.	byndes	bendes
*282.	boast] but	boastes] to
284.	ere] hope	have] hope I
285.	and	in
287.	bosiart	bovearte
289.	store	score
	3*us* proiicitur	proiiciat terciu*m* pastorem, et dicat Garcius
292.	I will	will I
293.	cup	curye
295.	all you	you all
*296.	and] taynt	as] attaynt
297.	this (*second*)] wake	with this] walke *Stage Direction:* Et sic recedat Garcius, et dicat prim*us* pastor.
	Heading.	*om.*
302.	harme	harmes
	Secundus	Secu*ndus* pastor
304.	here	here I
305.	weete	wayte
306.	this would	the wedder
	Tertius	Tertius pastor
309.	may we be] overthough] no wonder] apparebit stella	wee may bee] in thought] now vnder stella apparebit et dicat prim*us* pastor
	Heading.	*om.*
*312.	shynes	blasses
314.	sight	light
317.	Aferd	ffeard
324.	gleming	leeminge
325.	for to	*om.* for
*330.	se	seeke
*331.	fayle	fayle mee
*333.	stand	not fond
*334.	avayle	avayle mee
	dicat	dicat Garcius
	Heading.	*om.*
	After 338 Primus	Prim*us* pastor
340.	for to	*om.* for
	Secundus	prim*us* pastor
349.	to	for to
	Tertius	Tertius pastor
353.	well	will
354.	height	high
355.	ayre	eare
359.	why] fayre	why that] sent
	Primus	prim*us* pastor
*363.	Nor I	Ne fye
364.	it is	is it

Line.	MS. of 1607.	Dev. MS.
368.	or	or that
	cantabit	cantet
	Heading.	*om.*
370.	you	yee
371.	height	highe
		Heading: Secun*dus* pastor
372.	on (*twice*)	In (*twice*)
	Tertius	Tertius pastor
376.	I am	am I
377.	without	bowt
378.	strang	strange
379.	more I	is merye
	Primus	Prim*us* pastor
382.	Caelcis	selsis
	Secundus	Sec*undus* pastor
385.	wrecking	wreakinge
	Tertius	Tertius pastor
393.	Glorum, glarum	gror*us* glar*us*
After 394		*Heading:* Gartius

Then follows in Dev. MS.:

Nay yt was glor*us* glar*us* glorius
me thinke that note went over the howse;
a seemely man hee was and curiouse,
but soone away hee was.

Line.	MS. of 1607.	Dev. MS.
		Heading: prim*us* pastor
*401.	rowe	woo
	Secundus	Sec*undus* pastor
*403.	glee	glye
	Tertius	Tertius pastor
405.	it	hee
*408.	wondrous	worders
409.	come	came
410.	tayle	teale
		Heading: prim*us* pastor
*411.	and a glare	& on glay
412.	good	gurd
414.	for] bloting	*om.*] bletinge
	Secundus	Sec*undus* pastor
415.	my faith	god
416.	sang	sayde
417.	had I	I have
	Tertius	Tertius pastor
*419.	you	hee
*421.	sang	singe*s*
*422.	ner	ney
423.	upon	on
424.	on	and
426.	height] had howted	high] vp hent
	Primus	prim*us* pastor
*427.	of pax	a pax
428.	pie	a pye
*429.	ledden	loden
	Secundus	Sec*undus* pastor
*433.	quocke] while] shewted	quoked] when] whewted
434.	here] I	hede] yt
	Tertius	Tertius pastor
*436.	worth] founder	worthye] forder
438.	past	passeth
439.	and	&
440.	may	shall
446.	song to this	to this songe
	Primus	Prim*us* pastor
448.	unbrace	vmbrace
	Secundus	Sec*undus* pastor
*452.	for	*om.*
455.	Nowe sing on] us	Singe wee nowe] *om.*
456.	I will	will I
457.	singes	nowe singes
	Stage Direction.	Tunc cantabunt et postea dicat terti*us* pastor *In margin:* here singe troly loly loly loo
	Primus	Prim*us* pastor
463.	And	*om.*
465.	bend we *our* lynes	boyne the lymis
	Secundus	Secund*us* pastor
*467.	that hyeth] so	and hyes] full
468.	were us	vs were
	Tunc	Hic
	Tertius	Terti*us* pastor
471.	Stynt	Stynt nowe
472.	begins	beginneth
473.	here we	Harvye
474.		we seene by our savyour fonde
	Et apparebit angel*us*	hic apparet Angelus et dicat
	Heading.	*om.*
479.	goe	*om.*
480.	shall you	yee shall
482.	kever	cover
484.	wynde	wend
490.	kinges	kinge
	Secundus	Sec*undus* pastor
	Tertius	Terti*us* pastor
502.	thy	the
	Primus	Prim*us* pastor
509.	like	is like
	Secundus	Sec*undus* pastor
512.	he	him
514.	his head is	hee heedes
	Tertius	Terti*us* pastor
516.	heedes	hydes
522.	me in] tent	in mee] lent
*524.	ner	in

Line.	MS. of 1607.	Dev. MS.
527.	takes	take
*529.	as	vs
537.	or	nor
*541.	never to see	to have never seene
547.	goes! preach forth	goes forth and preach
	Prim*us*	Prim*us* pastor
553.	we	nowe wee
554.	here	this
	Secundus	Sec*undus* pastor
*557.	brush	brooche
558.	lets	lett
	Tertius	Terti*us* pastor
	Primus	Prim*us* pastor
560.	first goe	goe first
	Secundus	Sec*undus* pastor
*561.	you be fathers of age	yee be father in age
562.	must you	ye must
	Prim*us*	Prim*us* pastor
565.	to	vnto
*566.	all	full
570.	doth	do
[572].		I praye thee save me from hell
574.	fare well	serve thee
	Secundus	Sec*undus* pastor
*576.	als	alsoe
577.	thou shalt fall	shall thow fell
581.	blessedfullst barne that ever yet was borne	blessed*es* full baronne *Separate line.* that ever was borne
582.	I bring] flasket	Loe sonne I bringe] flackett
583.	and thereat	therby hanges
*584.	to] w*ith*all	for to] w*ith*
585.	oft hath	ofte tymes have
586.	take	to take
	Tertius	Terti*us* pastor
587.	peere	any pere
589.	soe	the fooe
591.	hayle] happes	Hayle the] hope
*592.	in	for one
*595.		This gifte, sonne, *that* I giue thee, ys but smalle
596.	though] came] hyndermost	and though] come] the hyndmost
*598.	then	yett
599.	Drury	dryrie
600.	flote] no lesse	state] not lose
601.	to	for to
602.	to	vnto
603.	jewell, sonne	Iewells, my sonne
,,	I haue] for	*Separate line.* have I] thee for
606.	do	doth

Line.	MS. of 1607.	Dev. MS.
	Between 606 & 607, *MSS.* B W h.	44 *lines as in MSS.* B W h.
2.	before	or that
8.	him	her
11.	the last	*om.* the
14.	nor	ne
23.	I haue	have I
25.	jewells	Iewell
27.	thou take	*om.* thou
29.	thee	thy father on hye
30.	for	for to give
31.	pipe	pype that soundeth so royallye
32.	no thing	have I no thinge at all
33.	rock*is* or in	rocke or in the valey a lowe
34.	pipe	pipe sound I trowe
35.	wood	world
36.	quiver] were	quaver] would fall
38.	god, thie self,	thy selfe god
40.	wilt	will
41.	peares, appells	apples, payres
42.	thombes	handes
	MS. of 1607.	
	Prim*us*	prim*us* pastor
610.	w*hi*ch] mast	*om.*] most
*613.	thou] me and for	hee] *om.*
614.	so	and
*615.	thy	his
	Secundus	Sec*undus* pastor
*618.	homewardes	homwardlye
*620.	Ever] crye	all] knowe
622.	alway	awaye
	Tertius	Terti*us* pastor
624.	about goe	goe abowt
625.	this	this thinge
627.	gree	agree
630.	to] whollie will I	and to] I wholey
631.	euer	aye
632.	here	*om.*
634.	to my] to wach	in my] *om.* to
	Prim*us*	prim*us* pastor
*636.	paye	praye
637.	wake	walke
640.	will	shall
641.	bare-foted	bare foote
643.	honestlie	alwayse
644.	will	fully
645.	for	*om.*
[646].		turne to thy felowes and kys
647.	my] and	*om.*] for
	Secundus	Sec*undus* pastor
651.	such	lowth

Line.	MS. of 1607.	Dev. MS.
652.	another	such another
653.	fremd] cought	frend] cowth
654.	geue	grant
	Tertius	Tertius pastor
655.	vs	you
656.	it	that

Line.	MS. of 1607.	Dev. MS.
657.	Amend] thinges that be amisse	Amen] singe you
658.	now] fares	*om.*] fare
	paginae septimae.	septim*ae* pagin*ae*.

VIII. The Vintners Playe, p. 160.

Line.	MS. of 1607.	Dev. MS.
		Heading: The Vintners Playe.
	Heading: Pagina] de Tribus Regib*us* Orientalib*us*.	Incipit pagina] tri*um* Reg*um* orientali*um*.
*2.	ruled	rules
3.	mercy	pittye
6.	we	I
11.	betokening	tokninge of
22.	that] hym	but] *om.*
27.	to	in
*33.	you	I
*37.	some	a
41.	fellowes	fellowe
	Before 45 *Heading.*	*om.*
	Stage Direction: Descendunt] ad	Hic descendunt de equis] in
		Heading: primus rex.
*49.	is	ys yt
51.	geve thou	thou give
*56.	kinges	knightes
		Heading: Tertius rex.
59.	counsaile	conceale
	Heading: Primus rex.	*In margin.*
61.	weale	well
*62.	thou shalt	that shal
*63.	deale	dwell
	stella apparet	apparebit stella
	Before 65.	*Heading.* primus rex.
65.	plaist	ploitt
66.	Gardez	gardes
68.	sur	syr
	Before 69.	*Heading:* Tertius rex.
69.	semblant] Aloys	vne semblant] Aloies
	Heading.	*om.*
74.	hast	hase
78.	well	well well
	Stage Direction: Et surgit.	Tunc Reges iterum genua flectent et angelus portans stellam.
86.	especially	speciallye
	Stage Direction.	*After* 84.
89.	A!	*om.*

Line.	MS. of 1607.	Dev. MS.
	After 96.	*In margin:* here the kinges ryse vp.
99.	abyde	byde
100.	till that	*om.* that
	Stage Direction.	*om.*
*108.	Corsers	beasts
109.	Lordes	Lord*es* and
111.	bringen	bringinge
	Stage Direction.	Then goe downe to the beastes and ryde abowt.
	Before 113.	*Heading:* Prim*us* rex.
123.	heere	there
124.	tydinges	tydinge
	Heading: Explorater	The messinger
126.	say ought	ought saye
127.	weare	beare
128.	Iewes] the kinge	the Iewes] *om.* the
129.	saw this	see the
	Explorator	Messinger
134.	hard	here
	Explorator	Messinger
139.	You	Yee
144.	thinges	tidinges
	Stage Direction.	Here the messinger must goe to the kinge. *In the margin:* minstrells here must playe.

After 144, *in Dev. MS., as in MSS.* B W h., *the following* 8 *lines.*

O noble kinge and worthye conqueroure,
Crowned in gould, sittinge on hye,
Mahound thee save longe in honoure;
license I require to speake to thee.
Tidings now my lord I shall you tell
That these three kinge doe shewe vnto mee;
From whense the binne I knowe not well.
yonder the stond as yee may see.

Line.	MS. of 1607.	Dev. MS.
145.	et	and
147.	Coynopent	Comoplent
	Between 148 *and* 149.	*In the margin:* staffe
150.	vesture	vetere

Line.	MS. of 1607.	Dev. MS.
151.	queramus] paret	querennes] parent
154.	your	such
165.	weale	weld
176.	if	and
181.	Nor (*first*)	Non
182.	destroy	him nye
184.	wil not	nyll
189.	well	wott and
	Baculum	staffe
192.	saith	sayes
	Gladius	sword
	Iace Gladium	cast vp
197.	royaltie	riallye
	Baculum et toga alia	*om.*
202.	reconed I have	I reconed
	adoratum	adorare
213.	prophesies	prophecye
215.	and	to
220.	shall none	non shall
225.	art cheife	cheife art
[227].		of Daniell, David, and Isaye
*228.	sees	seest
230.	them	*om.*
234.	that	what
238.	prophet	prophetes
239.	nothing	any thinge
*247.	to heare the truth	the trueth to here
254.	Abdias	*om.*
255.	and also	Abdias and
257.	on	vpon
	Heading.	*om.*
	Latin quotation. 49.	quadragessimo nono
263.	prophesies	prophecied
265.	shold neuer taken be	never taken should bee
266.	till] which	vntill] that
267.	Heaven	heavenly
271.	Romans	the Romans
274.	now is	is nowe
275.		a bill, *in margin.*
276.	all	*om.*
278.	his	hye
*279.	a] parage	*om.*] parentage
280.	for	*om.*
281.	sharpe] I shall	*om.*] shall I
	After 281.	Et dicat, read one.
	Danielis 9.	*om.*
*283.	before	alsoe
284.	which	that
285.	the	*om.*
287.	delyuer] all	to deliuer] *om.*
288.	pitiously] blynde	most pitiously] bynd

Line.	MS. of 1607.	Dev. MS.
291.	the	there
293.	shall	should
297.	sleeping	sleepie
*298.	befall	shall befall
299.	gedling	godlinge
302.	knightes	kinges
	Heading.	*om.*
	Iuda	*after* terra
	Iuda (*second*) qui	Iudae] qui reget
	Mich. 5 et Math. 2.	Michei quinto et Mathei secundo.
304.	prince	child
307.	lyving	beinge
308.	many other	divers others
*309.	their lyving was	they were livinge
	Esay 60.	Esaui sexagessimo
313.	from many a sondry coast	& from sundrye coasts
*314.	birth	death
	cum gladio	*om.*
	parvulum	paruulum istum
	After Latin.	*In margin:* cast downe the sword
318.	gedling	godlinge
*320.	Congeown	conninge
322.	a small	finall
323.	ilke	eke
326.	which] were borne	that] *om.* borne
327.	to	for to
328.	yonge	*om.*
	Insula	Insule
	Psal. 71.	Phalmo septuagesimo primo
332.	from	of
*333.	Lord	lord and prince
334.	descended	descendinge
336.	both	*om.*
337.	a	*om.*
338.	Lord	my lord
*339.	shall	should
	After Heading.	*In margin:* breake a sword
343.	these] all to	those] rent &
348.	getis non] nor	gett noe] or
	After 349.	cast vp, *in margin.*
355.	to] that	*om.*] *om.*]
	Iacet Gladium	cast vp
*366.	Beleave	By your leave
*373.	and	but
	Stage Direction.	the boye & pigge when the kinges are gonne, *in margin.*
378.	say well this	well say thus
	Baculum	staffe, *in margin.*

Line.	MS. of 1607.	Dev. MS.
*382.	greeues	greivouse
383.	thes	those
386.	tell	tell mee
387.	borne	then borne
388.	he and they	they and hee
	After 389.	sword, *in margin.*
393.	swap	choppe
394.	never	not
399.	will I	I will
405.	great	greatest
*406.	bost] great	boye] greatly
410.	Cup	Cuppes
412.	Quintely	curiouslye
	finis paginae Octavae.	*om.* paginae Octavae.

IX. The Mercers Playe, p. 177.

Line.	MS. of 1607.	Dev. MS.
	The Mercers.	*Heading:* The Merrcers Playe, *after the Latin.*
	Latin quotation.	*om.*
3.	is	yt
	After 12 *Heading.*	*om.*
21.	well I wot	wott I well
34.	vs (*first*)] betwixt	we] amongest
*40.	ere	or
47.		*om.*
*54.	mase	hasse
*55.	stench	stynke
62.	for	to
81.	you Sirrs twoo	syrs both two
*86.	roting	rowtinge
*93.	lasteth	lastlye
94.	geue	give him
*99.	there	these
*126.	his	this
128.	he is	is hee
129.	Sirres	*om.*
*134.	from o*ur*	in farre
136.	will I] Barne aperiet	I will] Baron appariet
138.	come	common
139.	bye	forbye
149.	Lord, here	here Lord
153.	thou	*om.*
154.	comen are	common [illegible]
157.	fayle	saye
167.	Lord, here	here, lord
170.	hast	hasse
*175.	through	though
197.	the	*om.*
209.	maide	mayden
226.	not you	you not
227.	send	send*es*
230.	ordaynt	ordayne
237.	loare	lere
245.	meete	to meete
*246.	offer	offered
248.	that	*om.*
*250.	vs	you
*252.	befall	may befall
254.	Landes	land
259.	is	*om.*
263.	two	to

X. The Gouldsmythes Playe, p. 186.

Line.	MS. of 1607.	Dev. MS.
	innocentu*m*	Innocensiu*m*
	The Gouldsmiths	*Heading:* The Gouldsmythes Playe *before the Latin.*
	Herode	Herodes
	Latin quotation.	*om.*
7.	under me	*om.*
9.	subiet*is*	subiectes all
13.	w*i*thout	w*i*thouten
15.	mar	marye
18.	come	commen
30.	againe	agaynst
31.	rocked	recked
*33.	none	noe
34.	that	but
*37.	knaves	knave
*38.	gilt	guile
41.	petty	prettye
	After 48 Doctor	Preco
50.	hestes	hest
*51.	and	or
*61.	swone	sowne
*66.	these	this
*70.	day	waye
*73.	in see	on hye
81.	Graund	Grant
84.	tyde	steede
90.	Resar	Reason
91.	w*hich*] worship	that] grace
92.	full] shall	*om.*] should
93.	we hym	him wee
119.	knaves childer	knave children
123.	Childer	children
129.	in	to
138.	hase	have
144.	they	there
145.	Conioyne	commen ?

Line.	MS. of 1607.	Dev. MS.
146.	thus	this
158.	might	*after* head
160.	good	great
167.	St	saynct
168.	in to	*om.* to
169.	or	nor
*173.	that	this
179.	years	yeere
*193.	Rewkes	But lookes you
195.	spart	speare
*197.	blabb lipped	blacke lypped
198.	mightie	*om.*
*199.	the	they
*201.	wot	wytt
206.	fawcon	faconne
208.	for	*om.*
216.	not] without scathe	non] bout scatche
219.	not] best	*om.*] boaste
227.	teenen	teene
230.	a hundred	an hundreth
233.	must	will
237.	gedlinge	geldinge
242.	this	thus
252.	right] shall	*om.*] should
253.	yet	yett yett
262.	warne	warne thee
263.	haue	have you
265.	must	most
266.	flee	flye
274.	shalt] now	shall] *om.*
*275.	till	that
	**Stage Direction.*	
	d*omin*us	d*omin*us ascendet
	ingredietur] cadet	ingrediatur] caldet
289.	Hase	Have
*291.	their] all to-thrast	the] in thrust
293.	all	*om.*
*297.	bitch	dogge
*298.	my] drister	thy] daystard
299.	stich	stike
306.	knaues	knave
*314.	stibbon] stickt	stitton] styck
	Secunda	*Secundus*
326.	abode	abyd
331.	nor	or
334.	and	or
	transfodiet] lancea	traffodiet] super lancea
346.	shalt	shall
355.	boote	bote
358.	you	thou
359.	you	thou
361.	shew] the] here	shewe thou] thy] there
362.	pon	vpon
363.	and if	*om.* if
366.	thou shalt	shall thou
*367.	he] II	hit] two
*369.	stockt	styck
370.	bode	or boad
371.	or	and
372.	you	yee
378.	all	*om.*
382.	wo be	who binne
385.	drye	drey
386.	myne	my
	After 392	*Stage Direction.* Tunc ibit ad Herodem
393.	Lord, lord, see see	Loe lord, looke and see
394.	to	*om.*
*395.	meny	contrey
*396.	they be	the bine
	irabit	iratus
401.	aright	right
402.	have bene	be
404.	wondrous	wonders
*411.	his aray	this daye
*414.	so	so farre
	Between 419 *and* 420	booteles is me to make mone
422 *and* 423		*Inverted.*
424.	for	after
*431.	I dye (*second*)	now
	Stage Direction.	Tunc faciet signum quasi morietur et veniet demon
*433.	you	your
434.	doe	rowe
437.	Croked Cambrock	crocked crambocke
438.	in a low	and lowe
440.	wholl	no right whole
*441.	hither	*om.*
443.	and] bringe	in] there to bringe
446.	be ther	there be
449.	Tapstars] lowty	trespas] lewtye
*452.	grace	grave
453.	bringe this	you bringe thus
455.	euer	*om.*
463.	whon	whome
467.	is dead] hath	is hee dead] hase
*469.	againe	a whome
*470.	at home	agayne
472.	good	great
475.	hath	hase
485.	root	hart roote
*487.	ryde	soonne ryde
	After 488	*Heading* Angelus
492	fone	foe
496.	hundreth	thousands

XI. The Blacksmythes Playe, p. 205.

Line.	MS. of 1607.	Dev. MS.
	The Black Smiths	The Black smythes Playe *before the Latin.*
1.	Might	Mightie
2.	are	art
7.	flitt	fytt
14.	sooth	the sooth
18.	no man	may no man
*19.	books	booke
*21.	What	When
23.	dyed	deed
	librum respiciens] parietur filium	respitiens librum] pariet filium, &c.
*32.	were	yt were
35.	shall	should
	librum fricabit] postea]	fabricabit librum] post]
	libro accepto faciet	accipiet librum faciens]
	scribendi]	quasi scriberet]
	libro clauso recedet	claudet librum et vnanesset
	Heading: Anna	Anna vidua
	MSS. B W h (*two leaves are missing from MS. of* 1607 *at this place*).	
45.	cometh] leve thou	comes] leaues you
48.	saue	salue
52.	thinketh	thinkes
60.	theron	therin
	Stage Direction.	*om.* et dicat
74.	for	forsooth
	Stage Direction.	*After* 82 *in margin.*
81.	by] yet	*om.*] yet eft
87.	since	syth
95.	mayden	mayd
97.	seith, lorde	lord, syth
102.	that	thy
108.	shalt	shall
111.	to	for to
112.		*om.*
114.	haste	hase
119.	Esayes boke procull	Esaues bookes plocul
	et dicat maria	*om.*
121.	trewe owine	owne trewe
132.	lawe	sawe
134.	we	*om.*
135.	also	too
136.	to	soe
138.	nowe	here
142.	birdes	bryddes
152.	from	of
153.	my Christe	*om.* my
155.	frute	fruites
168.	on	of
	in pace	etc.
173.	for	And
175.	light	lightninge
186.	not	non
194.	my	thy
195.	yeaire	yeares
196.	sente	send
200.	it	*om.*
203.	hath	have
204.	our	*om.*
207.	for	now and
212.	seeke	seech
	MS. of 1607.	
*213.	away	his waye
	Heading.	*om.*
217.	mirth	myrthes
*218.	betwene	betwixt
222.	has	hath
*223.	I red	I read, I read
225.	euer	that euer
227.	aye	any
229.	row	a rowe
*231.	me] learne	methinkes] will learne
234.	talke	talkinge
*245.	wold	wouldest
*247.	neuer	neither
248.	may	might
252.	they	that
254.	noynted	annoynted
257.	lead	learned
259.	thinke he saith	thinkes hee sayes
263.	will full sone	full sonne will
267.	as wyde	And wyde
268.	ferly a fare	farrely fare
275.	to me you	you to me
279.	thinges	thinge
280.	sawe	lawe
	[*Heading*]	Deus
282.	in	with
286.	doe	give *altered to* doe
287.	sooth	for
290.	goode	goodes
298.	whersoever	whatsoever
*306.	there] light	*om.*] bright
307.	sitteth	sittes that
320.	haue	*om.*
324.	neede	needes
325.	seale	heale
*326.	can I	*om.* I
*328.	they	the
331.	Esaie	Esau
332.	hath	hase
333.	lorde	lordes
334.	well	all
	Name and date.	*om.*

XII. The Butchers Playe, p. 217.

Line.	MS. of 1607.	Dev. MS.
	pagina de tentatione saluatoris	Incipit pagina qualiter Ihesus ductus est in desert*um* a spir*itu*. Incipiat Diabolus.
	The Butchers	The Bowchers Playe *before the Latin.*
	Sathanas	Diabolus
6.	about	abroad
*9.	man	mon
10.	in the world thus	nowe in world
13.	father] I not	*om.*] not I
*14.	ne] quaintyce	and] couintise
15.	he thought heaven were	that heaven all should be
17.	a	*om.*
*20.	neuer	*om.*
24.		his hasse him honoure youre
25.	Sith	Sythen
*27.	deadlish	deadlych
*28.	yet she is wemlesse	hee yet wembles
29.	the] doth	*om.*] dose
31.	he seemes to be	blotles eke
33.	ne no	nor any
*35.	hath	hase
36.	he	*om.*
40.	nother	neather by
41.	By] aye he put*is*	My] he puttes aye
42.	can I none	non can I
45.	For	And
46.	somewhat	somethinge
47.	saffe he is hungrie	save only honge he hasse
48.	I wot	wott I
50.	were	be
53.	will	would
*55.	hath fasted	hasse fast nowe
56.	now meat	therfore bread
	After 56.	*Heading:* Diabolus dicit
59.	that thou may	nowe lett
	Ies*us*	Deus
62.		bread man lives not only bye
74.	not	nought
77.	this	his
80.	avayle	thee avayle
	Sathanas	Diabolus
83.	for] that	*om.*] well
*84.	be	*om.*
85.	quoyntice	coyntise
86.	may	can
87.		that neede of any bodely blys
88.	hath	hasse
*89.	nye	of noye
91.	ever he wyn- [nes	aye hee winneth
93.	must	mott
*94.	Dosaberd	disobedient
95.	hath	hasse
96.	unhappely	vnhappingely
*98.	deceipt	discent
102.	ne	w*i*th
195.	But I will	yett will I
107.	unto the	to this
*110.	sone	well
111.	ordayne	shape
	statuet Iesu*m* templi	statuat Iesus templi et dicat diabolus
*113.	thou] there	thou nowe] *om.*
114.	be slye	by sleight
*115.	I see	in sight
116.	thee doe	thou diddest
117.	Angell] thee	Angells] to thee
118.	nether] nor	no] ne
120.	thou] honour	that thou] maistrye
	After 120.	*Heading:* Iesus dicit ad diabolu*m*
121.	sickerly	securlye
124.	mooved	ment
	Stage Direction.	Discendens de pinnaculo dicat Diabolus
	Sathanas	*om.*
125.	woe is me	that me is woe
126.	twise	this
127.	rowted	rent
128.	ne] reproued	ne halfe] reprived
	After 128.	*Stage Direction:* Tunc Sathan adducet Ihesu*m* super monte*m* et dicat diabolus
129.	But yet	Yett fellowe
130.	upon this	to a
131.	thou	I
134.	these realmes	this realme
136.	shalte	shall
137.	Sathan	Sathanas
139.	God thy Lord	thy lord god
*140.	it	*om.*
	Sathanas	Diabolus
141.	now	that
142.	mickle	great
*148.	quayntice	contyse
149.	out] must be shut	*om.*] mone be shitt
150.	pyned	punished

Line.	MS. of 1607.	Dev. MS.
151.	none] a	man] *om.*
156.	all to dyrt	to the fyre
157—160.		*om. Twelve lines substituted same as MSS.* B W h.
	Stage Direction.	*om.*
	Expositor	Doctour
162.	St.	*om.*
*166.	Covetuousnes	covetous
167.	thinges, without	poyntes, bowt
168.	hath overcome	hasse overcommen
171.	the	that
175.	to	and
*178.	het	hight
181.	covetous	covetousnes
*182.	not onely	nought greatly
186.	you	as yee
*188.	you saw	sleightely
190.	stones	the stones
191.	prone	move
192.	weere	a weare
193.	also	him alsoe
194.	excited	bade
197.	covetous	covetousness
199.	het] both	height] *om.*
200.	there	that
201.	Thus] Christe	This] thrise
*203.	*with* those	of the
204.	waued	weaved
207.	Sathanas	soothnes
	venint] Iudeorum]	venient] pharasei]
	cum muliere] deprehensa in adulterio]	adducentes mulierem] in adulterio deprehensam]
	ut Iesum tentarent; quare dicit primus]	dicat
	Heading: Iudeus	Pharaseus
209.	us	*om.*
212.	adultery	advowtrye
*214.	for	for so
	Iudeus	pharaseus
217.	Hit] redd	That] read fellowe
*218.	we may	mone we
222.	dothe	dose
223.	hath	hasse
224.	man shall	mon should
	Stage Direction.	Tunc adducent mulierem inter se coram Iesu et dicat *Heading:* primus pharaseus
226.		was wedded lawfully to yeare

Line.	MS. of 1607.	Dev. MS.
227.	man	*om.*
228.	was	we
230.	women	*om.* *Stage Direction as heading before* 238: Iesus scribens in terra dicat
234.	without	bowt
	Stage Direction.	*om.*
	Iew	pharaseus
237.	somewhat to	and somewhat
239.	here today	as thou maye
	Iew	pastor *altered to* phariseus
242.	wrytes *master*	writest thou
243.	save	spare
	Stage Direction.	*om.*
245.	wrytes] lett	writest] lett me
	Heading: Primus Iew	*om.*
247.	here] be	for] here be
	Between 247 *and* 248: I see my synnes so clearly	*om.*
248.	worlds	worldly *Stage Direction after* 248: Et fugiet et postea dicat primus pharaseus
*249.	by my	be thy
	Stage Direction.	*om.*
251.	not away	*om.* not
252.	behynde	beyonde
254.	I darr abyde	dare I chyde *altered to* abyde
255.	now	*om.*
256.	I haue	have I *Stage Direction:* Et fugiet et dicat Iesus ad mulierem
	Heading.	*om.*
257.	those	these
259.	is ther	nowe there is
260.	those	tho
	Mulier	Mulier adulteria
*263.		Nowe I dampne thee not, woman
*267.	from henceforth synne	hethen forth filth
270.	knoweth] all workes] done be]	knowes] worke] doe wee
271.	thee lord	*om.* lord
272.	I will	will I
	Expositor	Doctor
273.	lordings	lord*es*
273.	take hede	marke here

Line.	MS. of 1607.	Dev. MS.
274.	of	*om.*
276.	this thing] was	these thinges] were
277.	sayeth	speaketh
279.	Iohn	Iohns
280.	sayeth] this case	sayes] that case
*282.	sith	syns
283.	commaunded	commandeth
285.	trespassed] Adultery	trespassen] advowtrye
288.	blemishe	blenquyshe
*289.	Then] well	That] full well
290.	sett	hee sett
*291.	no synne hadd	synne had not
295.	eche one	Ichone
296.	ther lafte never one	they lefte hir alonne
299.	other	them
300.	owne	synnes
301.	were] way	the were] the waye
*393.	the	that

XIII. The Glovers Playe, p. 229.

Line.	MS. of 1607.	Dev. MS.
	Ceco	*om.*
	The Glovers	The Glouers Playe *as heading before the Latin.*
*4.	bereth	bearen
*9.	his	the
	Reference.	*om.*
20.	scriptureth	scripture
21.	ovibus	omnibus
	Reference.	*om.*
30.	oft	*om.*
	Reference.	*om.*
	cacum	caecum
	Chelidonius	Caecus
43.	me	*om.*
45.	blynd borne	borne blynd
51.		*om.*
53.	sinnes	synne
54.	nor	or
62.	coninge	comminge
	Reference.	*om.*
70.	and	there
	Chelidonius	Caecus
78.	Christ	god
	proximus	vicinus
87.	is	yt is
	Chelidonius	Caecus
95.	Now	*om.*
98.	seeth	seest
100.	to us therfore	therfore to vs
	Chelidonius	Caecus
106.	Siloei	of Siloe
109.	the	my
	Chelidonius	Caecus
118.	wouldst	would
	Chelidonius	Caecus
130.	came	come
*136.	It	I
138.	not	nought
	Chelidonius	Caecus
143.	and	that
144.	this	this is
147.	shalt	shall
156.	from] they loquitur	for] the adloquitur eos
165.	they	the
*166.	there	here
169.	cursse	coarse
*175.	that you	ere we
*177.	deceit	descent
184.	at] it is	of] *om.* it
192.	and	nor
	Chelidonius	Caecus
199.	this truth	this is trueth
	Before 202.	*Heading:* primus pharaseus
204.	you	hee
208.	all we	*om.* all
210.	we	I
	Chelidonius	Caecus
212.	whence	from whence
*213.	hath	*om.*
219.	to him is	is to him
222.	unto	to
225.	such	some *altered to* such
230.	Gods	god
	Chelidonius	Caecus
*234.	hear	I here
*236.	makes	makest
237.	any anye	*om.* any
240.	speak unto	spake to
	Heading: Iew	Iudeus
261.	anow	nowe
*266.	you	yea
	Heading: Iew	Iudeus
271—274.		*om.*
275 *and* 276.		*inverted.*
*275.	lyest foule and	lyes
279.	you may	may you
282.	which you now	that you may

to them belevinge takes yee
for nothing may be sother.

So you may know well and veray:
in my father that I am aye,
and he in me, [the] sothe to say,
and eyther of us in other.

(tunc colligent lapides, et statim evanescet Iesus.)

SECUNDUS IEW. (49)

Out, out, alas! wher is our fone?
quintly that he is heathen gone.
I would haue taken him *and* that anone,
and foull him all-to-frapped.

Yea, make we never so much mone,
now ther is no other wone;
for he and his men everichon
are from us clearly scaped.

PRIMUS IUDEUS. (50)

Now by the Deathe, I shall on dye,
may I see him with my eye,
to sir Cayphas I shall him wry,
and tell that shall him dere.

Se I never none, by my fay,
when I had stones, so sone away;
but yet no force, an other day
his tabret we shall fere.

MARIA. (51)

A lord Iesu, that me is woo
to wit my Brother sickly so;
in feble tyme Christ yode me fro;
well were we, and he were heer.

MARTHA.

yea, suster, about I will goe
and seeke Iesu, to and fro;

285 you may] maye ye B W h. may you D. evanescet] euanescit B W h D. Iew] Iudæus B W h D. 290 quintly] quicklye W h. 291 haue taken] atacken W h. 292 foull] woulde W h. all-to] to haue B. frapped] wrapped B, clapped W h. 294 ther] here W h. 296 scaped] escaped h. *Heading*] *om.* H. 297 Now] O. now B. 299 I shall him] I shall I him B. 300 dere] dare W h. 304 tabret] taberte W h. 307 tyme] teene B. 308 we] me W h. 309 I] we W h.

to help him he would be thro,
and he wist how it were. (tunc venit Iesus.)

(52)

A my lord, swet Iesu, mercy!
Lazar, that thou lovest tenderly,
lyeth sick a little hereby
and suffereth much teene.

IESUS.

yea, woman, I tell thee witterly,
that sicknes is not deadly,
but gods sonne to glorify,
by him as may be seene. (Tunc ibit martha ad mariam.)

MARIA. (53)

A! Martha, suster, alas! alas!
my Brother is dead since thou here was.
had Iesu, my lord, been in this place,
this case had not befalne.

MARTHA.

Yea suster, neer is god[e]s grace;
many a man he holpen hase,
yet may he doe for us in this case
and him to lyfe call.

MARIA. (54)

here will I sitt *and* mourninge make,
tyll that Iesu my sorrow slake.
my teene to hart, lord, [that] thou take,
and leech me of my woe.

MARTHA.

In sorrow and wo here will I wake,
and lament for Lazar my brothers sake;
though I for could and penance quake,
heathen will I not goe.

(tunc *pa*riter iuxta sepulcru*m* Lazari, sedebunt plorantes, et ait Iesus.)

313 A] O W h. 314 lovest] loved D. tenderly] so tenderly h. 320 by] loe! I am D. *Stage-direction*] *om.* H. 322 since] syth D. 323 place] *om.* D. 328 call] callen *is required by the rhyme.* 330 Iesu] my Iesu H. sorrow] soueraigne B. 332 leech] ease W h. 335 penance] paine h W, *the latter inverts* could *and* payne. pariter] pariet W. iuxta] Iusa? *or* Iesu? B. Lazari] *om.* B D W h. ait] *om.* W h, *pr*ocul ait B. Iesus procul ait D.

IESUS. (55)

Brethren, goe we to Iudy!

PETRUS.

Maister, right now thou might well see,
the Iewes would haue stoned thee,
and yet thou wilt agayne.

IESUS.

Wot you not well, this is veray,
that xij hours are in *the* day,
and who so walketh that tyme his way,
trespasseth not, the sooth to say.

(56)

he offendeth not that goeth in light,
but who so walketh about in night,
he trespasseth all against the right;
and light in him is none. St. Iohn XI, 9 and 10.

Why I say this, as I haue tight,
I shall tell you sone in height;
haue mynd on it through your might,
and thinkes well therupon.

(57)

To *the* day my self may likned be,
and to *the* twelue howers all ye,
that lightned bene through following me,
that am most lyking light.

ffor world[e]s light I am veray,
and who so followeth me, sooth to say,
he may goe no chester way,
for light in him is dight.

(58)

Oportet me operari opera eius, qui misit me, donec dies est; venit nox, quando nemo est operari; qua*m* diu su*m* in mu*n*do, lux sum mundi.
Iohannis Cap. 10 de Lazaro resuscitato.

337 *After* Iudy] H *has space for one line.* 338 now] *om.* W h. might] maye W. might well] well might D. well] *after* right W h. 339 haue] a h. 343 his] a D. 344 say] sayne *is required by the rhyme.* 346 who so] who soeuer B W h D. about] *om.* W. 347 he] *om.* H. trespasseth] trespassed W, *om.* D. 349 as] that W h. tight] toulde W h. 351 on] of W h. 352 well] *om.* W h. 353 *the*] *om.* B. may] *after* likned W h. 354 and] *om.* W h. twelue] xij. D. 359 chester] thester? Zupitza. est] potest D. *First* sum] *om.* H, sunt B. *Second* sum] fiunt B. mundi] *om.* h. Iohannis Cap. 10 *etc.*] *om.* B W h D, *in* H *in the margin.*

Brethren, I tell you tydinge : Iohn IX, 4 and 5. 361
Lazar my frend is slepinge ;
thider must we be goinge,
upon him for to call. 364

IOH*ANNES* EVA*N*GEL*IST*A.

Lord, if he sleep, safe he may be ; 365
for in his sleep no peryll is he.
therfore it is not good for thee
to goe thider for so small. 368

IES*US*. (59)

I tell you, Brethren, certaynly : 369
Lazar is dead and thyder will I ;
fayne I am, you wott that I
was not ther, as you may see. 372

THOMAS.

follow him, brethren, to his anoy, 373
and dye with him devoutly ;
for other it will not be.
goe we thider in hye ! 376

(tunc versus locu*m* ibit Iesus, ubi Maria et ma*r*tha sedent.)

MARTHA. (60)

A ! lord Iesu, hadst thou bene here leade, 377
lazar, my Brother, had not bene dead ;
but well I wott thou wilt us read,
now thou art with us here. 380

And this I leeue and hope aright : 381
what thing thou askest of god almight,
he will graunt it thee in height,
and graunt thee thy prayer. 384

IES*US*. (61)

Martha, thy Brother shall ryse, I say. 385

361 tydinge] tydinges B W h D. 363 we] *before* must B W h D. Evan*gelista*] *om.* B W h D. Ioh*annes*] Iohn D. 365—369] *om.* B. *Heading*] *om.* B. 368 to] *om.* D. 371 wott] wotte not W h. you] I D. that] *om.* W. 372] *in* B W h D *followed by what is* 376 *in* H. *Heading*] *after* 370 H. 374 *and*] and I W h. 375 other] non other W h. 376] *before the heading* Thomas B W h D, *inserting* anone *after* thider, D h *inverting* goe we. *Stage-direction*] *continued by:* et martha fuet obviam *in* W h D. fuet] fuit D. 377 Iesu] *om.* B. leade] layd H. 381 this] thus B. 384 thee] to thie B. 385 Martha thy Brother] Thi brother Martha B W h D.

MARTHA.

That leeve I, lord, in good fay, 386
that he shall ryse the last day,
then hope I him to see. 388

IESUS.

Martha, I tell thee, without nay, 389
I am rysinge *and* lyfe veray;
which lyfe, I say, shall last for aye,
and never shall ended bee. John XI, 25. 392

(62)

Whosoever leeveth stidfastly 393
in me, I tell the truly,
though he dead be, *and* down lye,
shall lyve and fare well. 396
leevest thou, woman, th*at* th*is* may bee?

MARTHA. (63)

Lord, I leeue, and leeue mon, 398
that thou art Christ, gods sonne,
and commen into th*is* world to woon,
mans boot for to bee. 401
Thus haue I leued stidfastly; 402
therfore on me thou haue mercy,
and on my suster eeke, mary!
I will fetch her to thee. 405

(64) (tunc martha ibit et vocabit mariam, dicens:)

A! mary, suster, leefe and deer, 406
hye thee quickly *and* come neare!
my swet lord, Iesu, he is here,
and calleth thee him too. 409

MARIA.

A! well were we, and it so were! 410
but had my louely lord of leere

391 I say] *om.* D. 396 *and* 397] *written as one line in* H. 397 leevest] Leeves D. bee] *om* D. 400 and] is B W h D. into] vnto h. this] the B. 402 Thus] this B W h D. 403 on] in B. ibit et vocabit] vocat H. *Stage-direction*] *followed by the heading:* Martha B W h D. 406 A leffe marye sister deare W. 408 is] was h. 409 and] *om.* D. 410 we] me h. so were] were so W h.

seene my Brother lye on Bere,
some Boot might haue bene done. 413

(65)

But now he stinketh, sooth to say; 414
for now this is the fourth[e] day,
since he was buryed in the Clay,
that was to me so leefe. 417
But yet, my lord I will assay, 418
and with all my hart him will I pray,
to comfort us, if that he may,
and mend all our mischefe. 421

(66) (tunc maria, videns Iesu*m*, pro*s*ternat se ad pedes, dicens:)

A! lord Iesu, hadst thou bene here, 422
Lazar, my Brother, thy owne dere,
had not bene dead in this maner;
much sorrow is me upon. 425

IESUS.

Wher haue you layd him? tell[e]s me! 426

MARIA.

Lord, come thither and thou may see;
for buryed in this place is he
four days now agon. (tunc veniu*n*t Iudei, quoru*m* dicat p*ri*mus:) 429

P*RIMUS* IEW. (67)

Se, fellow, for cock[e]s sowle! 430
this freak beginneth to reem and youle,
and make great dole for a gole,
that he loved well before. 433

SECU*NDUS* IEW.

If he had cu*n*ninge, me think, he might 434
from death haue saved lazar by right,

412 seene] since B. my] ny H. on] in B. 413 Boot] helpe W h. haue] a W h. done] *the rhyme requires the form:* do. 416 since] syth D. 417 leefe] deere h. 419 will] *om.* W h D. 420 if] and W h D. pro*s*ternat se] se pro*s*ternit H. pedes] pedes Iesus h. 426 you layd] yea done B W h. yee doune D. tells] tell it B, tell to W h. 428 is] was h. veniu*n*t] venient B h D, veniet W. p*ri*mus] prim*us* Iudeus W h. *Heading*] *om.* W h, primus Iudeus B D. 431 freak] fellow B. reem] weepe h. 432 a] *om.* W h D. 433 before] beforne *is required by the rhyme.* Iew] Iudeus B W h D. 434 If] *om.* D.

as well as send that man his sight,
that which so blynd was borne. 437

IESUS. (68)

haue done, and putt away the stonne! 438

MARTHA.

A, lord! iiij dayes be now gone,
sith he was buryed, blood *and* bone:
he stinkes, lord, in good fay. 441

IES*US*.

Martha, sayd I not to thee, 442
if th*at* thou leeved fullye in me,
gods grace soone shouldst thou see?
therfore doe, as I thee say. 445

(tunc deponent lapidem de sepulcro; et Iesus, tergum vertens, manib*us* levatis dicit:)

(69)

ffather of heaven, I thank it thee, 446
that so sone hast hard me!
well I wist, and soothly see,
thou hearest my entent. 449

But for this people that stand hereby, 450
speak I the more openly,
that they may leeue stidfastly,
from thee that I was sent. 453

(70)

Lazar, come forth! I bydd thee. 454

LAZARUS.

A! lord, blessed most thou be!
from death to lyfe hast raysed me
through thy mickle might. 457

Lord, when I hard the voyce of thee, 458
all Hell fayled of ther posty,

439 iiij] foure D. now] *om.* B W h D. gone] agone D. 443 leeved] loved H, beleeved B; *after* fully *in both, also in* D. 444 soone] soone that B. thou] *before* shalt B. shouldst] shalt B W h D. deponent lapidem] lapides deponu*n*t. levatis] elivat W. elavatis D. dicit] *om.* H, et dicat Iesus W h. *After stage-direction*] *heading* Iesus D. 446 it] *om.* W h. 450 stand] standeth W h. here] *om.* W. *Before* 454] *heading* Iesus D. 456 from] that from B. w*hi*ch from D. 457 thy mickle] thy great and mickle H, thie much B.

so fast from them my soule can flee,
all Devills were a frayd. 461

IESUS. (71)

Loose him now, *and* let him goe ! 462

MARTHA.

A ! lord, honored be thou oo,
that us hath saved from muche woe,
as thou hast ofte beforne ; 465
for well I wit, it should be so, 466
when you were full far me froe ;
the, lord, I honour, *and* no moe,
kneling upon my knee. 469

MARY. (72)

A ! lord Iesu, much is thy might ! 470
for now my hart is gladd and light,
to se my Brother ryse in my sight,
here before all thes meny. 473
Well I hoped, that soone in height, 474
when thou came, it should fare aright ;
thee, lord, I honour with all my might,
knelinge upon my knee. 477

MARTHA. (73)

A ! lord Iesu, I thank thee, 478
that on my Brother hast pitty ;
by very signes now men may see
that thou art god[e]s sonne. 481
Withe thee, lord, ever will I bee, 482
and serue thee with hart free,
that this day hast gladded me,
and alway with thee wonne. 485

460 can] could H. 461 a frayd] afright *is required by the rhyme.* 463 A] O B h. 464 hath] hast D. saved] waved H. 465 beforne] before W. 466 wit] wist D. 467 me] vs B, *om.* W h D. 469 knee] kneene D. *The similarity between* 468 *and* 476 *seems to have led the writers of all the MSS. to put* 477 *also after* 468, *while the rhyme requires here a line ending in* -orne. 470] O W h. 472 to] I B. my] *om.* B. 473 meny] men B W h D. 475 came] camest B. it] I W. fare] fall B. 477 knee] knees D. *Heading*] *om.* B W h D. 478 A] O W h. 480 signes] signe D. 481 that] *om.* h. 482 lord] *om.* H, *after* ever W D. 485 alway] alwayes h.

IESUS. (74)

Haue good day, my Deghter deer! 486
wherever you goe, farr or neer,
my blessinge I geue you here.
to Ierusalem I take the way. 489

finis Decimæ tertiæ paginæ.

---

pagina Decima quarta de Iesu intrante domu*m* Simonis Leprosi et de aliis rebus.

The Corv[i]sars.

IESUS. (1)

Brethren, goe we to Bethany, 1
to lazar, martha, and mary!
for I loue much that company,
thether now will I wend. 4

Symon, the leper, hath prayed me, 5
in his house to take Charity;
with them now it lykes me,
a whyle for to lend. 8

PETRUS. (2)

Lord, al ready shall we bee, 9
in lyfe *and* death, to goe w*i*th thee.
great ioy the may haue to see
thy cominge into ther place. 12

PHILIPPUS.

Lazar, thou raysed through thy posty, 13
and Symon also—messel was he—
thou clensed, lord,—that wotten we,—
and holpe them through thy grace. 16

Heading] *om.* D. 486 Deghter] daughter B, daughters W h, doughter D. 487 goe] *om.* H. or] and H. Decimæ tertiæ paginæ] deo gracias per me Georgi bellin W h (W *inserting* 1592 *after* gracias, h *reading* Georgiu*m*). paginae] *after* finis D.

The Corvsars] The coruisers pagent B, The Corvysors playe *put before the Latin* W h D. 3 that] their W h. 7 lykes] liketh D. 11 the] they D. *Heading*] philippe B W, phillippi h. 13 posty] pittie B W h D. 15 thou] then H h. *After* 16 *as stage-direction*] Tunc ibunt versus domu*m* Simonis leprosi B W h D.

SYMON. (3)

Welcome, Iesu, full of grace!
that me, that fowle *and* messel was,
all whole, lord, thou healed has,
over all for to show.

Well is me that I may se thy face,
here in my house, this poore place!
thou comforts me in many a case,
and that I full well know.

LAZARUS. (4)

Welcome, lord, [thou] swet Iesu!
blessed be the tyme that I thee knew!
from death to lyfe, through thy vertue,
thou raysed me not yore.

four days in earth when I had layne,
thou grant[e]st me, lord, lyfe againe;
thee I honour with all my mayne
now and evermore.

MARTHA. (5)

Welcome, my louely lord of leer!
welcome, my dereworth darling dere!
fayne may thy frend[e]s be in fere
to see thy frely face.

Sitt[e]s downe, if your will were,
and I shall help to serue you here,
as I was wont, in good manere,
before in other place.

(Tunc Ihes*us* sedebit et o*mnes* cu*m* ipso, et veniet maria magdalena cu*m* Alabastro vnguenti, et lamenta*n*do dicat:)

MARIA MAGDALENA. (6)

Welcome, my louely lord of leele!
welcome, my hart! welcome, my heale!

18 me] I W h. was] face B. 20 all for] all Lorde for B W. 23 case] place W. 29 had layne] lyne W, had lyne h. 30 lord] *om.* W, *after* lyfe h D. lord lyfe] helpe lord B. 33 of] and B W h D. 34 dereworth] deere W h. 36 frely] sweetlye W h. 39 in good manere] to serve you heare W. sedebit] sedebat W h. ipso] eo B W h D. veniet] venit W. cum] at cu*m* W, ac cum h. dicat] cica maria magdelena W, dicat maria magdalena B h. *Heading*] *om.* B. 42 my] in W.

welcome, all my world[e]s weale,
my boote *and* all my blisse! 44
from the, lord, may I not conceale 45
my fylth *and* my fault[e]s feale.
forgeue me that my flesh, so frayle,
to thee hath done amisse! 48

(7)

Oyntment here I haue ready 49
to anoynt thy swet body;
though I be wretched and vnworthy,
wayve me not from thy wonne! 52
full of synne and sorrow am I, 53
but therfore, lord, I am sory;
amend me through thy great mercy,
that make to thee my mone! 56

(Tunc pixidem aperiet, et faciet signu*m* vnctio*nis*, et rigabit pedes Iesu lacrimis, et tergebit capillis suis.)

SYMON. (8)

A, Iudas! why doth Iesus so? 57
me thinkes that he should let her goe,
this woman full of synne and woe,
for fear of world[e]s shame. 60
And if he very prophet were, 61
he should know her lyfe here,
and suffer her not to come him nere,
for payring of his fame. 64

IUDAS ISCARIOTA. (9)

Nay, Symon, Brother, sooth to say, 65
it is nothing to my pay,
this oyntment goeth so fast away,
that is so much of pryce. 68
This ilke Boyst might haue bene sould 69
for three hundreth penyes tould,

43 weale] Heale W. 46 fylth] fayth H. fayle D. 49 Oyntment] oyntement*is* B. here] *after* have D. 52 thy] the B. 55 great] *om.* B W h D. 56 make] makes B W h D. pixidem aperiet] aperiet pixidem B W h D. rigabit] capillis rigabit H h, *omitting all the rest of the stage-direction.* 58 thinkes] think H. 59 *and* 60] *inverted in* W. 61 were] be W. 67 so] to D. 69 ilke Boyst] oyle boxe W h. Iscariota] Iscariot*es* D.

and dealt to poor men, who-sere would,
and who-sere had bene wyse.

IHESUS. (10)

Symon, take good heed to me! Luke VII, 40.
I haue an arrand to say to thee.

SYMON.

Maister, what your will may be,
say on, I you beseech.

[IESUS.]

By an Exsample I shall thee showe,
and to this companye, on a roe,
wherby I saye, thou maie knowe,
to answere to my speache.

(11)

Two detters sometyme ther were,
oughten money to an vsurer;
the one was in his dangere
fyve hundreth penyes towld,
The other fifty, as I say here:
for they were pore, at ther prayer,
he forgaue them both in feer,
and nought take at them he would.

(12)

Whether of these two,—read if you can,—
was more beholden to *that* man?

SYMON.

Lord, as much as I can theron,
I shall say, or I passe.
fyve hundreth is more then fifty;
therfore me thinketh skilfully,
that he that forgaue more party,
more holden to him he was.

71 sere] so-ere B h, euer W, soever D. 72 sere] so Ever W h, so ere B, soever D. 75 your] you D. 76 Heading] *om.* B W h. Iesus D. 77—81] *om.* H. 79 maie] maist B. 81 sometyme] *after* ther were B. 84 penyes] poundes W. 85 the] they D. 87 *and* 88] *written as one line in* H. 88 them] *om.* H. take] toke B. at] of D. 89 you] thou B W h D. 89 *and* 90] *written in one line in* H. 91 as] as as H. 93 hundreth] hundrye B. 94 thinketh] thinke D. 95 forgaue] hee forgaue D. more] the more B.

IHESUS. (13)

Symon, thou deemes soothly, I-wisse. 97
sees thou this woman that here is?
sicker she hath not done amisse,
to work in this man*n*er. 100
Into thyne howse here thou me geet; 101
no water thou gaue to my feet,
she washed them w*i*th her teares weet,
and wyped them w*i*th her hear. 104

(14)

Kisse, since I came, thou gaue me none; 105
but since she came into this wonne,
she hath kissed my feet echon;
of wyping she never ceassed. 108
With oyle thou hast not me anoynt; 109
but she hath done, both foot and ioynt;
therfor I tell the one poynt:
much sinne is here released. (Ad Iudam Iscari*otam.*) 112

(15)

And Iudas, also to the I say, 113
wherto wouldest thou thee mispay
with this woman, by any way,
that eased me thus hase? 116
A good deed she hath done to-day; 117
for poor men you haue with you aye,
and me you may not haue, in fay, Joh. xii, 8.
but a little space. (Ad mariam magda*lenam.*) 120

(16)

Therfore, woman, witterly, 121
for thou hast loved so tenderly, Luke vii, 47, 48.
all thy sinnes now forgeue I;
belefe hath saved thee. 124
And all that preach the Evangely 125
through the world, by and by

100 in] on D. 102 gaue] gaue mee D. 103 teares] tear H. 105 me] *om.* B W h D. 108 wyping] weepinge B W h D. 109 anoynt] anoynted W h. *Stage-direction*] *in* H *in the margin, om.* B W h. 113 also] *after* the B. 114 thou] *om.* W h D. 116 thus] this D. 119 fay] good fay W. *Stage-direction*] *om.* W h D, ad mariam B.

of thy deed shall make memory,
that thou hast done to me.

MARIA MAGDALENA. (17)

My Christ, my comfort, and my kinge!
I worship thee in all thinge;
for now my hart is in lykinge,
and I at my above.

Seven Devills now, as I well see,
thou hast dreven now out of me,
and from foule lyfe vnto great lee
releved me, lord, for loue.

(Tunc surget Iesus, et stando dicat Discipulis suis, ut sequit*ur*:)

IHES*US*. (18)

Peter and Phillip, my Brethren free,
before you a Castell you may see;
goe you thither, and fetch anone to me
an asse *and* her fole also.

Loose them, bring them hither anon!
if any man gritch you as you gone,
and you say th*a*t I will ryde theron,
soone will the let them goe.

PETRUS. (19)

Maister, we shall doe yo*ur* biddinge,
and bring them sone for any thinge.
phillip, Brother, be we goinge
and fetch these Beastes two!

PHILIPP*US*.

Brother, I am ready bowne;
hye that we were at the Town!
great ioy in hart haue we mon,
on this Arrand for to goe.

(Tunc ibunt in Civitate*m*, et dicat petrus Ianitori:)

127 of] and of B W. 128 hast] hasse D. me] daye h (W *has* daie *crossed out*). 132 my] myne D. 133 as] *om.* h. 134 thou hast] hast thou B. dreven] removed H. now] *om.* B. out of] from H. 136 me] my B. surget] fraget W. discipulis suis] *om.* B W h D. 139 anone to] it B. 142 *first* you] ther H. 143 say] will saye h. 144 the] they D. *Stage-direction*] *om.* h, *in* H *in the margin.* petrus Ianitori] primuz Ianitor W. Ianitori] Ianitro D.

PETRUS. (20)

how! how! I must haue this Asse.

IANITOR.

here gets thou nother more or lesse,
But thou shalte telle me, or thou passe,
whether they shall goe.

PHILIPPUS.

My maister Iesu—leeve thou me—
thinks to come to this Citty,
and badd bothe brought to him should be,
hymself to ryde vpon.

IANITOR. (21)

All ready, goodmen, in good fay!
and sithe he will come to-day,
all this Citty I will say
and warne of his cominge.

Take Asse and fole, and goe your way!
for eche man of him marvayle may:
Lazar, that four days dead lay,
he raysed at his callinge. (Tunc ibit Ianitor ad Cives.)

(22)

Tydings, good men, every one!
the prophet Iesus comes anon!
of his disciples, yonder gone
twayn, that were now here.

for his marvayles aye leev vpon
that he is verye god[e]s sonne,
although he in this worlde wonne;
for ells it great wonder were.

PRIMUS CIVES. (23)

A! lord! blessed must thou be!
him will I goe now to see;

Heading] *om.* D. 154 gets] gettest D. thou] *before* getts B W h D. or] then D. 155 shalte] *om.* H D. thou] the B. 156] goe] gone *is required by the rhyme.* 159 to him] *after* brought B. 163 say] assaie W h. 164 cominge] conninge H. 167 Lazar] Lazarrous h. days] daye D. 173 aye leev] leeve aye B W h D. 174 verye] verylye H. 175 worlde] *om.* H D. 176 it great] *om.* B W h D. 178 to] and B W h D.

and so I redd that all we
hitherward take the way. 180

SECU*NDUS* CIVES.

ffellous, I leeue that Christ is he, 181
common from god in magesty;
ells such marvayels, as thinks me,
he ne dyd day for day. 184

TERTIUS CIVES. (24)

Lazar, he raysed, as god me save! 185
that iiij dayes hathe bene in grave.
therfore Devotion now I haue
to welcom him to this Towne. 188

QUA*R*TU*US* CIVES.

Branches of *the* palme Tree, 189
ech one in hand take we,
and welcome him to this Citty
with fayre procession! 192

QUINT*US* CIVES. (25)

with all *the* worship that I may, 193
I welcome will him to-day
and spread my Clothes in the way,
as soone as I him see. 196

SEXT*US* CIVES.

These mirackles apreven apeartly, 197
that from *the* father Almighty
he is common, mankynd to bye:
it may none other be. 200

P*RIMUS* PUER. (26)

ffellous, I hard my father say: 201
Ihe*sus* the prophet will come to-day;
thither I redd we take the way,
with Branches in our hand! 204

180 hitherward] thidderward D. the] our h. 185—189] *stand in* H *in the margin opposite to* 181—185, *as the scribe had omitted the four verses.* 185 raysed] saved W. as] so L W h. 186 iiij] foure D. hathe] had B. 194 will him] him will D. 195 the] his h. 197 apreven] approven B W h, preeven D. 200 none] no W, not D. 202 Ihesus] that Iesu B W h. 204 hand] Handes B W h.

SECUNDUS PUER.

Make we mirth all that we may,
pleasant to that lordes pay.
hosanna, I redd by my fay,
to sing that we fonde.

(Tunc ibunt pueri versus Ierusalem, cum ramis palmarum in manibus; et Cives prosternent vestimenta sua in via, et cantabunt "hosanna filio David! Benedictus, qui venit in nomine Domini! hosanna in excelcis!" Tunc Iesus, sedens super Asellam, videns Civitatem, flebit.)

IHESUS. (27)

Ha! Ierusalem, holy Citty!
vnknown to-day it is to thee
that peace thou hast! canst thou not see?
but Bale thou shalt abyde.

Much must thou dright yet some day,
when woe shall fall on every way
and thou begiled, sooth to say,
with sorrow on all syde.

(28)

Destroyed dilfully, dryven downe,
no Stonne with other in all this Towne
shall stand, for that they be vnleven
to keep Christes come,

And gods owne visitatïon,
done for mankynds salvation;
for they haue no Devotion,
ne dredë not his Dome.

(Tunc Iesus equitabit versus Ierusalem, et omnes cives pannos suos in via prosternent, et cum venerit ad Templum, de Asina descendens dicat vendentibus cum flagello.)

(29)

Doe away and vse not this thinge!
for it is not my lykinge.

205 Make] maye B. cum] cantantes hosanna cum B W h D. et cantabunt] *om.* B W h D. Iesus sedens] sedens Iesus W. *after* flebit] et dicat B D, et dicat Iesus W h. 209 Ha] A B W h D. 211 canst thou] thou canst D. see] fley h. 212 shalt] mvste W. 214 way] *om.* W, syde way H. 215 sooth] the south W h. 217 dryven] beaten W h. 218 this] the B. 220 come] coming B, commen D, commaundmente W, commaundementis h. 223 they] the D. 224 ne] nor W. drede] dreiden D. Ierusalem] civitatem B W h D. in] in in h. de Asina descendens] discendens de asina B W D, descendes de asina h. flagello] flagello et dicat Iesus h. 225 Iesus] *as heading before* doe A waye h.

you make my fathers wonninge
a place of marchandiye.

PRIMUS MERCATOR.

what freak is this that makes this fare,
and casteth downe all *our* ware?
came no man hither full yare,
that did vs such anye.

SECUNDUS MERCATOR. (30)

Out! Out! woe is me!
my Table with my monye
is spread abrode, well I see,
and nought dare I say.

Now it semës well that hee
would attaynë royalty;
ells thus bould durst he not be,
to makë such araye.

PRIMUS MERCATOR. (31)

It semës well he would be kinge,
that casteth downe thus our thinge,
and sayes, his fathers wonninge
in this Temple is.

Say, Iesus, with thy Iangling,
what Evidence or tokening
shewest thou of thy raygninge,
that thou darest now do this?

SECUNDUS MERCATOR. (32)

What signes shewest thou now here,
that thou prevës such power,
to shend our ware in this maner,
maisterly through thy mayne?

227 wonninge] dwellinge W h. 228 marchandiye] marchandise B W h, marchandize D. *Second* this] *om.* W h. 231 came] come W h D. *Heading*] Secundus mecator H. 233 woe is] woes W h. 238 attayne] attayne to H D. 239 thus] this D. 242 thinge] thinges D. 245 Iangling] janeling B. 248 now] *om.* H D, *after* thou W h. 249 signes] signe B W h. now] *om.* H, *after* signe W h, *after* signes D. 250 thou] *om.* W h D. such] of such B. 251 this] suche W B h.

IHESUS.

This Temple here I may destroy,
and through my might and my maystry
in dayës three it reedify,
and buyld it vp agayne.

PRIMUS MERCATOR. (33)

A, ha! Iesu, wilt thou so?
this word, as ever mott I goe,
shalbe rehearsed before mo,
and Cayphas I shall tell.

(Tunc Ihe*sus* eijciet cu*m* flagello eme*n*tes et ve*n*de*n*tes inquiens.)

Hye you fast this Temple fro!
for marchandise shall be here no mo;
in this place, be you never so thro,
shall ye no longer dwell.

IUDAS ISCARIOT. (34)

By deer god in maiesty!
I am as wroth as I may be,
and some way I will wreak me,
as sone as ever I may.

My m*aste*r Iesu, as men might see,
was rubbëd head, foot, and knee
with oyntment of more daynty
then I se many a day.

(35)

To that I haue great envy,
that he suffred to destroy,
more then all his good[es] thry,
and his Dam[e]s too.

Had I of it had maystry,
I would haue sould it soone in hye,
and putt it vp in Treasury,
as I was wont to doe.

255 reedify] Edifie B W h D. 257 A ha] Ah h. 258 this word] these word*is* B. 260 and] *om.* D. vendentes] videntes h. inquiens] *om.* B W h D. Iesus] *as heading before* 261 *in* B W h D. 262 marchandise] marchandes h. 266 *First* as] so W h. I] men h. be] see h. 269 might] maye W h. 271 oyntment] oyntmt*is* B.

(36)

What-seer was geaven to Iesu,
I haue kept, since I him knew;
for he hopës I be trew,
his purse alway I beare.

him had bene better, in good fay,
to haue spared Oyntment that day;
for wroken I will be some way,
of wast that was done theer.

(37)

Three hundreth penyes worth it was,
that he let spill[en] in that place;
therfore god geue me hard grace,
but him self shall be sowld

To the Iewes, or that I sytt,
for the tenth peny of yt;
and thus my maister shall be quitt
my grefe an hundreth fould.

(38)

Sir Cayphas and his company
conspyrne Iesu to anoy,
ther speach anon I will espye
with falched for to fowle him.

And if they gladly will doe, why!
I shall teach them to him in hye;
for of his counsell well know I,
I may best beguyle him.

(Tunc Iudas *pro* tempore discedit, et Cayphas loq*ui*tur.)

CAYPHAS. (39)

Lordinges, lookers of *th*e law!
herkins hither to my saw:
to Iesu all[e] men can draw,
and lyking in him hase.

281 seer] so Ever B W h D. 283 be] wilbe W h. 284 alway I] I alwaye D. beare] bare B W. 285 better] *before* had B. 286 to haue] had H W h D. 288 that] that that H. 289 penyes] peni B W h. worth] worthes W h. 299 espye] spie W h. 300 falched] falsshood D. him] his W. 301] they] the D. discedet] abiit B W h D. loq*ui*tur] dicit B W D, dicat h. 305 lookers] lokes W, looke h. of] on W h. 306 herkins] harcken W h. 307 can] maye W h. 308 lyking in him] lyken him in B.

If we letten him long gone, 309
all men will leeve him vpon;
so shall *the* Romans come anon,
and pryve vs of our place. 312

(40)

Therfore it is fully my redd, 313
we cast how he may be dead;
for if he longe on lyfe be lead,
our law goeth all to nought. 316
Therfore say ech one his counsayle, 317
what maner way will best avayle
this ilk shrew for to assayle;
some sleight ther must be sought. 320

ANNAS. (41)

Sir, you say right skilfully, 321
but need[i]ly men must espye;
by hym we catch no vilanye
to found and fowle to fayle. 324
ffor you know, as well as I, 325
ofte we haue fownded to doe him nye,
but ever he hath the victorye;
that no way may avayle. 328

PRIMUS PHARISEUS. (42)

yea, sir, in Temple he hathe beene, 329
and troubled vs [hathe] with much teene,
that, when we wended *and* did wene
of him to haue had our will, 332
Or ever we wist, he was away. 333
this maketh the people, in good fay,
to leue that he is Christ veray,
and our law for to spill. 336

SECUNDUS PHARISEUS. (43)

yea, lords, on poynt may doe gayne: 337
that lorden lazar should be slayne,

314 may be] best were B W D, were h. 317 one] *before* ech B. 318 way] a waye W h. of waye D. 319 ilk] same W. 322 need[i]ly] needesly D. 326 ofte] *om.* B. nye] anoye D. 328 no] we no W h. 332 our] our B, all our H &c. 337 gayne] againe W h.

for he raysed him vp agayne,
that iiij days had bene dead. St. Iohn XII, 10.

ffor that miracle, much of mayne,
to honore him ech one is fayne,
and Lazar, that dead was, will not layne,
and he on lyfe be leade.

CAYPHAS. (44)

No more, for sooth, will many mo
that he has made to speak and goe,
and blynd that haue ther sight also,
loven him stidfastly.

And followu him, both farr and near,
preching the people his power;
therfore my wytt is in a weer,
to ordayne remedye.

ANNAS. (45)

And remedy must ordayned be,
before this great Solemnity;
or ells may other, as well as we,
trusse and take our way. St. Iohn. XII, 13, 19.

for when he came to this Citty,
all *the* world, as you may see,
honoured him vpon ther knee,
as god had comen that day.

PRIMUS PHARISE*US*. (46)

Also, lordings, you saw theer
how he fared with our Chaffer,
cast it downe, god geue him care!
that was so great of pryce.

And also lowdly he can lye,
called the Temple apertly
his fathers howsë full falslye,
right as it had bene his.

340 iiij] foure D. 343 Lazar] Lazarus h. 349—353] *om.* B. 349 both] *om.* W. 350 the] to the W h D. 356 way] naye B D. 357 came] comes H D, come W. 358 may] might B D, *the reading of which is much corroborated by* came *and* honoured. 362 how] how that B W h D. fared] fareth W. our] *om.* B W h D. 367 falslye] falcsy H.

SECUNDUS PHARISEUS. (47)

Lordings, ther is no more to say, 369
but lost is our law, I dare lay,
and he come on our Sabaoth day,
that now aproches nye. 372

Heale he any, less or more, 373
all men will beleue on his lore,
therfore it is good to slay him before,
if that we will be slye. 376

CAYPHAS. (48)

Amonge our witt[e]s let vs see, 377
to take him with some subtilty:
he shall haue Siluer, gould, and fee,
this thing that would fulfill. 380

IUDAS.

Lordës, what will you geue me, 381
and I shall sonë help that he
Sleëly betrayëd bee,
right at your ownë will? 384

CAYPHAS. (49)

welcome, fellow, as haue I roe,
that Bargayn fayne would I goe to. 386

IUDAS.

Let me see, what you will do,
and lay downe siluer here; 388

for, *the* Devill Swapp of my Swyre, 389
if I do it without hyre,
other for Soverayne or Syre!
it is not my maner. 392

CAYPHAS. (50)

Say on, what we shall gevë thee, 393
to helpë that he taken be,
and here is ready thy money
to pay thee, or thow passe! 396

369 to] t ?, *or om.* ? B. 372 aproches] aprocheth D. 374 beleue] leeve B W h D. Iudas] Iudas Iscarioth h. 381 Lordes] lord H. 383 Sleely] Sleely that he B. 386] That bargane woulde I fayne knowe W. 389 Swapp] swope W h. 390 if] and B W h D. 391 *and* 392] *written as one line in* B. 391 Soverayne] swaine B.

IUDAS.

As ever mott I thryve or thee,
and I shew my subtilty,
Thirty pennyes you shall geue me,
and not a farthinge lasse.

PRIMUS PHARISEUS. (51)

yea, but thy troth thou must plight
for to serue[n] vs aright,
to betray thy maister through thy might,
and haue hear thy money!

IUDAS.

Haue here my troth, as I haue tight,
on fryday that, or it be night,
I shall bring him to your sight,
and tell [you] which is he.

PRIMUS PHARISEUS. (52)

you bene Brethren on a row,
which is he I can not know.

IUDAS.

now a very signe I shall you show:
aspyës whom I kysse,

and that is he, sooth to say;
takës him manly, as ye may,
And lead him sleëly away,
whether your lykinge is.

CAYPHAS. (53)

Now look thou serve[n] vs truly,
thy maisters cominge to espye.

IUDAS.

Trust well therto *and* sickerly,
that he shall not eschew.

397 ever] evill H. 398 *and* 399] *inverted in* H. 400 a] one h. 401 yea] nay B. thy] the B. troth] trueth D. plight] pighte W. 402 vs] is B. 405 troth] trueth D. tight] pighte W. 406 on] or H B h D. that] *om.* W. or] *om.* H D. 407 him] you B W h D. your] his B W h D. 411 now] *om.* H, noe D. 412 aspyes] espices W, aspyesye H. 414 manly] manfullye W. 418 maisters] maiste is W, master is B h. cominge] conninge H. to] vs to W h. 420 eschew] eskape W.

and, would god Almighty,
the kinge of ffraunce may so affye
In his realme or Bareny,
that they were all so trwe.

(54)

On fryday in *the* morninge,
espyës all on my cominge;
for wher that he is walking,
I will goe and espye.

with him I think to eate *and* drinke,
and after, Tydings to you bringe,
wher he shapës his dwellinge,
and come and tell you in hye.

finis Decimæ Quartæ paginæ.
Iulij 23. 1607.

Pagina decima quinta de cæna do*mini* et de eius p*ro*dicione.

The Bakers.

IHESUS. (1)

Brethren, all, to me right deere,
come hither to me, and you shall heare:
the feast of Easter, you know draweth neare,
and now it is at hand.

That feast need[e]s kepe must wee
with very great Solemnitye;
the pascall lambe eaten must be,
as the law dothe command.

421—425] *om.* W h. 422 may] might D. 423 his] this D. or] and D. 426 all] *om.* W h. cominge] conninge H. 427 that] as h. 427 *and* 428] *written as one line in* B. 428 espye] spye h. 430 bringe] to bringe D. 432 in] one B. paginæ] pagina *before* Decimæ B D. W *and* h *close with* finis deo gracias *per* me Georgi bellin, h *adding* 1600, W 1592 Come lorde Iesu Come quicklye 1592.

et de eius] et eius h. The Bakers] The bakers playe B W h D, *in the three latter MSS. before the Latin.* 4 now] how B. 5 need[e]s] *after* kepe B. 7 must be] mvste we W.

(2)

Therfor, peter, looke that thou goe, 9
and Iohn with thee shall be also;
prepare all things that belongeth therto,
according to *the* law. 12

PETRUS.

Lord, thy biddinge doe will we; 13
but tell us first wher it shall be,
and we shall doe it spedely,
and thither will we draw. 16

IHESUS. (3)

Goe into the Citty which you do se, 17
and ther a man meet shall yee
with a water-pott that beareth he,
for so you may him know. 20

Into what house that he shall goe, 21
into the same house enter you also,
and say 'the maister send you two,
his message for to shew.' 24

(4)

Say 'the maister to thee us sent, 25
to haue a place convenient,
the pascall lambe to eate ther is my intent
with my disciples all.' 28

a fayr parlor he will shew you; 29
ther prepare all things dwe,
wher I with my retinue,
fulfill the law we shall. 32

PETRUS. (5)

All ready, lord, even thy will 33
shortly we two shall fulfill,
and the fayr Citty we shall goe tyll,
as fast as we may. 36

(Tunc petrus et Iohan*n*es ibunt, et hom*in*em vas aquæ testaceu*m* portante*m* alloquerent*ur*, et an*n*untiabit eis domu*m* heri sui.)

10 be] *om.* B. 11 belongeth] longes B, longeth D. 22 enter] goe B. 23 the maister] *your* master B. 25 the maister] thie master B. 27 ther] *om.* B, *after* eate W h. my] his B. 28 my] his B. 29 shew you] you showe B W h D. *Heading*] Iohn W. et] ac D. alloquerent*ur*] alloquerentib*us* W. et an*n*untiabit . . . sui] *om.* D.

PETRUS.

all hayle, good fellow! hartely, 37
to thy maisters house, we pray the, hye,
and we must keep thee company,
our message for to say. 40

SERVUS. (6)

Come on your way, and follow me; 41
my maisters howse sone shall you se.
loe! here it is, verely;
say now what you will. (Tunc domu*m* intrant.) 44

PETRUS.

Sir! the maister saluteth thee, 45
and as messengers sent we be;
therfore we pray thee hartely,
take heed us untill: 48

(7)

The maister hath sent us to thee, 49
a place prepare for him must we.
the pascall lamb ther eate will he,
with his disciples all. 52

PATER FAMILIAS.

loe! here a parlour all ready dight, 53
with pavëd floors and windows bright;
make all things ready, as you think right,
and this, haue you shall. 56

IOH*ANNE*S. (8)

Now, brother Peter, let us hye, 57
the pascall lamb to make ready;
then to our maister will you *and* I,
as fast as we may. 60

PETRUS. (tunc, mensa pr*e*parata, reverte*ntur*.)

Thy commaundement, lord, done haue we: 61
the pascall lambe is made ready.

38 we] I W D. 39 must] will H. *Heading*] Servanns W h. *Stage-direction*] *in* H *in the margin*. 45 the maister] thie master B. 46 sent] send D. 50 prepare] preparde D. we] bee D. 59 then] and D. will] then will D. you *and* I] wee B. *Stage-direction*] *in* H *in the margin*, tunc adornant mensam et reuertunt (*sic!*) B W h D.

therfore come on, and you shall se,
and we shall lead the way.

IHESUS. (9) (tunc edunt.)

Now, brethren, goe to your seat;
this pascall lambe now let us eate,
then shall we of other things intreat,
that be of great effect.

ffor know you now, *th*e tyme is come
that signes and shadows be all done;
therfore make hast, that we may soone
all figurs cleane reiect.

(10)

ffor now a new law I will beginn,
to help mankynd out of his synne,
so that he may heaven wynn,
the which for synne he lost.

and here, in presence of you all,
an other sacrifice beginne I shall,
to bring mankynd out of his thrall,
for helpe him nede I must.

(tunc occu*m*bit Iesus, ac Iohan*n*es in suo gremio dormiet.)

IHESUS. (11)

Brethren, I tell you, by and by,
with great desyre desyred haue I
this passover to eate with you, truly,
before my passion.

ffor I say to you sickerly,
my fathers will, almighty,
I must fulfill meekly,
and ever to be bowne.

(tunc Ihe*sus* panem accipit, frangit, et suis discipulis dat, dicens.)

Stage-direction] *in* H *in the margin, om.* B W h D. 67 then shall we] and then we shall B W h D. 68 great] gretter H, greater D. 70 signes] figures H. 74 his] *om.* h. 78 an other] one other B. 79 his] *om.* H. *Stage-direction*] *in* H *in the margin.* occu*m*bit] accu*m*bit H, accumbet D. ac] et B. suo] *om.* B W h D. dormiet] dormit B W h D. 88 to be] to it be W h. *Stage-direction*] *in* H *in the margin.* panem accipit] accipit panem B W h, accipiet panem D. suis] *after* discipulis B W h D. dicens] dicens Iesus W.

(12)

this breade I geue here my blessinge, 89
take, eates, brethren, at my biddinge,
for leeve you well, without leasinge,
this is my body, 92

That shall dye for all mankynd 93
in remission of ther synne:
this geue I you, on me to mynd
aye after, euermore. 96

(tunc calicem accipiet in manib*us*, levatis oculis dicens.)

(13)

ffather of heauen, I thanke thee 97
for all that euer thou doest to me!
brethren, takes this with hart free,
that is my blood, 100

That shall be shedd on the tree; 101
for more togeather drink not we,
in heauen blis till that we be,
to tast that ghostly foode. 104

(tunc omnes simul edent, et Iudas Isca*riotes* manu*m* in patina habebit.)

(14)

Brethren, forsooth, I you say: 105
one of you shall me betray,
that eateth here with me to-day
in this company. 108

PETRUS.

Alas! Alas! and weale away! 109
who that may be, know I ne may,
for I it is not, in good fay,
that shall doe such anye. 112

90 take] takes D. eates] eates you H, eate D. 91 leeve] beleeve W h. 93 mankynd] mankyn *is required by the rhyme, and* myn *instead of* mynd. 95] *om.* W. 96 aye] here W. *Stage-direction*] *in* H *in the margin.* calicem] *after* accipit B W h D. levatis] *after* oculis B W h. elevatis *after* oculis D. dicens] dicit B, dicens Iesus h. 100 that] for this W, for yt h. 103 be] see h. *Stage-direction*] *in* H *in the margin.* omnes simul edent] edit et bibit cum discipulis B W h D. manu*m*] manus B, manibus h. habebit *before* manu*m* D. 110 ne] not B, nay D.

ANDREAS. (15)

hard it is for us all
to whom this case shall befall!
we be but twelue within this hall;
lord, tell if it be I.

IACOBUS.

Sorowfull for these words be we;
who it is I can not see.
if this case shall fall to me,
lord, tell me hastely. (tunc Iudas intinget in patina*m*.)

IHES*US*. (16)

Through his deceit I am but dead,
that in my cupp weets his bread:
much wo, for his wicked redd,
that wretch must thole, I-wis.

well were hym had he bene unborne!
for body and soule is both forlorne,
that falcely so hath done beforne,
and yet in will he is.

IUDAS. (17)

Leife maister, is it not I
that shall doe thee this villanye.

IHES*US*.

Thou hast read, Iudas, redely,
for sicker thou art he.

that thou shalt doe, doe hastely!

IUDAS.

ffarewell, all this companye;
for on an Arrand I must hye,
undone it may not be.

IHES*US*. (18)

Brethren, take up this meat anon,
to an other worke we must gone:

115 within] in W. 118 it is] ys yt D. *Stage-direction*] *in* H *in the margin.* intinget] intingit B D. patina*m*] patinam Iesus dicens W. 124 thole] hold B. 126 both] *om.* B h D. is] he is h D. 128 will] witt B. he is] is he W h. 130 thee] *om.* H. 132 sicker] suerlye W. 133 doe] doe it B. 138 we] we D, wo H.

your feet shall washen be echon,
to shew all charitye.

And first my selfe I will beginne,
and washe you all that be herein,
on this deed that you may mynne
and meker for to bee. (tunc Ihe*sus* pr*e*cinget corpus lintheolo.)

PETRUS. (19)

A! lord, shalt thou washe my feet?

IHES*US*.

That I do, peter, I the behight;
the whylë, more thou shalt not witt,
but thou shalt afterward.

PETRUS.

nay, lord, forsoth in no maner,
my feet shalt thou not washe here.

IHES*US*.

But I washe thee, withouten were,
of ioy getts thou no part.

PETRUS. (20)

Nay, lord, my feet may well be layd,
but washe my handës and my head.

IHES*US*.

All is clean, therfor doe my redd:
thy feet shall washen be;
and you are clean; but, not all.

PETRUS.

lord, of wayle thou art *the* wall;
and thoughe it do not well befall,
haue here my feet to thee.

(tunc lavabit pedes omniu*m* singulatim, et absterget lintheolo.)

139 washen] *before* shall B. 141 my selfe] my feete W h. 142 you all] all you B. pr*e*cinget] precingit B. lintheolo] lintheolo et dicite petrus W. 146 I do] doe I B W h D. 149 nay] No B. 150 not] ney W. 152 ioy] ioyes B. 153 layd] leade W h. 155 doe my] doe I B D, I doe W h. 157 are] *om.* B W h D. 159 do] *om.* B W D. *Stage-direction.* absterget lintheolo] abstergit lintheo D.

IHESUS. (21)

My deare brethren, well wytt ye, 161
that lord and maister you call me,
and well you say, as it should be,
I am and haue been yore. 164

Sith I haue washen your feet here, 165
lord and maister, in meeke maner,
doe echon so to other in fear,
as I haue done before. (tunc alius alios pedes lavabunt.) 168

(22)

My children and my brethren free, 169
little whyle I may with you be,
but thither shall you not goe withe me,
as I am now in way. 172

But this sothly is my biddinge: 173
you loue togeather in all thing,
as I before, without fleching,
have loved you truly aye. 176

(23)

So all men may know *and* see, 177
my disciples that you be,
falcehod if you allways flee,
and loven well in feer. 180

PETRUS.

Lord, whether art thou in way? 181

(IHESUS.)

Peter, thider as I goe to day,
come nye sickerly thou ne may,
this tyme, in no maner, 184

(24)

but thou shalt thider goe. 185

162 call] will call W h. 163 it] *om.* W D, I B. 166 lord] your lorde W h. 167 so] *om.* D. alios] *for* alius. *Stage-direction*] tunc Inuicem *omnes* aliorum pedes lavant B W h D. 169 children] brethren B, littill children W h D. 170 little] a littill W h. I may] maye I D. 173 is] *om.* B D. 175 I before] I haue before H. 177 may] *before* all B. 179 allways] ever h. 183 nye] *om.* D. 184 maner] mann*er* way B, manner a waye W h.

PETER.

Why shall it not, lord, now be so?
my lyfe I will [now] putt in woe,
and for thy sake be slayne.

IHESUS.

Peter, I say thee sickerly:
or the cocke hath crow[e]n thry,
thou shalt forsake my company,
and take thy word agayn.

(25)

Brethren, let not your harts be sore,
but leeve in god [for] evermore,
and in me as you haue before,
and care not for this case.

ffor in my ffather howse ther is — John xiv, 2.
many wonnings of great blisse;
and thider I will goe now, iwis,
to purvay you a place.

(26)

And though I goe from you away
to purvay a place to your pay,
I come agayne another day
and take you all with me.

THOMAS.

Lord, we wot not, in good fay,
what maner a gate thou wilt assay;
tell us, that we know[en] may
that gate, and goe with thee.

IHESUS. (27)

Thomas, I tell thee, without stryfe:
in me is way, soothenes and lyfe;
and to my father, no man ne wyfe
may come with-out[en] me. — John xiv, 6.

186 it not] not it W. lord now] *om.* W h. now] *om.* D. 190 hath] haue B W h D. 197 howse] *om.* h. 202 *second* to] for W h. 206 maner] *om.* W h. a] of B D. 210 way] very H. 212 me] *om.* W.

And if thou knew me verely
my father you might know in hye;
from hence forth, I say you sickerly,
know him all shall ye.

PHILIPPUS. (28)

lord, lett us see thy father anon,
and it sufficeth us euerychon.

IHESUS. John xiv, 8.

A long tyme you haue with me gone;
phillip, why sayest thou so?

Sickerly who seeth me,
seeth my father, I tell it thee;
why wills thou my father to se,
whyle I with you goe?

(29)

Phillip, leevest thou not this,
that my father in me is
and I in him also, I-wis,
and, both we be one?

The workes that I doe are his,
for his help may I not misse;
therfore, to win you heaven blis,
my deeds you leeve upon!

(30)

what so ever you aske my father deere
in my name, in good maner,
to fulfill it I haue power;
all that is to my pay, Iohn xiv, 13.

That my father in magesty
By me gloryfied may be;
and eyther, as I say to thee,
for one haue bene aye.

213 thou] you W h D. knew] knowe D. 214 might] maye h. 215 you] *om.* W. 221 Sickerly] suerly W. 223 wills] willest D. 229 that] *om.* W h. 231 therfore] wherfore W. 233 you] *corrected out of* I, *which is crossed out in* H. 235 it] it in W h. 236 to my] to his H.

(31)

If that you loue me hartely,
keep my byddinge tru[e]ly,
and to my father pray will I
to send you *the* holy ghost,

To abyde with you euermore,
for *the* world knoweth not his lore;
but you that haue known me yore,
in you he shall be moste.

(32)

Though I goe now to distres,
I will not leaue you comfortles;
but leev[e]s this well and expres,
eft I will come agayne.

And then yo*ur* hartes, on a roe,
shall gladly be my bliss to know,
which ioy shall no man take you fro,
would he neuer so fayne.

(33)

Ryse up! and goe we heathen anon; Iohn xvi. 5.
to my prayer I must gone,
but sit you still euerychon,
my father whyle I call.

Wakes, and haue my benison
for falling into tentation!
the spirit aye to bale is bowne, Matth. xxvi, 38.
and the flesh aye ready to fall.

(Tunc Iesus oratu*m* ibit, et Discipuli præ dolore dormient.)

IHES*US*. (34)

ffather of heauen in maiesty, Iohn xvii, 1.
glorify, if thy will be,
thy sonne that he may glorify thee
now, or I heathen wend.

241 hartely] hartefullie B W D. 242 byddinge] bidding*is* B. 245 you] *om.* B. 253—257] *om.* B. 253 roe] vow H. 254 be] *after* shall W h. 255 shall] *after* man W h D. 257 and] *om.* B. we] *om.* W h D. 259 euerychon] everych wonne D. 264 *and*] but B. aye] ever W, *om.* D. Iesus oratu*m* ibit] iit Iesus oratum B W h D. dormient] dormiunt B W h D. *Heading*] *om.* B W h. 268 heathen] hence B W h.

In earth thou hast geuen me posty, 269
and I haue done with hart[e] free
the worke that thou charged me, Iohn. xvii, 4.
and brought it to an ende. 272

(35)

Thy name haue I made men to know, 273
and spared not thy will to shew
to my disciples on a row,
that thou hast geuen me. 276

and now they know[en] verely 277
that from the father sent am I;
therfor I pray thee especially,
saue them through thy mercy! 280

(36) (Tunc ad discipulos redit, eos dormientes inveniens.)

What! slepe you, Brethren, all heer? 281
ryse up, and makë yo*ur* prayer
lest tentatïon haue power,
to make you for to fall. 284

The fleshe is, as I sayd before, 285
inclyninge aye to synnë sore,
and ghost occupied euermore,
therfore now wakës all! 288

(37) (Tunc iteru*m* ad oratione*m*, et alta voce loquit*ur*.)

My hart is in great mislyking Math. xxvi, 42. 289
for death that is to me cominge;
father, if I dare aske this thing:
put it away from me! 292

All thing to thee possible is; 293
neuertheles, now in this,
at your will I am, iwys;
as thou wilt, let it be. 296

277 now] that H. *Stage-direction*] Tunc venit ad discipulos et invenit dormientes et ait B W h D (ait] dicit W D, dicat h.) dormientes] eos dormientes D. 286 inclyninge] enclyned B. aye] *om.* W. 287 and] *and* so is B. 288 wakes] wake you B. loquit*ur*] loquitor dicit W. 291 this] thes H. 292 it] this W h D. 293 All] Eych D. thing] thing*is* B h. 294 now] yet W. 295 your] thy h.

(38) (Tunc redit ad discipulos.)

you slepen, brethren, yet, I see; 297
sleep[e]s on now all[e] yee!
my tyme is come, taken to be;
from you I must away. 300

He that hath betray[e]d me, 301
this night from him will I not flee;
in sory tymë borne was hee,
and so he may well say. 304

(Tunc Iudas cu*m* militu*m* cohorte, laternis, facib*us*, et armis veniet.)

IHES*US*. (39)

You, men, I aske: whom seek ye? 305

MALCHUS.

Iesus of Nazareth; him seek we. 306

IES*US*.

here, al ready; I am he!
what haue you for to say? 308

IUDAS ISCA*RIOTES*.

A! swet maister, kyssë me, 309
for it is long sith I thee see;
and, togeather we will flee,
and steal from them away. 312

IHES*US*. (40)

What seke you, men, with such a breath? 313

P*RIMUS* IEW.

We seeke Iesus of Nazareth 314
. . . . . . [eth]
. . . . . [ill] 316

IHES*US*.

I said yore, and yet I say: St. Iohn xviii, 8. 317
I am he! [and] in good fay,

discipulos] discipulos iteru*m* B W h D. 298 all yee] lette see h. 299 come] common D. 301 hath] *om.* B. veniet] venit illuc B W h D, W h *continuing:* et dicat. *Heading*] *om.* h. *Heading* Iesus] *om.* H. Iscar*iotes*] *om.* B W h D. 309 kysse] kysse thou D. 310 for] *om.* H. Iew] Iudæus B W h D. 314] *the apparent omission of two lines is not indicated in any of the MSS. by a blank space.* 317 said] say H W h D.

suffer thes men to goe ther way,
and I am at your will.

MALCHUS. (41)

ffalcë thefë! thou shalt gone
to Bishop Cayphas, and that anon,
or I shall break thy body and bone,
and thou be to late.

PETRUS.

Thefe! and thou be so bowld
my maister so for to howld,
thou shalt be quit a hundreth fould,
and onward take thou that!

(42)

Be thou so bould, as thryve I,
to hould my maister here in hye,
full dear shalt thou it abye,
but thou thee heathen dight.

Thy eare shall of, by god[e]s grace,
or thou passë from this place.
(tunc gladium extrahet, et Malchi auriculam abscidet.)
goe! playnt now to Cayphas,
and bydd him do the right!

MALCHUS. (43)

Out! alas! alas! alas!
by Cockes bones, myne Eare he has.
me is betyde a hard[e] case,
that ever I came here!

IHESUS.

Peter, putt up thy sword in hye! Math. xxvi, 52.
whosoeuer with Sword smiteth gladly,
with Sword shall perish hastely,
I tell thee withouten were. (Tunc Ihesus tangit auriculam, et sanat eam.)

323 and] or h. 326 so] *om.* h. 328 that] this W h. 330 hould] handle h. 331 thou] *before* shalt B W h D. *Stage-direction*] tunc extrahit gladium et abscidit auriculam malchi B W h D (extrahit] extrahet W h D.) abscidit] abscindet D. 335 playnt] *om.* W. 338 Cockes] Cocke H. 340 came] come D. 342 with] with the W D. smiteth] *before* with h. tangit] tetigerit B W h D. sanat eam] sanabit B W h D.

MALCHUS. (44)

A! well is me, well is me!
my eare is healed, now I see.
so me*r*ciful a man as is he,
knew I never non.

PRIM*US* IEW.

yea, though he has healed thee,
Shut fro*m* us shall he not be,
But to Sir Cayphas, as mot I thee,
with us shall he gone!

IESUS. (45)

As to a thefë ye come here,
w*i*th swords, *and* stauës, and armyre,
to takë me. in foule maner,
And end your wikked will. Luke xxii, 52, 53.

In temple whyl I was w*i*th you aye,
no hand on me would you lay;
but now is commen tyme and day,
your talent to fulfill.

PRIM*US* IUDEUS. (46)

Come, Caytafe, to Cayphas,
or thou shalt haue a hard[e] grace;
trott uppon a prowder pace,
Thou vyle pop[e]lard!

Though Belzebub *and* Satanas
Come to help thee in th*i*s case,
Both thy handës that thou hase,
shall be bounden hard!

finis paginæ decimæ quintæ.

From 345 *to the end*] H *writes two verses in one line* *Heading*] Malchus *om.* B. 346 now] well W. 347 as] now B, *om.* W h. 349—365] *om.* B, *without any apparent indication that it means the play to be ended by* 348. Iew] Iudeus W h D. 349 has] haue W h D. 352 gone] goe H D. 353 ye come] you came D. 354 swords] sworde W D. armyre] armerer W, armerye D. 357 whyl] when B h. whyl I was w*i*th you] w*i*th you when I was D. 364 vyle] vilde D. 367 handes] hand D. paginæ decimæ quintæ] deo gracias W h; W *adding:* *per* me Geo bellin 1592.

Pagina decima sexta de passione Iesu Christi.

The Boyers, fletchers, *and* Iremongers.

PRIMUS IEW. (1)

Sir Bishopps, here we have brought
a wretch, that much wo hath wrought,
and would bring our law to nought,
for it he hath spurned.

SECUNDUS.

yea, wyde-wher we haue him sought,
and dere also we haue him bought,
for, here many man[ne]s thought
to him he hath turned.

ANNAS. (2)

A! Ianglinge Iesu, art thou here?
now may thou prouë thy power,
whether thy cause be clean *and* clear,
thy christhod we shall knowe.

CAIPHAS.

me thinke, a maister if he were,
eyther for peny or prayer,
to shunt him[self] of this danger,
and such a sleight to show.

ANNAS. (3)

Sir Cayphas, I say sickerly,
we that bene in company,
must needs this Disabeard destroy,
that wickedly hath wrought.

Heading] The fletchers, bowers, Cowp*ers*, stringers, and iremongers pagina XVI B W h (stringers] and stringers W h. and iremongers pagina XVI] playe W h), The fletchers, Bowiers, Cowpers and Stringers Playe D, *followed by* Incipit pagina decima sexta et de passione Ch*risti* et primo venient Iudei, adducentes Iesu*m* ad annam et caypham, et primo incipiet, *om. first* et D. Iew] Iudeus B W h D, *so in all the headings throughout.* 2 hath] hase D. 4] right so at it hath he spurned B W h, right soe hath hit spurned D. *Heading*] Secund*us* Iudeus D. 5 we] *after* haue B. 7 mans] mens B W h D. 8 hath] hase D. 9 here] now here B W h D. 10 may thou] thou may D. power] postee power B W h D. 12 shall] must D. 13 maister if he] maistrye that it B W h D. 15 shunt] shutt B W h D. this] his W h D. 16 a] *om.* B W h D. sleight] sleight*is* B, *om.* h. 17—21] *om.* W D.

CAYPHAS.

It is nedefull, this say I,
that one must dyë, verely,
all the people to forbye,
so that they perishe nought.

TERTIUS IEW. (4)

Sir Cayphas, herken now to me:
this Babliant, *our* king would be,
what-sere he sayeth now before thee;
I hard him say full yore,

That prince he was of such posty,
destroy the Temple well might he,
and buyld it up in day[e]s three, **Matth. xxvi, 61.**
right as it was before.

QUART*US* IEW. (5)

yea, sicker, that I hard him say,
he may deny it by no way;
and also that he was god veray,
Emanuell, and Messy.

He may not nicke this nor say nay,
for mo then twenty, in good fay,
that in the temple were that day,
hard him as well as I.

CAYPHAS. (6)

Say, Iesus! to this what say yee?
thou wottest now what is putt on thee.
put forth, princë, thy posty,
and perceave what they preven.

What the Devill! one word speakes not he!
yet, Iesus, here I coniure thee,
if thou be gods sonne, before me
answare to that they meven!

Cayphas] Annas D. 21 It] S*ir* it B W h D. 22 must dye verely] man die witterly B W h D. 23 all] then all B. 24 so] and H. they] the D. nought] not H. 25 now] *om.* H. to] unto h. 26 Babliant] bablavant B W h, babelavaunt D. *our*] that h. would] *before* our D. 27 what-sere] whatsoever D. sayeth] sayes D. now] *om.* B. 29 such] *om.* H. 33 that] *om.* H. 34 deny it] not denie B W h D. 37 nicke] denye h, nye W. 38 twenty] fourtie B h D. 40 hard him] harden B W h D. 41 say] sayne D. 44 they] the D. preven] sayne H. 45 the] *om.* B W h D. Devill] devell of hell W. not] *before* on W h. 47 before] here before W. 48 they] the D.

IHESUS. (7)

As thou sayest, so say I:
I am gods sonne Almighty,
and hear I tell[e] thee truly,
that me yet shalt thou [i]se
Sit on god[e]s hand, him bye, Matth. xxvi, 64.
mankynd in clowd to iustifye,

OMNES SIMULL.

witnes all this company
that falcely lyeth hee!

CAYPHAS. (8)

You herken all what he sayeth here!
of witnes what need were?
for, before all this folk, in fear,
lowd[e]ly thou lyes.
what say you, men, that be here?

PRIMUS IEW.

Buffetts him that makes this Beer!
a new[e] law we shall him leer,
that our law so destroyes!

CAYPHAS. (9)

Destroy shall he not yt!
you, wretches without witt,
found this freak a fytt,
and gurd him in the face!

ANNAS.

Despyse him! spurne and spitt!
let se, or you sytt,
who hath happ to hitt
that us thus harmed hase!

(Tunc Iudei statuent Iesu*m* in cathedra, dicentes ut seq*uitur*.)

49 so] right so B W D, soe righte h. 52 shalt] shall D. 53 hand] right hand D. 54 clowd] cloud*is* B W h, clowdes D. *Heading*] *om.* B W h D. 55 *and* 56] *om.* h, *in* B W D *under the heading* Cayphas *and after* Iustefie, mary, fie on thie, fie (mary] *before* Iustiffye W). fie] fye fye D. all] of all B W D. 56 lyeth] lyes D. 57—62] *om.* h. 57 herken] heren B W D. 58 what] now what B W D. 59 this] these D. 61 that] that now B W D. 63] for to god maye he not be dere B W h D (maye he] he maye W.) 64 law] lawes B. 66 without] ye wanten B W h D. 67 this] that B W h D. 68 in] on W h. 70 let] let*is* B. 71 hath] hase D. 72 us] *after* thus B D. cathedra] cathedram B W h D. dicentes ut seq*uitur*] et dicat torquendo B W h D.

PRIMUS IEW. (10)

ffor his harmes here, 73
nigh will I neare
this same lewd feere,
that makes our law falce. 76

SECUNDUS IEW.

he is, but a were, 77
to the devill dȝer.
Spitt we in feere,
and Buffet him als! 80

TERTIUS IEW. (11)

you hard in th*is* plac now, 81
How he lyed has now;
in midds of his face now
fully will I fowle him. 84

QUARTUS IEW.

Passe he shall a pace now, 85
for god he him makes now;
getts he no grace now,
When I begyle him. 88

PRIMUS IEW. (12)

ffye on thee, freake! 89
Carpe now and breake!
thy breans will I breake;
am I ready bowne. 92

SECUNDUS IEW.

His face will I streake 93
with Cloth, or he break,
and us all wreak
for my waryson. 96

73 harmes] harming B W h D. 74 nigh] nygnahe D (?). will I neare] well I were B. 75 same lewd] fameland B W h D. feere] frere B D. 77 but] without B W h D. a] *om.* D. 78 deer] full deare B W D. 80 als] all B, elles W h. *Heading*] tertius Iudeus Exputans B W h D. 81 hard] harcken W h, herden him D. 83 midds of] mydest D. 84 fully] fowle D. fowle] fielle B h, fyle D (*probably right, as the rhyme shows*). *Heading*] Quartus Iudeus Exputans B W h D. 86 makes] *the form* mase *is required by the rhyme.* 88 I] I may B W h D. *Heading*] primus Iudeus dans alapam B W h D. 89 on] vpon D. thee] this W h. 90 Carpe] stowpe B W D, stope h. now] nowe nowe D. breake] creake D. 91 will I] to B W h D. 92 am] as B. *Before* 93] *as stage-direction:* tunc Secundus Iudeus dans alapam, velando faciem Iesu B W h D, W *adding:* et dicat Secundus Iudeus. 93 streake] steeke B W h D. 94 with] with a B W h D. or] ere D. break] creake D. 95 all] all to H.

TERTIUS IEW. (13)

And thou be Messy,
and loth for to lye;
who smott thee, Cry,
if thou be christ.

QUARTUS IEW.

ffor all his prophesy,
yet he fayles thry.
though my fist fly,
gettes he a fust!

PRIMUS IEW. (14)

though he him beshitt,
a Buffet shall bytt!
may no man me witt,
though I doe him woe.

SECUNDUS IEW.

he fayles for to flyte,
or ought to despyte.
for he has to lyte,
now must he haue moe!

TERTIUS IEW. (15)

And moe, if I may,
I shall soone assay:
haste thou large pay,
thou prince on thy pate!

QUARTUS IEW.

If he say nay,
I shall in fay
lay one; I dare lay,
it is not to late. (tunc cessabunt ab Alapis.)

100 if] yf that D. *Heading*] Quartus Iudeus percutiens B W h D. 101—105] *om.* W D. 104 gaue I not a fist H. *Heading*] *om.* W D, primus Iudeus percutiens B. 105 beshitt] skrike B W h. him beshitt] sore scrike D. 107 me witt] myne white D. *Heading*] Secundus Iudeus percutiens B W D. 109—113] *om.* W D. 109 he] him B h. for] *om.* B h. 110 despyte] despice B. 112 haue] hame H. *Heading*] *om.* W D, tertius Iudeus percutiens B h. 113 moe] moe yet B W h D. if] *om.* D. 115 haste thou] *and* shew B W h D. 118 in] hym W h. 119 one] *om.* H. 120 late] laike B. Alapis] alapis et dicat Cayphas B W h D (Cayphas] *om.* W).

CAYPHAS. (16)

Lordings, what is your best redd?
this man hase served to be dead;
and if he lightly thus be ledd,
our law clean will slepp.

ANNAS.

Sir, it is fully myne advyce,
lead we him to the hye justice,
Sir Pylat, that is ware *and* wyse,
and hase the law to keep.

(tunc Cayphas et Annas et Iudei adducent eu*m* ad pilatu*m*.)

CAYPHAS. (17)

Sir pylate! here we bringen one
that falce is, and our Elders fone,
Tribute may be geuen none Luke xxiii, 2.
to Cesar, for him here.

whersoeuer he and his fellows gone,
they turne the folk to them echone;
now aske we dome him uppon
of thee that hath power.

ANNAS. (18)

Sicker he is our Elders foo;
whersoever he goeth to or fro,
that he is Kinge and Christ also,
he preacheth apertly.

Wist Cesar th*at*, he would be woe,
such a man and we lett goe.
therfore to dome him we be throe,
lest he us all destroy.

127 that] *om.* B W h D. is] is both B W h D. *Stage-direction*] *in the margin in* H. adducent] adducant B W h D. eu*m*] Iesu*m* B W h D. pilatu*m*] pilatu*m* dicat caiphas B W h (caiphas] *om.* h.) Cayphas *as heading* D. 135 dome] donne here D. 136] lest he us all destroy H; *cf.* 146. thee that hath] that he hasse D. 137 foo] fone H. 139 Kinge and Christ] Christ and kinge D. 142 and] if W h. 143 dome] dampne D. *Between* 144 *and* 145] *under the heading* pilatus B W h D *insert:*

per vos, sir cayphas, 1
die vos, sir annas,
et sum desepte Iudas
vell atres in fuit. 4

cu*m* up, lordinges, I you pray, 5
and wee shall here what he will saye
amonest this fellowshipe here. 7

(1, 1 vos] vous W h D. 1, 2 vos] vous W h. 1, 3 desepte] dispte W, despte h, de septe D. 1, 4 vell] vel W h D. atres] a tres D. *Before* 2] pilatus W. *In* B h D *the two first, and two last lines of* 1 *are written as one line.*) 2, 7 amonest] amonge D.

PILATUS. (19)

What sayest thou, mon in misse aray ?
and thou be Kinge of Iewes, say.

IHESUS.

So thou sayes, as men heare may,
a kinge that thou me mase.

PILATUS.

No cause fynd I, in good fay,
to doe this man to death to-day.

CAYPHAS.

Sir, the people follow his way,
perverted them all he hase.

ANNAS. (20)

yea, all the land of Galaly — Luke xxiii, 5.
cleane turned to him hase he ;
therfore dome now ask we,
this falce man to doe downe.

PILATUS.

sith he was borne ther, as sayn ye,
to herode sone send he shall be,
ells reft I him his royalty,
and blemish his renowne.

(21)

Goes ! lead him to Herode in hye,
and say I send to iustifye
this man of which he hase maistry,
at his owne lykinge.

PRIMUS IEW.

him shall he haue hastely,
for lead him thider anon will I.

Heading] *om.* D. 145 misse aray] misserye W, mystarye h, miseraye D. 146 say] then saye B. 147 thou] *om.* B. as] *om.* D. 151 follow his way] us to mispaye B W h D. 152 perverted them] converted to him B W h D. 154 him] them H. 155 dome] downe D. now] *before* doome B. ask] of him aske B. 156 doe downe] be done H. 157 sayn] seene B W, sceyne D. 158 he shall] soone shall he B W h, shall he D. sone send] send soone D. 159 reft] waste D. 160 blemish] blemished D. 161 lead] leades D. 162 send] send him B W h D. 164 lykinge] lykonge H. 165 he] you W h. hastely] full hastelie B W h D. 166 for] and B W h D. will I] in hye h.

come then forth with thy sigaldry,
and speak[en] with the kinge ! 168

(tunc ibunt Duo Iudei cu*m* Christo ad Herodem.)

(22)

Sir kinge, here pilate hath you sent 169
a shrew that our law hase shent,
for to haue hye Iudg[e]ment,
or he heathen wende. 172

HERODES.

A ! welcome, Iesu, verament, 173
I thank pilate for this present,
for ofte tyme I haue bene intent,
after thee to sende. 176

(23)

Iesu, much I haue hard of thee ; 177
some sygne now fayne would I see ;
Giff thou from god in maiesty
be commen, tell us here. 180

I pray thee that thou say to me, 181
and proue here some of thy posty,
and much the gladder I must be,
truly all this yeare. (nihil respondet.) 184

(24)

What ! I ween this man is wood, 185
or ell[e]s dumbe, and can no good ;
Such a Stanold before me never stode ;
and stowt *and* stearn is hee. 188

Speak on, Iesu, for Cock[e]s blood ! 189
for pilate shall not, bye my hood,

167 then] thou B W h D. sigaldry] ribaldrye B W h D. 168 the] our B W D. cu*m* Christo] adducentes Iesu*m* B W h D. Herodem] Herodem et dicat B W h D, B D *and* W *adding as heading:* primus Iudeus. 169 pilate] sir pilate W. 171 hye] his B W h D. 172 heathen] hence a waye B W h D. 174 I] and I B W h D. for] of B W h D. this] his D. 175 tyme] tymes B W h D. I] *after* haue B. intent] in that intent B W h D. 176 to] for to B. sende] haue sent B W h D. 177 I] *after* haue B W h D. 178 sygne] vertue B W h D. now] *after* faine W B h D. 179 giff] yf B W h D. 181 that] *om.* B W h D. thou] *om.* D. say] saye now B W h D. 182 here] *om.* B W h D. 183 I must] would I B W h D. *Stage-direction*] *in* H *in the margin.* Iesus nihil respondebit D. respondet] resondet H ; B W h D *continue:* et Herodes dicat (Herodes] *om.* D (dicat] dicit W, *before* Herodes *as in* h). Herodes] *heading* D. 185 this] that B W h D. 186 no] not h. 187 Stanold] stalward B W h, scalward D. never] *om.* W *before* before B D. 188 and] So B W h D.

doe thee amisse. now mend thy mode,
and speak somewhat to me.

(25)

alas! I am near wodd for woe!
me think, this man is wondrous throw,
dumbe and deafe as a doted doe,
or frentick, in good fay.

yet since that pilate hath done so,
the wrath that was betwen us two, Luke xxiii, 12.
I forgeue him, no more his foe
to be after this day.

(26)

Cloth him in whytë for this case,
to pilate it may be solace,
for Iews custome before was
so to cloth men that be wodd,
(tunc induunt eu*m* veste albâ.) Luke xxiii, 11.
Or madd, as he now him mase,
as well semes by his face;
for him that hath lost his grace,
that garment is full good.

PRIM*US* IEW. (27)

haue this, Iesus, uppon thee,
a worshipfull weed as thinken we,
of the kingës leverye,
that on thee now is lifte.

SECUND*US* IEW.

putt thee forth, thou may not flee;
now art thou in thy royalty

191 thee] thie non B W h, the non D. now] but B W h D. 192 and] then B. to] with W h D. 193 near] ney W h B, *in the latter after* I. nigh D. 194 wondrous] wonder B W h, wonders D. throw] froe H. 197 since] sythen D. that] *om.* B. 198 betwen] betwixt B. 199 him] *om.* B W h D. 200 to be] *after* more W, *before* more h. 201 for] in B W h, for in D. 204 so] *om.* B W h D. be] were B W h D. *Stage-direction*] *after* 208 *in* B W h D. tunc induunt] tunc Iudei induent D. alba] alba et dicat B W h D. 205 madd] wood h. now] *om.* W, *after* as B D. him] hym selfe h. 206 semes] seemed h. 208 that] this B W h D. 210 thinken we] think*is* me B W h. 212 now is] *after* that B W h D. lifte] light B W h D. 214 thou] *before* arte B W h D.

Sir kingē herode—beleeue will ye !—
and grant mercy this gifte !

(Tunc redeunt ad Pilatu*m* cu*m* Christo.)

PRIM*US* IEW. (28)

Sir pilate, here the king hath sent
Iesus agayne, and sith he went,
he hath forgeuen his male intent
for thy deed to-day.

PILATUS.

yea, fault in him can I fynd none
nor herode, as seen is here upon,
therfore is best we lett him gone
whether he will his way.

SECUND*US* IEW. (29)

Nayle him ! we cry with on voyce,
nayle him, nayle to the crosse !

PILATUS.

you men, for shame ! be still your noyce !
my counsell will I say :

you know echone the maner,
deliuered must be a prisoner,
this feast that now aprocheth nere,
for honour of the day.

(30)

will you Iesus deliuered be ?

TERTIUS IEW.

Nay to suffer death worthy is he
and therupon cry all we,
and "Barabbas reserved."

215] S*ir* herod king, beleeve of thie B W h D. (of] on D. 216 this] *om.* W h. gifte] guyse h, guyste D. *Stage-direction*] tunc exeunt duo Iudei ad pilatu*m*, adducentes Iesu*m* in veste alba et dicat B W h D. 218 he] we D. 222 nor] ne B W h D. as] has W h. is] *om.* W h. seen is] seemes D. 225 Nayle him] nay nay B W h. Nay all all D. we] we all W, all we h. 226 him] *om.* h. nayle to] naile him to B D. crosse] *a form* croice *is required by the rhyme.* 227 be still] let be B W h D. noyce] naye B. 234 to] *om.* B W h D. death] the death B W h D. 235 all] *before* cryen B W h D.

PILATUS.

What shall I doe with Iesus here, 237
that Christ is called and kinge in fere?

QUARTUS IEW.

nayle him on Crosse, in all manere,
for so he hath deserved. 240

PILATUS. (31)

now since I see you so fervent, 241
and shapen that he shall be shent,
wash will I here, you all present,
waxe you neuer so wood. 244
you shall all witt, verament, 245
that I am cleane and innocent,
not for to sheed, in no intent,
this rightwyse mans blood. St. Matth. xxvii. 24. 248

(32) (tunc Pilatus manus suas lavabit et postea dicat.)

you prelates, here everychon, 249
what will you doe? lett him gone!

CAYPHAS.

Nay! nayle him to the crosse anone,
and dome him, or thou leave! 252

PILATUS.

take yee him that bene so gryme, 253
and after *your* law deme you him!

ANNAS.

Nay, it is not lawfull lyfe ne lymine
for us no man to reave. St. Iohn. xviii, 31. 256

PILATUS. (33)

what the devill of hell! is this to say? 257
Iesus tell me, I thee pray:

239 on] on the B W h D. 243 will I] I will D. you] in *your* B W h. you all] in *your* D. 246 cleane] clear H. 247 not] *and* B W h D. *Stage-direction*] tunc pilatus lavabit manus, et caiphas et annas recedent a pilato, et dicat B W h (manus] manibus W h. a] cu*m* W h D. dicat] dicat pilatus h D.) *Before* 249] *as heading* Pilatus B W h D. 252 dome] deme B W h D. 253 *and* 254] *om.* H *together with their heading.* 255 it] that D. lyfe] lyth B W h D. lymine] lymme D. 257 the] *om.* B W h D.

art thou kinge—say yea or nay!—
of Iews by Ancetry?

IHESUS.

whether hopes thou it so be,
or other men towld thee of me?

PILATUS.

Ma fay! thy self may know *and* see
that no Iew am I. St. Iohn xviii, 35.

(34)

men of thy owne nation
shewe for thy Damnation
with many accusation,
and all this day so han.

Art thou kinge, say for all ther cry.

IHESUS.

My realme in this world, as say I,
is not, but if it weer, witterly,
with Iewes were I not tane.

(35)

And if my realme in this world were,
stryve with you I would now here,
and lead with me such power,
should pryve you of your pray.

But my might in this manere
will I not proue, ne now appear
as worldly kinge, my cause unclear
were then, in good fay.

PILATUS. (36) St. Iohn xviii, 37.

ergo a king thou arte or was.

IESUS.

That thou saies, it is no lesse,
But now I tell thee here expresse
That king I am *and* be maye.

262 thee of me] it thie B W h D. 263 Ma] May B, naye W h D. 266 shewe] shuen (*for* suen?) h. 267 many] many an D. 268 so] *om.* D. han] haue B W h D. 269 say] *om.* B. 268 *and* 269] *written as one line in* H. 271 not] nowe D. if] *om.* B W h D. it] *after* were B W h, *om.* D. 274 I would] *before* with B h D. 277 my] *om.* H. 278 ne] nor W h. 281—289] *om.* H. 284 be maye] maye be W.

In world I came to bere witnes
of southnes, therfore borne I was;
And all that lyven southnes,
Take heede to that I saye!

PILATUS. (37)

what is sothnes, tell thou me.

IHESUS.

Soothnes comes from Gods see.

PILATUS.

In earth then truth hath no posty
By thyne opinion?

IHESUS.

How should truth in earthe be,
whyle so demed in earth is he
of them that haue Aucthoryty
in earth agayne reason.

PILATUS. (38) St. Iohn xviii, 38.

lordes, I fynd no cause, iwys,
to dome this man that here is.

CAYPHAS.

pilate, he hath done much amis;
let him neuer passe.

By Moyses law leeven we,
and after that law dead should he be,
for apertly preached has he
gods sonne that he was.

ANNAS. (39) St. Iohn xix, 12.

yea, pilate he that makes him peere
eyther to kinge or kings feere,
withsayes Cesar of his power,
and so he hath with him;

286 therfore] and therfore D. 287 lyven] leeven D. 290 comes] came B W h D. 291 hath] *after* then B W h D. 292 By] in W. 293 truth] *om.* D. in] *om.* D. 295 haue] haue non B W h D. 297 lordes] lording*is* B W h D. 298 dome] dampne D. here] now here B. 301 leeven] liven D. 302 should] shal B W h D. 305 peere] a pere B W h, appere D. 307 withsayes] doth faith W. 308 so he hath] wee haue done B W h. so we have donne D.

for who so calls him kinge hear, 309
depryvis Cesar of his power.

PILATUS.

anon goe scourge this losenger,
and beat him leith and lym! 312

FIRST IEW. (40)

Come now, with care, 313
ffreak, for thy fare
on thy body bare
stroks shalt thou beare! 316

SECOND IEW.

cast of th*is* ware 317
of all thy clothes yare,
start now and stare!
thee, stanold, I steer. (tunc spoliabunt eu*m* et ad Columna*m* ligabunt.)

THIRD IEW. (41)

Now is he bownden; 321
be he never so wounden,
sone shall he be fownden
with flapps in feere. 324

QUARTUS IEW.

In woe shall he be wonden, 325
and his graynes grownden;
no ladd unto London
such law can him leere! 328

(tunc flagellabunt eu*m* et postea induent cu*m* purpura sede*n*te*m* in Cath*edra*.)

FIRST IEW. (42)

Now since he king is, 329
quaynt his clothing is;

309 for] and B W h D. him] him self a B W h D. 310 depryvis] reves B W h D. 312 leith and lym] limm *and* lithe H B D. *Heading*] primus Iudeus D. 314 for] with H. *Heading*] Secund*us* Iude*us* D. 317 th*is*] thie B W h D. 318 of] *om.* B D. 320] this stalward I would stere B W h D (would] will W h). eum] ip*sum* B W h D. ligabunt] *before* ad B W h D. *Heading*] *preceded by* et dicat B W h D. Terti*us* Iudeus D. 321 is he] he is B W h D. 322 wounden] wondon D. 323 shall he be] he shalbe B W h D. 325 shall he be] he is B W D, he was h. wonden] wounden D. 326 graynes] graue is B W h D. *Stage-direction*] *om.* W h. tunc postq*uam* flagellauerunt eum, postea induu*nt* purpurea potentes in cathedram et dicat primus B D. (postq*uam*] postea qua*m* D. (induunt] Induunt eu*m* D. (potentes] ponentes D. (primus] prim*us* Iudeus D. 329 king] konge H. 330 quaynt] whainte B, whante h, whyte h D. clothing] clothis H.

Begger, to thee I bringe this,
for this thou shalt beare.

SECOND IEW.

All of Heathing this is,
and of owld spinge is,
of thorns the thing is,
thee for to weare. (Cu*m* Corona spina.)

THIRD IEW. (43)

now thou hast a weed,
haue heer a reede,
Scepter I thee beede,
a king for to be. (tradet sibi ar*un*dinem.)

FOURTH IEW.

hark! take heed:
this must I need
for my fowle dede
knele on my knee. (tunc flectant genua.)

FIRST IEW. (44)

hayl, kinge of Iews,
that so many shrews!
ribald the rwes
all this reuerence.

SECOND IEW.

with spowld on him spues,
and his hyde hewes,
annoynting thy brows
for thyn offence.

331 I bringe] *before* thee B W h D. to] *om.* B W h D. 332 for this thou shalt] thie for to B W h D. beare] weare B W h D. *before* 333 *as stage-direction*] tunc secu*n*du*s* Iudeus ponens coronam spina*m* sup*er* caput eius et dicat B D. (spina*m*] spineam D. (caput] capite D. *Heading*] Secu*n*du*s* Iudeus D. 333 Heathing] lething B, lythinge h D, *a word ending in* -ing *ought to stand before* is. of] in B h D, ye W. 334] That of old sprong is B W h D. 335 the] this B W h D. *Stage-direction*] *in* H *in the margin, om.* W h D. *Heading*] Tertiu*s* Iudeus D. 339 Scepter] a scepter D. *Stage-direction*] *in* H *in the margin, om.* B W h D. *Heading*] Quartu*s* Iudeus D. 341 hark] hevie B, Harvye W h D. 342 this] thus D. 343 my] thy H. 344 on] upon B W h D. my] *om.* D. *Stage-direction*] *in* H *in the margin, om.* B W h D. *Heading*] primu*s* Iudeus D. 346 many] manie men showes B W (showes] rewes W), many men D. 347 the] now thie B h D. rwes] reaves B. 348 all] with all B W h D. this] thy D. *Heading*] Secu*n*du*s* Iudeus D. 349] with yron on him hewes B W h D. 351] anoyntment the newes B W h D.

THIRD IEW. (45)

to spitt in thy face, 353
that thee kinge mase,
now my nose hase
good spice, of the new. 356

FOURTH IEW.

with a hard grace 357
thou came to this place;
pass now the rase,
sore shalt thou rewe! 360

PILATUS. (46)

lordinges, here you may see 361
your kinge all in his royalty!

CAYPHAS.

Nay, sir, for sooth no king haue wee **St. John xix, 15.** 363
saue *the* Emperour of Rome.

but thou neile him to the tree,
the Emperour full wroth will be. 366

ANNAS.

All we say, right as sayeth he:
deme him whyle thou hast teme 368

PILATUS. (47)

whether of them would ye hane, 369
Christ Iesu or Barabban?

CAYPHAS.

Nay Iesu, that traytor that is tane,
must neiled be on the tree, 372
and let Barabbas goe his way. 373

Heading] Tertius Judeus D. 353 to spitt in thy] to write in his B W h D. 354 that thee] the that B, thou that W h, thou that the D. mase] then was B. 356] good Ostern (?) . . . new H. *Heading*] Quartus Iudeus D. 359 now the] thou this B W h D. 360 sore] so euer H. 361] Come hether lordingis ye may see B. 363 haue wee] is he H. 364 Rome] Rome perdee B W h D. 365 but] and but W h D. to] unto B. 366 full] *om.* B W h. 368 teme] tyme B W h D; *the rhyme requires* tome. 369 would] will B W h D. 370 Christ Iesu] Iesus Christ D. 371 that] this B W h D. tane] here h. 372 on] unto B, to D.

PILATUS.

takes him forth then, as you say;
for saue him, I see, I ne may,
undone but I should be. (tunc Iudei capiunt Iesum.)

FIRST IEW. (48)

This Dome is at an ende;
now I redd us to wende,
this shrew for to shend,
a little here besyde.

SECOND IEW.

heer shalt thou not lend,
come hither *and* be hend,
thy back for to bend,
here may thou not abyde. (tunc ibunt versus montem Calvariæ.)

CAYPHAS. (49)

Now of this Sager we bene sicker,
against vs him boots not to bicker,

374 forth then] to you now B W h D. you] I B W D. 375 I see] *om.* B W h D. 376 should] would B W h D. *Stage-direction*] *om.* B W h D. *Heading*] primus Iudeus D. 377 Dome] donne D. 378 I] *after* read B W h D. us to] that wee B W h D. *before* 381] Secundus Iudeus ponens crucem super dorsum eius dicat B h D (ponens] ponet h, eius] et h.) *Heading*] Secundus Iudeus D. 382 be hend] behind D. 384 here] he B, hit W. *Stage-direction*] *om.* W D, *in* H *in the margin.* *after* 384] B W h D *insert the scene of Christ's betrayal by Peter, with which in these four MSS. the* 16*th pageant ends.*

THE DAMSELL DOTH SPEAK TO PETER.
was not thou with Iesus of nazareth?

PETER.

I know him not nor what thou saith.

DAMSELL.

Sires, seckerly, I tell you plaine:
this man here is one of them,
That was with him in the garden,
I know it to be true.

PETER.

It is not true, so mote I thee!
I know him not, by any degree.

THE IEW.

One of them thou arte assuredlie,
and thou art also of gallilie,
thie spech clerelie bewrayeth thie
in witnes of us all.

PETER.

In faith *and* truth, that is not so.
shame haue I *and* mickle woo,
yf euer I did him before know
or kepe him companie!

B W h *add:* Thende of this story is finished in the next leaf; D *adds* finis paginae decime sextae. This storye is finished in the leaves followinge. W *and* H *adding, besides that:* finis deo gracias; *and* W *alone:* per me Georgi Bellin. Come lorde Iesu, Come quicklye, 1592.——(1*st heading* doth speake] *om.* B h D. 2 saith] sayest D. Damsell] the damsell D. 9 them] then D. 13 not] no D. finished] begannan W. leafe] leafes h, B *and* h *adding:* folowinge.)—385 *begins a new play in* B W h D, *under the following superscription:* The Iremongers play. Incipit pagina de crucifixione christi et de his que fuerant in eundo versus locum calueri et incipit Caiphas. (Iremongers] Irenmongers D. (que fuerant] qui fuerunt D. 385 Sager] segger D. 386 against] all againste W h. him boots not] bote he not B W h D. bicker] lecker ? B.

though he flyte, flatter, or flicker,
this fytt shall he not flee.

Thou, Iesu, would thou be our kinge?
goe forth! evill ioy the winge!
for wrocken on thee at *our* lykinge
full sone shall we be.

(50)

Gurde him fast, *and* make him goe,
this freak that hath bene *our* foe,
for all his wiles from th*i*s woe
shall no man him weare.

ANNAS.

him semes wery of his way;
some help to gett I will assay,
for this crosse, in good fay,
so farr may he not beare.

(51)

Come hither Symon of surrey,
take this crosse anon in hye,
and to the mount of Calvary
helpe that it were borne.

SIMON DE CIREN.

The devill speed all this companye!
for death he is not worthy.
for his sake, sickerly,
I howld you all forlorne.

(52)

To bear no Crosse is my entent,
for it was neuer my assent
to p*ro*cure this prophetts Iudgment,
full of the holy ghost.

387 flyte] flyre D. or] and D. 388 fytt] fiste D. 389 *second* thou] *om.* B W h D. 390 ioy] Iohn B. winge] wringe D. 391 on] of h. 393 1st him] one B W h D. make] lett H. 394 hath bene *our*] is *our* Elders B W h D. 395 his wiles] this whyle H. 396 weare] warne B W h D. 397 of] on W. 400 may he] he maye B W h D. 401 of surrey] Sirrye H. 402 take] *and* take B W h D. 403 and to] unto B W h D. de Ciren] *om.* B W h D. 405 all] *om.* W h D. 409 is my] ame I B W h D.

CAYPHAS.

Symon, but thou wilt be shent, 413
and suffer payne *and* prisonment,
this crosse upon the backe thou hent,
and lett be all thy boast! 416

SIMON DE SIREN. (53)

alas! that ever I hither come! 417
would god I hadd bene in Rome,
when I the way hither nome,
thus to be anoyed! 420

but lord I take to witnes 421
that I doe this by distres.
all Iewes for this falcenes
I hope will be destroyed! (tunc Cruce*m* accipiet.) 424

ANNAS. (54)

haue done! bring forth those theues two! 425
on eyther syde of him shall they goe,
this Sir shall be honored so
with fellowship in feere. 428

Takes him here bounden fast, 429
while a whipcord here will last.
pryme of the day is past,
how long will you be here? 432

(tunc Iesu*m* et duos latrones abducent et venient mulieres, quaru*m* dicat prima.)

PRIMA MULIER. (55)

alas! alas! and woe is me! 433
a dolefull sight is it to se:
so many sick saved hath he,
and now goes thus a way! 436

414 prisonment] Imprisonment W h D. de Siren] *om.* B W h D. 418 in] at W. 419 nome] come B W h D. 421 lord] god B W h D. 422 *and* 423] *inverted in* H. 423 Iewes] I wise B W h D. for this] through yo*ur* B W h D. *Stage-direction*] *in* H *in the margin*, *om.* B W h D. 425 those] these W h. 426 on] *om.* h. syde] halfe B h D. of] *om.* B W h D. they] *before* shall B W h D. 427 Sir] freke B W h D. honored] handled B W h D. *Before* 429] *as heading* primus Iudeus B W h D. 429 him] them B W h D. 430 a] this B W h D. here] *om.* B D. will] may B W h D. 431 pryme] for the prime B W h D. 432 will you] shall wee B W h D. *Stage-direction*] *om.* B W h D. *Heading*] prima Maria B W h D. 434 dolefull] dilfull B W h. is it] this is B D, is this W h. 435 sick] *om.* H. 436 thus] his H, this W h D. a way] waye D.

SECUNDA MULIER.

Sorowfull may his mother be 437
to witt the flesh, so fayr and free,
nayled so fowle upon a tree,
as he must be to day. 440

IHESUS. (56)

yee women of Ierusalem, 441
weeps not for me, nor makes no swem,
but for your own Barnteame
you may wepe tenderlye. 444

ffor tyme shall come, without weer, 445
ye shall blesse Belye th*a*t never Child beare,
and papps that never milk came neare,
so much is your anoy. (tunc ibunt sup*er* mo*n*tem.) 448

CAYPHAS. (57)

haue done, ye Tormentors, tyte!
spoyl him that hath done us spyte! 450

PRIMUS IEW.

yea, though he both pisse and shyte,
out he shalbe shaken. 452

be thou wroth, be thou fayne, 453
I will be thy Chamberlayne:
this Coat getts thou never agayne,
and I be waken. 456

SECUND. (58)

This Coat shall be myne 457
for it is good *and* fyne,
and Seam is ther none within,
that I can see. 460

Heading] the second mary B, Secunde Maria W h. Sec*un*da maria D. 438 witt] see B W h D. the] thy W D, his h. flesh] flecke W. 439 so] *om.* W h. 440 must] mon B W h D. 442 weeps] weepe D. nor makes] ne make D. swem] mone B. swene D. 444 may] mon B W h D. wepe] reme W D, rue B. 446 ye] they H. 447 Belye] ball B W, bale h. 448 much] nigh B h D, niche W. *Stage-direction*] *om.* B W h D, *in* H *in the margin.* 449 haue] hase W, haste h. ye] you D. 450 spoyl] and spoyle B W h D. us] you B. Iew] Iudeus D. 451 pisse and shyte] growne and skrike B W h D. 453 wroth] wroth or B W h D. 456 I] I may B W h D. Secund] Sec*undus* Iudeus B W h D, *and so everywhere, where* H *has the English number.* 459 ther none within] non therein B W h D.

THIRD.

yea, god geue me pyne,
and that shalbe thyne!
aye thou art enclyne
to draw toward thee.

FOURTH. (59)

nay, fellow, by my fay,
at the Dyce we will play,
and ther we shall assay
this weed for to wynne.

FIRST.

yea, fellow, by my fay,
well canst thou say!
lay forth thes Cloths, lay
on Board, or we blinne!

(tunc spoliabunt Iesu*m* vestibus, et stabit nudus, q*u*ovsq*ue* sortiati *sunt.*)

SECOND. (60)

fellow, now letts se,
here are Dyce three,
which of all we
shall wynne this ware.

THIRD.

Nay parted it shalbe—
for that is equitye—
in fowr p*ar*ts as mott I thee,
or we heathen fare.

FOURTH. (61)

this coat with out seame
to break it were sweme;
for in Ierusalem
ther is none suche, verament.

463 aye] for B W h D. art] art euer B W h D. 465 fellow] fellowes h D. my fay] this daye B W h D. 469 yea] A, B W h D. my fay] this daye B W h D. 470 canst] can D. 471 thes] those W h D. *Between* Cloths *and* lay] *there is a little hole in the page, but nothing seems to be lost.* 472 we] you W. *Stage-direction*] *om.* B W h D. 473 fellow] fellowes B W h D. letts] let D. 477 parted] departed H. it] they D. 478 equitye] egallie B W h D. 479 in fowr parts] therefore B W h D. 481 with out] bout B W h D. 482 sweme] shame B W h D. 483 in] in all B W h D. 484 ther] *om.* B W h D. verament] a garme*n*t B W D, one other h.

FIRST.

his Dame now may dream 485
for her Barnteam,
for neyther Aunt nor Eame
getts this garment. 488

SECOND. (62)

his other Clothes all 489
to vs fowr mon fall,
first part them I shall,
and after Dice for this. 492

This Kirtell myne I call, 493
and take thou this pall,
each man in this hall
wotts I do not amisse. 496

(63)

this corsett take to thee, 497
and thou this to thy fee
eche man may see
that all we be served. 500

THIRD.

yea, I redd now that we 501
sytt down, so mott I thee!
and loke whos this shall be,
that is here reserved. (tunc sedebunt om*ine*s.) 504

1 FYRST. (64)

now will I beginne 505
to cast, or I blynne
this coate for to wynne,
that is good and fyne. (Iacet et perdit.) 508

486 her] her owne B W h D. 487 neyther] nother D. 488 this] this gay B W h D. 490 mon] can W h D. 491 part] depart H. 492 Dice] play B W h D. 494 and] *om.* B W D. 497 corsett] kirtell B W h D. 497 *and* 498] *have in* W *in the margin the stage-direction:* ad Secundus, *and* ad Tercium; *in* D, ad tertiu*m and* ad quartu*m*. 499 may] now may B D, maye nowe W h. 501 now] *after* yea B W h D. 502 so] as B W h D. 503 loke] *om.* H. *Stage-direction*] *om.* W, tunc omnes sedent B h D, B D *continuing:* et dicat primus Iudeus, iactans alias (alias] decios D. 506 to] for to B W h D. 508 good] both good D. *Stage-direction*] *om.* B W h D, *in* H *in the margin.*

2 Second.

By my father kynne 509
no part hast thou in!
but or I heathen twynne,
this coat shall be myne. 512

(65)

Take here, I darr lay, 513
a Rowndfull, in good fay. (Iacet et perdit.)

3 Third.

Thou fayles, by my fay,
to haue this to thy fee. 516
for it was Cater trey, 517
therfor goe thou thy way,
and as well thou may,
And leave it with me! (Iacet et perdit.) 520

4 Fourth. (66)

fellows, verament, 521
I redd, you all assent,
this gay garment,
that is with out seame, 524
you geue, by my Iudgment, 525
to me, this vestament;
for since god has sent,
think ye neuer so swem. (Iacet et vincit.) 528

First. (67)

as haue I good grace, 529
wonne it thou hase,
for synnes ther was,
ech man might see. 532

509 father] fathers D. 510 hast] hasse D. in] there in B W h D. 511 twynne] wine B W h. wynne D. 514] are Dublett*es* in good array B W h D. *Stage-direction*] *om.* B W h D, *in* H *in the margin.* 515 by] fellow by B W h D. 517 it was] her is B W h D. Cater] Sater H. trey] tray B W, tree h. 519 and] for B. 519 *and* 520] *written as one line in* H. 520 it] this B W h D. *Stage-direction*] *om.* B D, *in the margin in* H. 522 you all] wee be at one B W h D. 524 with out] boute W h D. 525 you] nowe W. my] *om.* B W h D. 526] *om.* W h. 527 since] syyes H, synnes W h D. has] hath me B W h D. 528 so swem] to wine B, so sweene D. *Stage-direction*] *in* H *in the margin*, *om.* B W h D. 530 wonne] well wonne B W h D. 531 synnes] synke D. 532 ech] that eu*er* B, that everye W h D. might] maye W h.

CAYPHAS.

Men, for Cockes face! 533
how longe shall poydrace
stand naked in this place?
goe, neyles him to the Tree! 536

SECOND. (68)

anon, maister, anon; 537
a hammer haue I one,
as farr as I haue gone,
ther is not such an other. 540

THIRD.

and here are, by my pon! 541
neiles, very good wone,
to neyle thervpon,
though he were my Brother. 544

FOURTH. (69)

Goe we to hit fast! 545
this Caytyfe I have cast,
shall be wronge wrast,
or I wend away. 548

FIRST.

here is a rope will last 549
for to draw a maste.
this Poplard neuer past
so perilous a play. 552

SECOND. (70)

Lay him thervpon, 553
this ilke mased mon,
and I shall dryve on
this neile to the ende. 556

534 poydrace] powderas B, pewdreas W, pewdras h. peweears D. 535 this] that B W h D. 536 neyles] nayle D. to] on D. 538 one] wonne D. 540 ther] *om.* B W D. 541 pon] bones H. 542 very] *om.* B W h D. wone] ones H. 543 thervpon] him vpon B W h D. 544 though] *and* B W h D. 545 hit] as B W h D. 546 I have] have I D. 547 shall] he shal B W h D. 550 for] *om.* W. draw] draw hym W h. a] at the B W h D. 553 Lay] Layes D. 554 ilke] madde W D. 555 shall] drive W h. 556 ende] head B.

THIRD.

As broke I my pon, 557
well cast him I can,
he shall be well wonne,
or I from him wend. (Tunc ponent Iesu*m* sup*er* Crucem.) 560

FOURTH. (71)

ffellows, will ye see 561
how sleight I will be,
this fyst or I flye,
here to make fast? 564

FIRST.

yea, but as mott I thee, 565
short Armed is he;
to bringe to this tree
it will not long last. 568

SECOND. (72)

ha! therfore care thou nought, 569
a sleight I haue sought,
Ropes must be brought,
to strean him with strength. 572

THIRD.

a Rope, as behight, 573
you shall haue, vnbought;
take here one well wrought,
and draw him on length. 576

(tunc ligabunt Corda*m* ad sinistra*m* manu*m* quia dextra erat pr*i*us fixa.)

FOURTH. (73)

Draws, for your father kynne! 577
whyle that I dryve in
this ilke Iron pinne,
that, I dare lay, will last. 580

559 he shall be well] *and* make him full B W h D. wonne] wan B. *Stage-direction*] *om.* W h D. 562 will] shal B W h D. 563 flye] flee D. 565—597] *om.* B. 567 bringe] boweringe W, booringe h, the booringe D. to] of D. 568 it] he W h. long] well W h D. 569 ha] and W h. A, D. 571 brought] bought D. 572 strean] strayne D. with] *om.* H. 573 as] as I D. 574 vnbought] in broughte W h D. 575 here one] it heare W h D. *Stage-direction*] *om.* W h D. 577 father] fathers D. 579 ilke] same W.

FIRST.

as ever haue I wynne,
his Arme is but a fynne;
now dryves on, but dyn,
and we shall draw fast.

(Tunc tres trahent et quartus transfiget Clavem.)

SECOND. (74)

ffellows, by this light!
now if his feet were pight,
this Gommon went aright,
and vp he should be raysed.

THIRD.

That shall be done in height,
anone in your sight;
for my trothe I plight:
I deserve to be praysed. (Tunc pedes transfigent.)

FOURTH. (75)

fellows, will ye see,
how I haue stretcht his knee?
why prayse you not me
that haue so well done?

FIRST.

yea, help now that hee
on height raysed he;
for, as mott I thee,
almost it is none.

(Tunc Pilatus, Tabulam habens in manu, tradet vni militum.)

PILATUS. (76)

Come hither, thou! I commande thee!
goe neile this Table on the Tree;
Sith he kinge of Iews will be,
he must haue Cognisaunce.

583 dryves] drive D. on] in h. but] bowten D. dyn] dimme H. *Stage-direction*] *om.* W h D. 585 this] this daye W. 586] nowe were his feete dighte W h D. 587 aright] on righte W D. 589 height] hye W h. 591 for] for by W h D. 592 deserve] serve W h D. *Stage-direction*] *in* H *in the margin, om.* W h D. 600 none] noone D. *Stage-direction*] tunc pilatus habens tabulam in manu dicit B W h D. (manu] manus W. dicit] dicat W h, h *adding* pilatus). 602 on] upon W h, unto B D. 603 will] *after* he B W h D. 604 haue] have a B W h D.

"Iesu of Nazareth" men may see, 605
"kinge of Iews" how lykes ye?
I writt theron, for so sayd he,
without variaunce. 608

SECOND IEW. (77)

Now, Sir Pilat, to vs take hede: 609
kinge he is not, as god me spede!
therfore thou doest a sory deed;
that writinge many one rews. 612

Thou should wryte *that* many might reade, 613
how he lyed to eche leede,
and towld ouer all wher he yeede,
that he was kinge of Iewes. 616

PILATUS. (78)

That is written, that haue I written. 617

THIRD. St. Iohn xix, 22.

yea, would god thou were beshitten! 618
for all men shall well witten,
that wrong thou hast wrought. 620

What the Devill! kinge is he none, 621
but falcsly ther as he hath gone,
towld Leasings to many one,
that full dear shall be bought! 624

(tunc omnes Crucem exaltabunt et veniet Maria.)

MARIA, MATER IESU CHRISTI. (79)

Alas! my love! my lyfe! my lee! 625
Alas! mowrning now madds me.
Alas! my Boote looke thou be,
thy mother that thee bare! 628

606 ye] thee B W h D. 607 I writt] is written B W h D. 608] *withowten* varyens D. 609] Nay *sir* pilate to us thou bede B D. (thou] *om.* D. Naye yf pilate to us byde W h. 610 he] *after* is B W h D. not] non D. as] so B W h. 612 that] this B W D. one] a man B W D. 613 many] men B D, man W h. 614 lyed] lyes D. 615 wher] theras D. 617 that] that that B W h D. that haue I] I haue B W h D. 618] And in good faith that is foule written B W h D. 619 all] eu*ery* B W h D. men] mon B W h D. shall] may D. 620 hast] hasse D. 621 is he] he is B. none] mon D. 623 towld] he hath told B W h D. to] *om.* W D. 624 full] *om.* B W h D. shall] they shal h, they should B W D. *Stage-direction*] tunc venit maria lacrymans B W h D, B *adding in its margin:* the mother of Iesus. *Heading*] maria W h, Marye D. 625 lee] lere W h D. 626 now] *after* alas B W h D. madds] woe is B W h D. 627 alas] alas son B W h D. looke] *om.* B W h D.

Thinke on my freut! I fosterd thee,
and gaue the sucke vpon my knee;
vpon my payne haue thou pitty!
thee faylës no power.

(80)

Alas! why ne were my lyfe forlorne?
to fynd my foodë me beforne
Tugged, Lugged, all to-torne
with Traytors, now this tyde?

With neilës thrust, *and* Crown of Thorne,
therfore I madd, both even *and* morne,
to see my birth that I haue borne,
this bitter Bale tc byde.

(81)

[My sorrow, sweet Sonne, thou cease,
or of my lyfe thou me releace!
how should I apayd be or in peace,
to se thee in such Penaunce?

Sith thou me to thy moder chose,
and of my body borne thou was,
as I conceived thee wemlesse,
thou graunt me some legiaunce!

(82)

Alas! the sorrow of this sight
marrs my mynd, mayne and might,
but aye my hart me think is light,
to looke on that I love.

And when I looke anon right
vpon my Child that thus is dight,
would Death deliuer me in height,
then were I all aboue.]

630 knee] brest B W h D. 631 thou] *before* haue B W h D. 632 thee fayles] thou feiles B D, thou feeleste W h. 633 ne were] will B W h, nyll D. 634 foode] sonne B W h D. me beforne] me here beforne B, heare me beforne W h D. 635 all] and all B W h D. 637 thrust] thast H. 638 madd] mone W h, made D. both] *om.* W. 640 bide] abyde W h. 641—657] *om.* B W h D. 645 chose] *the form* ches *is required by the rhyme.*

(83)

alas! my sorrow why wilt thou not slake,
and to thes Traytours me betake,
to suffer death, Sonne, for thy sake,
and doe as I thee say?

alas! Theefes, why doe ye so?
slay me, and let my Sonne goe!
for him suffer I would this woe,
and lett him wend his way.

MARIA MAGDALENA. (84)

Alas! how should my hart be light,
to see my semely lord in sight
dilfully drawn and all to-digt,
that did nevar man grevance.

Marred I am, mayne *and* might,
and for him me fayles to feight,
but god that aye rules the right,
he geue you much mischance!

MARIA IACOBI. (85)

alas! sorrow settes me sore;
mirth of thee gett I no more;
why wouldst thou dye, Iesus? wherfore?
that to the Dead gaue lyfe.

Help me, Iesu, with some thinge,
and out of this bitter bale me bringe,
or ells slay me, for any thinge,
and Stint me of this stryfe.

MARIA SALOME. (86)

Come, lord, downe, *and* breake thy Bandes!
loce and heale thy lovely handes!

657 why] when B W h D. not] *om.* B W h D. 662 slay] sleas you B h, slayes ye D. and] *om.* W h. 664 his] a B W h D. 667 dilfully] deolfully D. drawn] torne W h. all] *om.* B W h D. to] so B W h D. 670 me] *after* fayles B W h D. 671 aye] *after* rules B D, ever W h, *after* rules. 672 he] *om.* B W h D. much] mickell B W h D. 673 settes] syttys D. 674 gett I] I gett B W h D. 675 wherfore] therfore W h. 681—684 *and* 685—689] *inverted in* H, *but the mistake is corrected by a* hic come lord *after* 680 *and a* Thes verses must come before *in the margin opposite to the heading.* Lord] *after* downe B W h D.

or tell, Iesu, for whom thy woundes,
since thou art god and man. 684

Alas! that ever I borne was, 685
to se my lord in such vnpeace,
my sorrow will never slake ne cease,
such sorrow is me vpon. 688

ANNAS. (87)

Now this shrew is hoven an height, 689
I would se for all his sleight,
for his Croune how he would feight,
and fownd from vs to flee. 692

He that hath healed so many one, 693
now saue him selfe, if *that* he can, St. Matth. xxvii, 42.
and we shall leeve[n] him vpon,
that god[e]s sonne is he. 696

(Tunc Iesus in lignu*m* pendens, ait vt seq*ui*tur.)

IH*ESUS*.[1] (88)

[1] MS. Ihc.

ffather of heaven, if thy will be, 697
forgeue them this they done to me! St. Luke xxiii, 34.
they be blynd, *and* may not see,
how fowle the do amisse. 700

CAYPHAS.

If thou be of such posty, 701
and god[e]s sonne in maiesty,
Come downe, *and* we will leeve on thee,
that soothly so it is. 704

P*RIMUS* LATRO. (89)

If thou be Christ veray, St. Luke xxiii. 39 ff. 705
and gods sonne, now assay,
saue vs from this death to day,
and thy selfe also! 708

683 tell] tell me B W h D. thy woundes] wonnes W, woones h. thou wond*es* D. 686 my lord] thy bodye D. vnpeace] a case B W h D. 687 ne] nor B W h D. 689 is] we H D. hoven] hauen B. 690 would] will W h. 691 would] can B W h D. 692 fownd] fare h, farr B W, ferre D. 693 hath] hasse D. so] *om.* W. one] a one B. 694 if] give D. 695 and] *and* then all B W h D. shall] will W. him] thee h. 696] that it sothely so is B W h D. (it] is B). *Stage-direction*] *om.* B W h D. 697 of heaven] *om.* H. 699 they] for they B W h D. 700 fowle] *om.* B. the] they D. do] haue done B, donne D. 704 it] *after* that B W h D. *Heading*] The first Thefe B W h, *in margin* D. 706 assay] as I say B W h D.

SECUNDUS LATRO.

Ah! man, be still, I thee pray! 709
dreed god, I read thee, aye;
for folishly thou speaks, in fay;
make not thy frend thy foe! 712

(90)

Man, thou knows well, iwysse, 713
that righteously we suffer this,
but this man hath not done amis,
to suffer so great anoye. 716
But, lord, I beseech thee, 717
when thou art in thy maiesty,
then that thou wilt thinke on me,
and on me haue mercy. 720

IHESUS. (91)

Man, I tell thee in good fay, 721
for thy beleefe is so veray,
in paradice thou shalt be to day,
With me in my blisse. 724
And to thee, woman, also I say: St. Iohn xix, 26 ff. 725
ther thy sonne thou se may,
that clean virgin hase bene aye,
lyke as thy self is. 728

(92)

And, Iohn, thy moder ther may thou se! 729

IOHANNES EVANGELISTA.

Yea, lord, her keper I will be;
welcome Mary, mother free!
to geather we must goe. 732

Heading] The secund Theeffe B W h, *in margin* D. 710 I read] or I dreed H. 711 folishly] foullie B W h, folylye D. speaks] speakest D. 713 knows] wottest B W h D. 714 righteously] right wisely D. 715 but this man] for he B W h D. amis] so mych amis D. 716 so] such W h. 718 thy] *om.* B. 719 wilt] wouldest B. 722 thy] this W h. 723 *and* 724] *written as one line in* H. 724 me] me there B W h D. 725 woman] *after* And B W h D. 726 ther] by thy B W, by the D. thou] ther thou B W h D. 728 lyke] right B W h D. self] selvon B W h D. 729 ther] *after* Iohn B W h D. thou] *before* maist B W h D. Iohannes] Iohn D. evangelista] *om.* B W h D. 730—737] *om.* h. 730 will] shal B W D. 731 mother] *after* welckome W.

MARIA.

Alas! my hart will break in three!
alas! Death, I coniure thee!
my lyfe, sonne, thou take from me,
and twin me from this woe!

IHO*ANNES* EVANG*ELISTA*. (93)

Comfort thee, swet mary!
though we suffer this anye,
I tell the, suster, sickerly,
on lyfe thou shalt him see,

and ryse vp with full victory;
when he hath fulfilled the prophesy,
thou shalt him se, full sickerly,
with in thes day[e]s three.

IH*ESUS*. (94) St. Matth. xxvii, 46.

Hely! hely! hely! hely!
my god! my god! I speak to thee!
Hely, lama sabachthany?
why hast thou forsaken me?

FIRST IEW.

A! hark, he cryes vpon hely,
for to deliuer him hastely.

SECOND.

Abyde, and we shall witt in hye,
whether hely dare come here, or noe.

IH*ESUS*. (95) St. Iohn. xix, 28.

My Thirst is sore, my thurst is sore.

THIRD IEW.

Yea, thou shalt haue a drink, therfore,

Heading] Marye the ffirst B W D. 733 break] burst B W, brast D. 735 my] the B W D. Iho*annes*] Iohn D. Evang*elista*] *om.* B W h D. 737 thee] thie now B W h D. 738 though] for though B D. 739 suster] *before* I B W h D. 741 up] *om.* B D. 742 hath] hasse D. 743] thie sonne thou shalt see seckerly B W h D. (thou *as* tho] *after* shalt B.) 745 *and* 746] Eloy, Eloy, my god I speake to thie B W h D. 747 lama sabachthany] lama zabathanie B h D, lazama bathanye W. 748 hast] hasse D. . . . thou] thou thus B W h, thou thys D. *Heading*] Primus Iudeus D. 749 hark] hark how B W h, herke, herke how D. 750 for] *om.* B W h D. hastely] from his anoye B W h D. (from] of W h D). *Heading*] Secundus Iudeus D. 751 we] well B. witt] see B W h D. 752 come] come I B. or noe] *appears to be a later addition*, here *would rhyme with* 756. 753 my thurst is sore] *om.* H. *Heading*] Tertius Iudeus D. 754 a] *om.* B W h D.

that thou shalt list to drink no more
of all this seven yeare.

IESUS.

Almighty God in maiesty,
to worch thy will I will neuer wond;
my spirit I betake to thee; St. Luke xxiii, 46.
receiue it, lord, into thy hand!

CENTURIO. (96)

Lordings, I say you sickerly,
that we haue wrought wilfully,
for I know by the prophesy,
that god[e]s sonne is he.

Therfore, sirs, very ferd am I
to hear this noyce *and* this crye,
I am ashamëd, verely,
this vncooth sight to see.

CAYPHAS. (97)

Centurio, as god me speed!
peace, and speak not of *that* dede,
for of him thou getts no meede;
what needes the so to say?

But, Longeus, take *this* spear in hand,
to pearce his hart look thou ne wond!

LONGEUS.

A! Lord, I see neither sea nor land
this seuen year, in good fay.

755 to] *om.* B W h. 757 Almighty] mightie B W h D. 758 worch] worke D. will] would B W D. neuer] ever h. wond] wende W D. 759 spirit] speete D. 760 hand] hand*es* D. *Before* 761] B W h D *insert from St. John* 19, 30, "consum*m*atu*m* est."

762—765] *in* B W h D:
this was god*es* sonne, allmightie,
no other, for soth, leve will I,
for need*es* it so must be.

765—769] *in* B W h D:
I know by mann*er* of his crye,
he hath fullfilled the p*ro*phecie,
and godhead showed ap*er*tly
in him all men may know.

769 as] so B W h. 770—773] *in* B W h D:
thou most be smvtted, thou canst not read;
but when thou seest his hart blede,
lettes see what thou canst saye.

773 But] *om.* D. longeus] Longis B, Longes h, Longys D. *this*] the W h. 774] *in* B W h D, *and* put from thie, looke thou ne wonde (looke] *om.* W h.) 775 A] O W h. neith*er*] nay B W, no h, ne D. nor] nay B, ne D.

FOURTH IEW. (98)

take this spear, and take good heede,
and do, as the Bishopp thee badd,
a thing that is great need;
to wonne I hould thee wood.

LONGEUS.

I will do as you bydd me,
but on your perill it shall be,
what I doe I may not see,
wher it be ill or good.

(99)

High king of heauen, I call thee here,
what I haue done well wott I near;
but on my handes *and* on my Spear
whott water runnes ther throe;

And on my eyes some can fall,
that I may se you, some and all;
A! lord, wher ever be the wall,
that this water came froo? (Tunc sursum Aspicit.)

(100)

Alas! alas! and weele-a-way!
what dede haue I done to day!
a man, I see, sooth to say,
I haue slayne in this affray;

But this, I hope, very Christ be,
that sick *and* blynd, through his pitty,
hath healed before in this Citty,
as thou has me to day.

Heading] Quartus Iudeus D. 777 *First* take] haue B W h D. and] thou must B W h D. 779 great] of full great B W h D. 780 wonne] warne B W h D. thee] you W h. 781 you] ye D. 784 wher] whether B W h D. ill] evell D. *Before* 785] *as stage-direction:* tunc lunzius perforat cum lancia latus christi dicens B W h. (cum lancia] lancia *before* perforat W h D. dicens] dicens Longeus h.) 785 king] god h. call] *om.* B W h D. here] praye W. 787 handes] hand D. 788 whott] out B W h D. runnes] runneth D. ther] *om.* B W h D. 790 you *om.* D. some] both one B W h D. 791 a] O W h. the] this D. *Stage-direction*] *om.* B W h D. 795 see] see now B. 796 this] the W h. affray] steede B, streete W h, stead D. 797] very Christ be] be Christ verey D. 798 through his pitty] hath healed aye B W h D. *Before* 799] B W h D *insert:*

Of mercye, lord, now I thie praye
For I wist not what I did.
Iesu, much haue I hard of thie,
That sick and blinde through thy pittie.

1 now] *after* I thee D. 3 hard] hard speake D.

800 has] has done H.

(101)

Thee will I serue, *and* with thee be;
for well I leeue, in day[e]s three
thou wilt ryse through thy posty,
and saue that on thee call.

IOSEPH AB ARAMATHEA.

A, lord god! what harts haue ye,
to slay this man that I now se?
vengeanc vppon you, witt*er*ly,
I warrand sone shall fall.

[Alas! how should I be mery,
to se his Body, fayr and fre,
all to-torne vpon a tree,
that was so principall?

(102)

Nichodemus, Sir, both you and I,
haue cause to worship him, witterly,
and his body glorifye,
for god[e]s sonne he is.]

Therfore goe we, by and bye,
and worship him devoutly;
for we may therwith, perdy,
win vs heaven blisse!

NICHODEMUS. (103)

Ioseph, I leeve this sickerly:
that he is gods sonne Almighty.
goe aske of Pylate his Body,
and Buryed it shall be.

803 through thy] in thye W, in full B, full in h D. 804] from Enemyes, lord, I thie praye B W h D. *Heading*] Ioseph B W h D. 806 now] here B W h D. 807 *and* 808] *in* B W h D dead hanging one rood tree, that neuer yett did amis. (one] vppon W h D.) 809—817] *om.* B W h D. 817—821] *in* B W h D:

for sickerly god*es* sonne is hee, (sickerly] suerlye W.)
therfore a tombe is made for me,
there in his bodie buried shalbe,
for he is king of blisse.

821 Ioseph] S*ir* Ioseph B W h D. leeve] say B W h D. this] *om.* B W h D. 822 that he] this B W h D. 823 goe] to H. of] at B W h D. 824 it] he W, he *after* shall B h. it shall be] shall hee bee D.

I shall help thee, witterly, 825
to take him downe devoutly,
though Cayphas goe wood therby,
and eke also his meny. 828

IOSEPH AB ARAMATHEA. (104)

To Pilate, Brother, will we gone, 829
you and I togeather alone,
to ask his body of our fone,
if that it be thy read. 832

A Sepulchre I wott ther is one, 833
well graved in a stonne;
he shall be buryed, flesh and bone,
his body that is dead. 836

(Tunc venint simul ad pilatum, et Ioseph flectando dicat:)

(105)

Ben avoose, Sir Pilate in hye! 837
as you sitt in your Sea,
a boone graunt for Charity
to my Brother and me! 840

The body of my lord Messy, 841
that you neiled on a Tree,
graunt vs, lord, in suffraynty,
and buryed it shall be. 844

PILATUS. (106)

Ioseph, I tell thee without nay, 845
that body thou shalt haue to day;
but let me know, I thee pray,
whether his lyfe be gone. 848

hark! Centurio, is Iesus dead? 849

827 wood] horne wood B W h D. 828 eke also] all B W h D. *Heading*] Ioseph D. *Before* 829] *as stage-direction in* B W h D. tunc venit Ioseph ab Aramathia ad pilatum *et* dicit. (dicit] dicat Iosephe W h, dicat D. 829—833] *in* B W h D:

Sir pilate, speciallie I thie pray,
a boone thou graunt me, as thou maye:
this prophett that is dead to daye
thou graunte me his bodie.

833—845] *om.* B W h D. 845—849] *in* B W h D:

Ioseph, alreadie, in good faye,
yf that Centurio, he will saye
that he is dead, withouten naye
him will I not denie.

849 hark] *om.* B W h D.

CENTURIO.

yea, Sir, as ever break I bread, 850
in him is no lyfe lead,
nor never a whole vayne. 852

PILATUS. (107)

Ioseph, then take him to thee; 853
goes *and* let him buryed be;
but look thou make no sigaldry,
to rayse him vp agayne! 856

IOSEPH.

Graunt mercy, sir of Dignity! 857
you need not for to warn it me,
for ryse he will of his posty,
and make vs all full fayne. (Tunc ibunt p*er* iter super monte*m*.) 860

(108)

A! swet Iesu! Iesu! swet Iesu! 861
that thou must dye, full well thou knewe!
lord, thou graunt vs grace and vertue,
to serve the in our lyfe! 864
That they to thy Blisse renew 865
All *tha*t euer to thee be true!
for Emperour, kinge, knight ne Iew,
with thee they dare not stryve. 868

850 euer] *om.* D. break] broke B h D, eate W. bread] my head B h D. 851 is] ther is B W h D. 852] For I stoode therby B W h D. vayne] bone?? 853 then] *om.* B W h, *after* him D. 854] *and* bury him wher thie wilbe B W h D. 856 *and* 857] *om.* B W h D. *Heading*] pilatus h. 857 of Dignity] pardie B W h D. 858] I thank you hartefullie B W h D. (hartefullie] hartelye W h.) 859 *and* 860] *om.* B W h D. *Stage-direction*] tunc ibit Ioseph sup*er* montem et dicit Ioseph B W h D. (dicit] dicat W h D.) 861 *Second* Iesu] *om.* B W D. 862—864] *in* B W h D:

as thou arte good, faithfull *and* true
in a tombe is made full new
thie bodie shalbe laid. (shalbe] shall in be W h D.)

865—868] *are substituted by the following* 12 *lines in* B W h D:

shouldest thou neu*er* haue had such vertue, 1
As thou hast showen, since I thie knew,
But that godhead thie deedes should show,
As thou before hast said; 4
Therefore Iesu, come hether to me, 5
thie blessed bodie buryed shalbe
w*i*th all worshipe *and* honestie,
and menske, all that I may. 8
yett hope I w*i*thin these dayes three, 9
In flesh *and* blode, one lyve to see
thie that art nayled one a tree
Vnworthelie to daye. 12

(1 had] *om.* W h D. 2 showen] shewed W h D. 3 that] yf D. deedes] deed W h. 5 Therefore] Therwith W h D. 6 shal] *before* buryed W h. 8 menske] mirth W h.) 10 one lyve] alyue D. 11 thie] thou D.

865 *and* 866] *written as one line in* H.

NICODEMUS. (109)

Sir Iosephe, Brother, as well I se,
this holy prophett is geuen to thee;
some worship he shall haue of me,
that is of might most.

ffor as I leev, by my luteye!
very god[e]s sonne is he;
for very sightës men may se,
when that he yeeld the ghost:

(110)

ffor *the* sonne lost his light,
Earthquake made men afright,
the Roch that never had cleft
did cleev then, as men might know.

Sepulchrs opened in mens sight,
dead men rysen ther by night;
I may say he is god Almight,
such Signës that can show.

(111)

Therfor brought here haue I
an hundreth pownd of Spicery:
mirhe, Aloes, *and* many mo, therby
to honour him will I bringe;

ffor to Balme his swete body,
in Sepulchre for to lye,
that he may haue on me mercy,
when he in heaven is kinge.

Amen.

finis Decimæ sextæ pagine. Iulii 27 : 1607.

69 Sir] *om.* B W h D. I] *after* as B W h D. 872 might] mightes h, myghtest B, myghtiest D. 875 very] *om.* D. sightes] wonders sightes B D, wounderous sighte W, wounderous sighte h. may] might B D. 877 his] all his B W h D. 878 made] *om.* B. 879 Roch] rockes B h. neuer] neuer before D. had] before B W h. 880 did] *om.* B W h D. cleev] clayue D. then] *om.* D. as] that B W h. might] dyd H. 881 Sepulchrs] Graues B W h D. 882 rysen ther] did rise therefore B W h D. night] righte W h. 883 he is] this was B W h D. god] godes sonne B W h D. 884 such Signes that] that so great sygnes B W h D. 885 here] *om.* W, *before* brought B h D. 886 pownd] poundes W h D. 887 *and*] *om.* B W h. 888 will] w*hi*ch B, w*i*th D. 891 on] of W, *in* H *a former* on *is crossed out.* 892] in heauen where he is kinge B W h D. Amen] *om.* B W h D. Decimæ sextæ pagine] *om.* B W h, *the two latter continuing* Deo gracias, p*er* me Georgiu*m* bellin *whereto* h *adds* 1600, W. Come lorde Iesu, Come quicklye an*no* 1592. (paginæ] *before* decimæ D. *Date*] *om.* D.

Pagina Decima Septi*m*a de Descensu Christi ad Inferos.

The Cookes *and* Inkepers.

ADAMUS. (1)

A! lord and Severayne Saviour, 1
our Comfort and our Counseler,
of this light thou art Author,
as I se well in sight. 4
This is a Signe, thou would succour 5
thy folke that bene in great langour,
and of the Devill be Conquerour
as thou hast yore behight. 8

(2)

Me thou madest, lord, of Clay, 9
and gaue me paradice in to play;
but after my Sinne, sooth to say,
deprived I was therfro; 12
And from that weale putt away, 13
and here haue lenged sithen aye,
in Thesternes, both night and day,
and all my kynd also. 16

(3)

Now by this light that I now se, 17
ioy is com*m*en, lord, through thee,
and of thy people thou hast pitty,
to putt them out of payne. 20
Sicker it may none other be, 21
but now thou hast mercy on me,

Pagina] Hic incipit pagina B W h D. Decima septi*m*a] *om.* B. Christi] *om.* D. in feros] in ferna B W h D, *all four MSS. continuing,* et de his qui ib*id*em fiebant, sec*und*um evangelium nicodemi, et primo fiat lux in inferno materialis aliqua subtilitate machinata et postea dicat adam. (in] *om.* h.) and Inkepers] playe B W h D, *and before the Latin. Heading:* Adamus] *om.* B, Adam D. A] O B W h D. 3] *om.* B. 5 would] will B W D, wylte h. 6 folke] folkes B W h D. 6 bene] lyven B D, lyne W h. 7 be] *om.* W. 8 yore] earst B, eyer W h, yere D. 11 after] through B W h D. sooth] the south B W h D. 12 deprived] pryved H. 14 lenged] longed B W h, longett D. sithen aye] south to saye W. 15 Thesternes] this distres B, the stearnesse D. 18 ioy is] joyes are B. lord] now B. 19 of] one h D. hast] *om.* D. 20 putt] take B.

and my kynd, through thy posty,
thou wilt restore agayne.

ESAY. (4)

Yea Sickerly, this ilke light
comes from gods sonne Almight,
for so I p*ro*phesyed aright,
whyle that I was lyvinge.

Then I to all men beheight,
As I ghostly sawe in sight,
this word that I through gods might
shall rehearce without tariinge:

(Populus q*ui* ambulabat in tenebris vidit luce*m* magnam.) Isa. lx, 3.

(5)

The people, that tyme I sayd expresse,
that went about in Thesternes,
se a full great lightnes,
as we done now, echone.

Now is fulfilled my prophesy,
that I, the Prophet Esay,
wrott in my Books that will not lye,
who so will looke theron.

SIMEON IUSTUS. (6)

And I Symeon, sooth to say,
will honor god, all that I may,
for when Christ a Child was, in good fay,
in Temple I him tooke.

And as the holy ghost that day
taught me, or I went away,
these wordes I sayd to god[ë]s pay,
as men may fynd in Booke:

Heading] Esayus D. 25 sickerly] securely B, suerlye W, secker h. ilke] same W. 30 sawe] se H. 31 this word] thes wordes B W h D. through gods] shall to my B W h, shall to D. 32 shall] *om.* B W h. vidit] videbat B. ambulabat] ambulat H. 33 I sayd] *after* people B W h D. 34 went] yeaden B D, eylden W h. 35 se] seene B D, seithen W h. 36 we] you W. 37 fulfilled] filled H. 39 Books] boke B W h D. 42] *om.* W h. 43 a] *om.* B W h D. 48 as] that B W h. may] might B.

(7)

(Nunc dimittis servu*m* tuu*m*, D*omi*ne, secu*n*du*m* verbu*m* tuu*m* in pace.) St. Luke ii, 29.

Ther I prayd, with-out[ë] lesse, 49
that god would lett me dye in peace,
for he is Christ that Commen was,
I had both feld *and* seene; 52

That he had ordayned for mans heale, 53
ioy to the people of Israell,
nowe is it wonnen, that ilk weale,
to vs, withouten weene. 56

IOHA*NN*ES BAPTISTA. (8)

Yea, lord, I am that ilk Iohn, 57
that followed thee in flood Iordan,
and that in world about can gone
to warne of thy co*m*minge. 60

And with my finger I shewed expresse 61
A meke lamb in thy lyknes,
in token that thou common was
mankynd of Bale to bringe. 64

(Ecce agnus Dei, ecce q*u*i tollit peccata mu*n*di.)

SETH. (9)

And I, Sethe, Adams sonne, am here, 65
that lyvinge went, without[en] were,
to aske at Paradyce a prayer
at god, as I shall say. 68

Nunc] tunc B. 49 without] withowten D. 50 would] will B W h. dye] be B W h D. 51 he is] swet H. 52 feld] felte B. 53 heale] health B. 54 the] *om.* H. 55 nowe is it] that he hath H. that] with H. ilk] eke W. 57 lord] lord and H. ilk] p*ro*phett B W h D. 58 followed] baptised B W h D. 59] and preached to Everye nacion B W h D. (preached] prophesied B D. Everye] many a h.) 60 cominge] conninge H.

Between 60 *and* 61] B W h *insert:*

to bringe the people to salvacion,
by mirrette of thy bitter passion,
through faith and pennance to have remission,
and with thee to haue woninge.
penetenciam agite, appropinquat enim regnu*m* celorum, (et dicat.)

(mirrette] merit B, merrytt D. (et dicat] *om.* h D.)

61 finger] fingers h. shewed] shewe W. 62] *is preceded by* when I lyued in wildernes *in* B W h D. meke] *om.* B W h D. in] in token of B W h, in tokeninge of D. 63] *om.* D. 64] our ransome for to be B W h D.

Between 64 *and* 65] B W h D *insert:*

at thie coming wee had forgiuenes,
mercye concludeth rightwisenes,
therfore thes wordes I doe rehearse
with honour vnto thee.

(therfore] wherfore B.) concludeth] concluded D.

68 at] of B.

That he would graunt an Angell in hye, 69
to geue oyle of his mercy,
to anoynt my father in his nye,
in sicknes when he lay. 72

(10)

Then to me appered Michaell, 73
and bade me travell never a deale,
and sayd wepinge nor prayers fell
avayled me nothing to seeke. 76

Nay, of that Oyle might I haue none, 77
made I neuer so much mone,
vntill fyve Thousand years were gone,
and fyve hundreth eeke. 80

DAVID. (11) (Omnes Genu flectantes.)

A! high god *and* king of blisse, 81
worshiped be thy name, iwis!
I hope that tyme now come[n] is
to deliuer vs of danger. 84

Come, lord! come to Hell anone, 85
and take out thy folk, everychon,
for those years are fully gone
sith mankynd first came heare. 88

(Tunc Sathan sedens in Cathedra dicat Demonib*us*.)

SATHAN. (12)

Hell hownds, all that be here, 89
make you bowne with Bost and Bere,
for to this fellowship in feere
ther hyes a fearly freak. 92

A noble morsell you haue mon: 93
Iesu, that is gods sonne,

69 an] the H. 70 geue] give me D, geve to me W h. 71 his] *om.* H. nye] anoye D. 75 wepinge] for reminge B W h D. nor] nyf D. 76] that graunte me not to seeke B W h D. (graunte] graunted W.) 77 Nay] nor W h, nyf D. oyle] *om.* D. might] migh H. 78 neuer] neue H. 79 vntill] tell B W h, tyll D. 80 eeke] yeeke D. *Heading*] *om.* D. *Stage-direction*] Omnibus flectentibus dicat dauid B W h D, *before the heading.* flectentibus] flectib*us* D. 83 come] commen D. 84] delivered to be of langure B W h D. 86 folk] folkes D. 87 those] the B W h D. are fully] al be comon and B W h D. al be] be all D. 88 first came] came firste W h. dicat] dicens W. *Heading*] *om.* B W h D. 90 make] makes D.

comes hither with vs to wonne;
on him now ye you wreake!

(13)

a man he is fullye, in faye,
ffor greatly Death he dredd to day,
and these wordes I hard him say:
"my soule is thirste vnto Death:"
(Tristis est anima mea vsq*ue* ad mortem.)

Such as I made halt and Blynd,
he hath healed into ther kynd,
therfor that Boyster looke that you bynde
in Bale of hell Breath!

SECUNDUS DEMON. (14)

Sir Sathanas, what man is he
that should thee pryve of thy posty?
how dare he doe agaynst thee
and dread his Death to day?

gretter then thou he semes to bee,
for Degraded of thy Degree
thou must be soone, well I see,
and pryvëd of thy pray.

TERTIUS DEMON. (15)

Who is this, so stiff and stronge,
that maisterly comes vs amonge,
our felowship that he would fonge?
but therof he shall fayle.

wete he vs with any wrong,
he shall singe a sory song;
but on the, Sathanas, it is long,
and his will ought avayle.

95 hither] he heither W, he there h. 97 *om.* H. 100 is thirste] thirst H. is threst D. vnto] to B W h D. *Latin passage*] *om.* B W h D; *forms the fourth line of stanza* 13 *in* H. 102 hath] hath them B W h D. into] to W h. 103 that Boyster] this bolster B W h D. 104 hell] hells B. 108 his] the H. 109 he] hym W h. 110 degraded] degradit D. 113 this] he B W h D. 114 that] that so B W h D. maisterly] maysterlyke D. 115 that] as B W h D. 117] *in margin in* H. 119 Sathanas it is] sathan that it B W h D. that] or D.

SATHAN. (16)

Against this Shrew, that comes here, 121
I tempted the folke in fowle manere;
ayesell and Gall to his Dinner
I made them for to dight, 124
And hange him on a Rood Tree. 125
now is he dead right so throw me,
and to Hell, as you shall se,
he comes anone in height. 128

SECUN*DUS* DEMO*N*. (17)

Sathan, is not this that Syre 129
that raysed Lazar out of the fyre?

SATHAN.

Yea, this is he that will conspyre
anone to reave vs all. 132

TERCIUS DEMON.

Out, out! alas, Alas! 133
hear I coniure the, Sathanas,
thou suffer him not to come to this place,
for ought *that* may befall. 136

SECUN*DUS* DEMO*N*. (18)

Yea, sickerly, and he come here, 137
passed is cleane our power,
for all this fellowship in feere
he may take away when he would; 140
ffor all be at his Commandment: 141
Lazar, that was with vs lent,
mawger our Teeth away he went,
and him might we not howld. 144

(Tunc veniet Ih*esus* et fiet Clamor vel sonitus materialis magnus, et dicat Ih*esus*: "Attolite portas principes vestras et elevamini portæ æternales, et introibit Rex gloriæ.")

121 comes] sittes W, commys D. 125 And] And sithen to B W h D. a] *om.* B W h D. 127 as] *om.* H. 128 heighte] heigh B. 129 Sathan] Sir Sathan B W h, Syr Sathanas D. 130 out] one B. 131 will] would B W h D. 132 reave] repe W, rulle B. *Heading*] *om.* H. 133-4] *as one line* H. 133 out out] out one B. alas, alas] out alas h. 135-6] *as one line* H. 135 to] *om.* B W h. not] *after* come B. to come] *om.* to D. *Second* to] in B W h D. 140 haue whom a waie he woulde B W h D. (whom] home D.) 141 all be] *om.* B W h D. 142 was] *after* vs B W h D. 143 away] *om.* B W h. went] hent B h D. veniet] venit B W h D. fiet] fiat B W h D. materialis magnus] magnus materialis B W h D. et dicat Iesus] Ih*esus* ait H. portæ] portas D. introibit] introibis H. gloriæ] glorie et dicat Iesus h.

IHESUS. (19)

Open hell Gates anone! 145
you princes of payn, every chon!
That Gods sonne may in gone,
And the kinge of Blisse! 148

SECUNDUS DEMON.

Goe hence, Poplard, from this place! 149
or thou shalt haue a sory grace;
for all thy Boste and thy manase
these men thou shalt[ë] misse. 152

SATHAN. (20)

Out! alas! what is this? 153
see I never so much blisse
toward hell come, iwisse,
sith I was prince here. 156

My maisterdome now fares amisse, 157
for yonder a stubborn fellow is,
right as wholly hell were his
to reve me of my power. 160

TERTIUS DEMON. (21)

Yea, Sathanas, thy Soverainty 161
fayl[e]s cleane, therfore flee,
for no longer in this See
here shalt thou not sytt. 164

Goe forth! feight for thy degree! 165
or ells our Prince shall thou not be,
for now passeth thy postye,
and hence thou must flitt. (Iaceant tunc Sathanam de sede sua.) 168

SATHAN. (22)

Out! Alas! I am shent. 169
my might fayles verament,

Heading] *om.* B. 145 Open] Open vp D W, open open B. 149 from] of B, out from W h, owt of D. 150 or] for H. 152 misse] a myse W h, amys D. 154 see] seaghe D, seinge W h, sith B. 156 prince] warden B W h D. 157 now] *om.* B W h D. 159 hell] all H. 160 reve me of] pryve H. 162 flee] thou flee B W h D. 166 thou] *before* shall B W h. 167 passeth] passys D. 168 hence] hethen D. *Stage-direction*] Tunc surgens sathanas de sede et dicat B W h D. (et] *om.* D.) *Heading*] *om.* B.

this Princ that is now present
will spoyle from me my pray.

Adam, by my Intycement,
and all his bloud through me were blent;
now hence they shall all be hent
and I in hell for aye.

IHESUS. (23)

Open vp hell gates, yet I say,
you Princes of pine that be present!
and lett the kinge of bliss this way,
that he may fulfill his intent!

SATHAN.

Say, what is he, that Kinge of blisse?

IHESUS.

That lord the which Almighty is;
ther is no power lyke to his,
of all ioy he is kinge.

(24)

And to him is none lyk, iwis,
as is soothly seene by this,
for man, that sometyme did amis,
to his blisse he Will bringe. (Tunc Iesus accipiet Adam *per* manu*m*.)

172 spoyle] powle B W h, pull D. 174 me] hym h. blent] shente B W h D. 175 hence] hethen D. 176 for aye] for ever W. *After* 176] B W h D *insert:*

DAVID REX.

I, kinge david, nowe well maye saye,
my prophesye fulfilled is in faye,
as nowe shewes in sighte verrye
and southlye here is seene.

I taughte men this here in my life daie,
to worshipe god by all waie
that hell gates he shall affraye,
and wone that his hath bene:

Confiteantur d*omi*no misericordie eius et mirabilia eius, filius ho*mini*s contrivit portas æreas et vectes ferreas confreget.

(Rex] *before* dauid h.) 5 this] thus D. daie] dayes B. 6 waie] wayes B. 7 shall] should D. æreas] proreas W h. confreget] *continued by* Tunc item dicat W h). Tunc item dicat Iesus D.

177 vp hell] the H. 178 pine] peace H. 181 Say] Staye W h D. what] what what B D. he] *om.* H. Iesus] David rex B W D, rex Dauid h. 183 ther is] in warre B W h D. 184 ioy he is] blesse is greatest B W h D. 187 man] men B W h D. his] this h. 188 will] will them B h D, will vs W. *Stage-direction*] Hic extrahuntur patriarchi B W h D, *followed by* Here God doth take out addam in W h. (doth take] taketh h.), *by* and here must God take out Adam *in* B D. (and] *om.* D.)

IESUS.

Peace to the, Adam, my Darlinge,
and eke to all thy ofspringe,
that righteous were in eirth lyvinge;
from me you shall not sever.

(25)

To blis[se] now I will you bringe,
ther you shall be without endinge;
Michael, lead these men singinge
to ioy that lasteth ever.

MICHAELL.

Lord, your will done shall be.
come forth, Adam, come with me!
my lord vpon the Rood Tree
your sinn[e]s hath forbought.

(26)

Now shall you haue lyking and lee,
and be restored to your degree,
that Sathan with his subtilty
from bliss to bale hath brought.

(Tunc Michael adducet Adam et Sanctos ad Paradisum, et in obviam venient henoc et helias, Latro salvatus, et Sathan dicat:)

SATHAN.

Out, alas! now goeth away
my Prisoners and all my pray,
and I might not stirr one Stray,
I am so streitly dight.

(27)

Now comes Christ; sorrow I may
for me and my meny for aye.
never sith god made the first day,
were we so fowle of right. (Tunc Adam videns Enock et heliam ait.)

Heading] *om.* H. 191 righteous] ryghtwise D. eirth] ther H. 192 you shall] shall they H. 193 you] them H. 196 ioy] blesse B W h D. 197 your] thy h. 204 hath] hade W h D, you H. *Latin passage*] *om.* B W h D. 205 goeth] goes D. alas] out H. 206 all] *before* my prisoners B W h D. 207] and I my selfe maie not starte a waie B W h D, *but with* sture *instead of* starte B. 208 dight] tyed B W h D. 210 for] to H. and] and to H. 211 made the] *om.* H. 212 fowle of right] sore a freayde B W h D. (sore] *om.* h.) *Stage-direction*] Heare mvste adam speake to Enocke and Ely B W h D. (mvste] *om.* h. speake] speaketh h.)

ADAM*US*.

Say, what maner men bene yee, 213
that bodely meten vs, as I see,
and Dead come not to hell as we,
since all men Damned were? 216

(28)

when I trespassed, god hett me 217
that this place closed alway should be
from earthly man to haue entry,
and yet fynd I you here. 220

ENOCH.

Sir, I am Enocke, sooth to say, 221
putt into this place to gods pay,
and here haue lyved euer since that day,
at lyking all my fill. 224

(29)

And my fellow here, in good fay, 225
is Hely the prophett, as you se may,
that ravished was in that aray,
as it was god[e]s will. 228

HELIAS.

Yea bodely death—leeue thou me— 229
yet never suffred we,
but here ordaynd we are to be,
till Ante Christ come with his. 232

(30)

feight against vs shall he, 233
and slay vs in the holy Citty;
but sickerly with in days three.
and half one we shall ryse. 236

213 Say] Sires B W h D. men] of men B W h D. 215 and] that B W h D. as] as well as B W h. 216 since] sythen D. 217 hett] height D. trespassed] treaspaseth B W h. me] *om.* W. 218 alway] *om.* B W h D. 219 earthly] earthy h. man] men B W D. 220 I] *after* yet B W h D. 221 sooth] the sooth B W h D. 222 into] in B W h D. to] for h. 223 that day] aye B W h D. 224 all] at h. 226 as you se] se you B W h D. 227 that] this B W h D. *Heading*] Hely prophette B W h, Helias propheta D. 231 we] *om.* H. 232 with his] *om.* B, in haste h, with hise D. 233 feight] to feight B W h D. 234 slay] sleay B W h D. the] this B W h D. 235 sickerly] suerlye W. with] *om.* W. 236 half one] an half B W h D. (an] a D.)

ADAM.

And who is this that comes here 237
with Crosse on shoulder in such manere?

LATRO.

I am that Theefe, my fader deere,
that honge on Roode tree; 240

(31)

but for I leeved, without weere, 241
that Christ might saue vs both in feere,
to him I made my prayer,
the which was graunted me. 244

When I see signes veray 245
that he was gods sonne, soth to say,
to him devoutly I can pray,
In his Realme when he come, 248

(32)

To think on me by all way; 249
and he Aunswered and sayd: "this day
in Paradice with me thou shalt be aye,"
So hither the way I noome; 252

And he betooke me this tokeninge, 253
A Crosse vpon my backe hanginge,
The Angell michael for to bringe,
that I might haue entrye. 256

ADAMUS. (33)

Goe we to blisse, then, owld and yonge, 257
and worship god, alway weldinge,

Heading] *om.* H. 237 this] that H. 238 with Crosse on shoulder] that lives with you B W h D, *but in the latter simply before* with Crosse. such] this B W h D. 240 honge] hanged H. 241 but] *om.* B W h D. leeved] beleved B W h D. 242 saue vs bouth] us both saue B. 245 signes] synnys D. veray] fully verey h, full vereye B D, *perhaps to be taken into the text.* 247 I can] did I B W h D. 248 realme] region B W h D. he] I H. 249 To] that he woulde B W h D. by] *om.* B W h D. 250 this] to H. 251 be aye] playe B W h D. thou shalt] *before* with me D. 252] heitherwarde anon W h, hederward I nome D. so hither] heitherwarde B. 253 And] then B W h D. betooke] betaughte B W h D. 254 A] this B W h D. 255 The Angell michael] to Michell angell B W h D. 256 entrye] entrance h. 257] Now goe we to blesse bouth oulde and yonge B W h D. (bouth] *om.* D.) 258 alway weldinge] all willing W, all willinglie B h D.

and Afterward, I read, we singe
with great solemnity.

("Te Deu*m* laudam*us*, te D*omi*nu*m* co*n*fitemur." Et sic Ibunt glorificantes Deu*m*, ca*n*tantes "Te Deu*m*.")

Finis Paginæ Decime Septimoe.

[*The four MSS.*, B W h D, *continuing after the stage-direction as follows:*]

[MVLIER.

wo be to the tyme that I came heare!
I saye to thee nowe, lucifier,
with all thy felowshipe in feare,
that p*re*sente be in in place,

(34)

woful am I, with thee to dwell,
sir sathanas, sergante of hell!
endles paines and sorowe cruell
I suffer in this place.

sometyme I was a tavernere,
a gentill gossipe and a tapstere,
of wyne and ale a trustie brewer,
w*hi*ch wo hath me wroughte.

(35)

of cannes I kepte no trewe mesuer,
my cuppes I soulde at my pleasuer,
deceavinge manye a creature,
tho my ale were naughte.

and when I was a brewer longe,
with hoopes I made my ale stronge,
ashes and Erbes I blende amonge,
and marred so good mavlte.

(36)

therfore I maye my handes wringe,
shake my cannes and cuppes ringe,

259 Afterward] theiderwarde B W h D. *Stage-direction*] Tunc eant *omnes* et incipiat michell, te deum laudamus, dicat B W h D. (eant] eunt h, cantant B. incipiat] Incipiant W h, dicat] *om.* h B D.) finis] *om.* B D. paginæ Decime Septime] *om.* B D, deo gracias h W, *the latter adding:* p*er* me georgi bellin 1595. 261 (to] *om.* B D. 265 am I] I ame B. sergante] s*er*uant B. 267 paines and sorowe] sorrow *and* paynes B D. sorowe] sorowes h. 268 place] case B D. 273 kepte] kepe h. 278 hoopes] hoppes D. 282 cannes and cuppes] cupes *and* canes B D.

sorowfull maie I sicke and singe,
that ever I so dealed.

Taverners, tapsters of this cittie
shalbe p*ro*moted heare by me
for breakinge statut*es* of this cuntrey,
hurtinge the common welth;

(37)

with all tipplers, tapsters *that* are cunninge,
mysspendinge moche maulte, brewinge so theyne,
sellinge small cuppes, moneye to wyn,
against all truth to deale.

therfore this place ordeyned is
for suche ylle-doeres, so moche amisse;
here shall the have ther Ioye and blesse,
exsaulted by the neck;

(38)

with my mayster, mightye mahounde,
for castinge mavlte besyddes the combe,
moche watter takinge for to compounde
and litill of the secke;

with all masters, minglers of wyne in the nighte,
brewinge so blendinge against daye lighte:
suche newe made clarrytte is cause full righte
of sicknes and desease.

(39)

this I betake you, more and lesse,
to my sweete mayster, sir sathanas,
to dwell with hym in this place,
when it shall you please.

SATHANAS.

welckome, deare darlinge, to vs, all three;
though Iesus be gone with our meanye,

283 sorowfull] sorowfully h. sicke] syke D. 284 dealed] dalt D. 285 Taverners] Tavernes D. 286 by] w*i*th B D. 288 hurtinge] and hurtinge h. common] citie h. 289 tipplers] toppers h D, tiplinge W. tapsters] tappers h D. 293 ordeyned] nowe ordayned D. 294 for] so B. 301 minglers] mengers B D. 302 lighte] bryght B. 305 this] thus B D. 307 this] his W D. 309 darlinge] daughter D.

yet shall thou abyde heare still w*i*th me,
in paine with oute Ende. 312

SECUNDUS DEMON. (40)

welckome, dere ladye, I shall thee wedd! 313
for manye a heavye and droncken head,
cavse of thy ale, were broughte to bed,
farre worse then anye beaste. 316

TERCIUS DEMON.

welckome, dere darling, to endles balle; 317
vsinge cardes, dice, and cupes smalle,
with manye false outhes to sell thy ale;
nowe thou shalt haue a feaste!] 320

Pagina Decima Octava De Resurrectione Iesu Christi.

The Skinners.

PILATUS. (1)

Per vous, Sir Cayphas, 1
Et vous avous, Sir Annas
Et sum Disciple Iudas,
Gule Treison fuite. 4

Et grande luces de lucite, 5
A moy perfeyt deliuere,
Nostre Dame fuit Iudge,
per loys Roy estreit. 8

(2)

You lordinges and ladys so louely and leere, 9
You kempes, you known knights of kynde,

311 shall] shalt D. 313 dere] sweete h D. shall] will h D. 314 droncken] drinken B. 317 darling] daughter W. 320 shalt] shall W h. D *has at end:* finis huius paginae.

Christi] Christi 1600 h. Skinners] skinn*ers* playe B W h D, *in* W h D *before the Latin.* 2 vous avous] vous evous W h D. 3 Disciple] discipule W. 4] cule treison fuite W h. Ou le treison fuite D. vbi treson fuite B. 5 luces] lices W h, lucide B. 6 perfeyt] per foyet Iudge W, per foyte D. deliuere] deliuerie D. 7] mostre dame fint B W, *the latter adding* deliverie. 8 loys] loes W, loer h D. estreit] distreite h. 9 lordinges] lordes B W h D. louely] loving B. 10 kempes] kennes B W.

herkens all hitherward my hestes to here,
for I am most fayrest and freshest to fynde, 12

And moste highest I am of estate, 13
for I am Prince pereles most Royall man of Riches ;
I may deale and I may dresse,
my name is Sir Pilate. 16

(3)

ffor Cesar, lord moste of Posty, 17
honored my estate and my degree,
when that he sent Iesus to me,
to deliuer him to the dead. 20

They cryed on me all with one voyce, 21
the Iews on me made piteous noyce,
I gaue them leave to hange him on Crosse ;
this was through Iews redd. 24

(4)

I dreed yet lest he will vs greeve, 25
for that I saw, I may well beleeue ;
I saw the Stones began to cleeue,
and Dead men vp can ryse 28

In this Citty all about ; 29
was none so sterne ne so stowt,
that durst look vp for great doubt,
they could so sone agryse. 32

(5)

And therfor, Sir Cayphas, yet I dreed 33
lest ther were Peryll in that deed ;
I saw him hange on Rood and bleed
tyll all his bloud was shedd. 36

And when he should his Death take, 37
the wedder waxed wonderous blacke,
Layte, Thunder, and Earth began to quake,
therof I am a-dread. 40

11 herkens] harken B W. 12 fynde] fyne H. 13 *and* 14] *ought to be inverted.* 17 lord] prince W. 21 They] The D. 22 piteous] greate W h D. 24 Iews] Iesus h. 25 lest] lost H. 30 ne] nor h. 31 durst look vp] vp durst looke D, vp loked B W h. 32 agryse] agrie B. the were so sore agased W. 34 were] be W. 38 wedder] wedders D.

Cayphas. (6)

And this was yesterday abowt noone. 41

pilatus.

Yea, Sir Bishopp, this is one, 42
to speak therfor we haue to done,
for I leet bury him soone
in a Tomb of Stonne. 45

And therfore, Sirs, amongst vs three 46
let vs ordayne and oversee
if ther any perill be,
or we hence gone. 49

Cayphas. (7)

Sir pilate, all this was doone, 50
as we saw after soone,
but belyve, at after noone
the wedder began to cleare. 53

And, Sir, if it be your will, 54
such wordes you lett be still,
and speak of an other skyll,
lest any man vs here. 57

Annas. (8)

Yea, Sir Pilate, nought for-thy, 58
I saw him *and* his company
rayse men with Sorcerye,
that longe before were dead. 61

ffor and ther be any more such lafte 62
which can of any such wichcraft,
if that body be from vs rafte,
advyse you well, I redd. 65

Cayphas. (9)

Yea, Sir Pilate, I tell thee right, 66
lett vs ordayne many a harde Knight,
well armed, to stand and feight
with power and with force. 69

44 soone] full soone B W h D. 52 belyve] be tyme B W h. 55 be] to be B. 62 lefte] lafte B D. 63 any] *om.* B W h D. 66 thee] you B W h D. 67 harde] hardye H B.

That no shame to vs befall, 70
lett vs ordayne here amongst vs all,
and trew men to vs call,
to keep well the Coarse. 73

PILATUS. (10)

Now by Ih*esus*, that dyed on roode, 74
me think your counsell wonderous good;
the best men of kynne and bloud
anone I will call in. 77

Sir Colphran, and Sir Ierafas! 78
Aroysat and sir Gerapas!
we pray you, Sirs, here in this case,
anone looke you ne blinne. 81

(11)

A! my knights, stiffe and sterne of hart, 82
you be bowld men and smart;
I warne you now at word[ë]s short,
with you I haue to done. 85

PR*IMUS* MILES.

Sir, we be here, all and some, 86
as bowld men all ready bowne
to dryve your enemyes all adowne,
whyl that we may stande. 89

(12)

We be your knights, everichon; 90
fayntnes in vs ther shall be none.
we will be wroken vppon thy fonne,
wher euer he may be fownd; 93

and for no dred *that* we will wond! 94

71 amongst] amonge B W h D, *the reading of which eases a little this very rough line.* 75 counsell] consel is W h. 77 I will call in] loke ye no blyne W. call] haue h, *om.* D. 78—82] *om.* W. Ierafas] Ieregas B, Ieragas h D. 79 sir] *om.* H. Aroysat] Aroysiat B h D. Gerapas] gerophas h, Ierophas B D. 80 here] *om.* H. 82 A] and W h. 85 with] for with W h. I] we h. 86 all] both all B. 87 all] *om.* B W h D. 88 adowne] downe W. 89 whyl] why W. 91 fayntnes] fayntynes H. 93 *and* 94] *written as one line in* H. 94 wond] wounde B, wonne W h, wend D.

PILATUS.

That I am well to vnderstand : 95
you be men doughty of hand,
I loue you without lacke. 97

(13)

Butt *that* prophett that was done *and* draw 98
through *the* recounting of your law,
but yet some thinge me stands in awe
of wordës that he spake. 101

for sooth, this I hard him say, 102
that he would ryse the third day;
now surly, if he so may,
he hath a wonderous tatch. 105

SECUNDUS MILES. (14)

Yea, lett him ryse if that he dare! 106
and I may of him be warr,
he bode neuer a worse Charr,
or that he wend away. 109

I helped to slay him ere-whyle; 110
wenes he to do vs more guyle?
nay, it is no perayle,
my head here dare I lay. 113

TERTIUS MILES. (15)

Yea, lett him quicken hardely; 114
whyle my fellows here and I
may awak and stand him bye,
ne scapeth not vncought; 117

for and he once heave vp his head, 118
but that he be soone dead,
shall I neuer eate more bread,
ne neuer more be saght. 121

98 draw] drawes B W h D. 99 law] lawes B W h D. 100 me stands] we stand W h. awe] awes W h D. 102 I hard] harde I B W. 104 if] and B W h D. 106 he] hym W h D. 107 and] and yf B, for and W h D. may] *after* him, B W h, *om.* D. warr] aware B W h D. 110 ere] her B, yerre D. 113 here] their B W h. 117 scapeth] skaped W. 118 once] ofte W, one B. heave vp] leaue vs B. *After* 121] H *has a blank space for four verses more.*

PRIMUS MILES. (16)

Haue good day, Sirs! we will gone. 122
Geue vs our Charge, every one.

CAYPHAS.

Now fares well, the best of bloud *and* bone! 124
now takes heed vnto my saw!

for as I am a treue Iew, 126
yf that you any Treason sue,
ther is none of you all shall it eschew,
but he shall be to-draw. 129

SECUNDUS MILES. (17)

Now, fellows, we be charged hye; 130
our Prince hath sworne that we shall dye,
with out any prophesy
or any other enchare, 133

But if we done as the wyse; 134
I redd vs, we right well advyse,
though he be bowld he shall not ryse
but one of vs beware. 137

TERTIUS MILES. (18)

Sir, the most witt lyeth in thee, 138
to ordayne and ouersee;
you bene *the* eldest of vs three,
and man of most renowne. 141

The Tombe is here at our hand, 142
sett vs ther as we shall stand;
yf that he ryse we shall fond
to beate him all adowne. 145

PRIMUS MILES. (19)

And I shall now sett vs so, 146
yf that he ryse and would goe,

122 Sirs] syr D. will] wilbe B W h D. 123 every one] everye eich one B W h. Cayphas] pilatus B W h D, *and also in* H *there is, though crossed out, a* pilatus *besides* Cayphas. 124 fares] fare W. 125 now] and B W h D. heed] good heede B W h D. 127 sue] shewe W. 128 it eschew] esue W. 133 enchare] encure B, in charge W, encharre D. 134 we] the W h. 135 vs] *om.* W. we] here h. 139 and] and to B W h D. 141 and] a H. 144 fond] found D. 145 all] *om.* B W h D.

one of vs, or ell[ë]s two,
Shall see of his vprist. 149

Stand thou here and thou ther, 150
and I my selfe in middle mere.
I trow our hart[ë]s will not feer,
but it were stowtly wyst. 153

(Tunc Cantabunt duo Angeli, "Christus resurgens a mortuis, &c.," et *Christus* tunc resurget ac Cantu finito dicat vt sequitur :)

IESUS RESURGENS. (20)

Earthly man, that I haue wrought, 154
awake out of thy sleepe!
Earthly man, whom I haue bought,
of me thou take no keepe. 157

from heauen mans sowl I sought 158
into a Dongeon deepe;
my deere Lemmon from thence I brought,
for ruthe of her I weep. 161

(21)

I am very prince of peace 162
and kinge of free mercy;
who will of sinnës haue releace,
on me the call *and* cry. 165

And if they will of synnës cease, 166
I graunt them peace truly,
and therto a full riche messe
in Bread, my own body. 169

(22)

I am very bread of lyfe, 170
from heauen I light *and* am send.
who eateth this Bread, man or wyfe,
shall lyue with me, without ende. 173

149 vprist] uprise W. 150 ther] here W, here *and* there] *transposed* D. 152 *and* 153] *om.* h. resurget] resurgit B. ac] ac postea B W h D. sequitur] sequitur Iesus resurgens et pede omnes milites quatiat B W h D, *in the latter as heading* (pede] pedes B, omnes] eos B D). *Heading*] Iesus B W h. 156 Earthly] earth B. whom] that D. 157 take] haue W h. 161 of] or W. 164 sinnes] Sinmes H. 165 the] *altered into* they *by a later hand in* H. 166 synnes] Sinmes H. 168 therto] threto H. messe] messye W h. 172 this] that B W h D.

And that Bread that I you geue,
your wicked lyfe to amend,
becomes my flesh through your beleife,
and doth release your sinfull Band.

(23)

And who so ever eateth that Bread
in synne or wicked lyfe,
he receiveth his owne death,
I warne both man *and* wyfe.

The which bread shall be seene insteade,
ther ioy is aye full ryfe,
when he is dead through fooles redd,
then is he brought to payne *and* stryf.

(Tunc duo Angeli postq*uam* C*hristus* resurrexit, sedebunt in Sepulcro quo*rum* alter ad Caput, alter ad pedes sedeant.)

PRIMUS MILES. (24)

Out Alas! wher am I?
so bright about is hereby,
that my hart wholly
out of Slough is shaken.

So fowle feared with fantasye
was I neuer in none anoy,
for I witt not witterly
whether I be on slepe or waken.

SECUNDUS MILES. (25)

Wher art thou, Sir Bachler?
about me is wonder cleare.
witt me wants, without were,
for fearder I neuer was.

To remove, farr or neer,
me fayles might and power;
my hart[e] in my body heer
is hoven out of my Brest.

175 to] for to B W h. 178 eateth] eathe H. 179 or] and D. 182 in steade] stydd H. 183 ther] the D. ryfe] rafte W. 184 fooles] *om.* H. postq*uam*] posteaq*uam* D. resurrexit] resurrexisit H. 189 slough] my breste W. 192 witt] wott D. *Before* 194] D W *and* h *have:* tunc sociu*m* surgere cogett. (cogett] cogit D.) 195 wonder] wondrous B. *Line* 201 *is followed in* B W h D *by lines* 210—217.

TERTIUS. (26)

Alas! what is this great light,
shininge here in my sight?
marred I am, bothe mayn *and* might,
to move haue I no meane.

Thes two Beastes that are so bright!
power I ne haue to ryse aright;
me fayles with them for to feight,
would I neuer so fayne.

PRIMUS MILES. (27)

Yea, we ar shent sickerly;
for Iesu is risen, well wott I,
out of the Sepulcre mightely,
and therof I haue in mynd.

And as dead here can I lye,
speak might I not, ne espye
which way he tooke truly,
myne eyes the were so blynd.

SECUNDUS MILES. (28)

Yea, I will Creep forth on my knee,
tyll I this perill passed be,
for my way I may not see,
neyther earth nor stonne.

Yea, in a wicked tyme we
nayled hym on the Rood Tree,
for as he sayd, in day[ë]s three
Risen he is and gone.

TERTIUS MILES. (29)

Hye we fast we weer away,
for this is gods sonne veray;
stryve with him we ne may,
that maister is and more.

Heading] Tertius miles D. 204 bothe] *om.* W. 205 meane] mayne D. 207 I ne haue] have I non B W, non I haue h. 208 fayles] fayle D. *Before* 210] *as stage-direction*, Tunc tangett socium somno Desurgere cogett B W h D. (tangett] tangit B, cogett] cogett dicat W.) (somno desurgere cogett] et de somno surgere coget D). 212 out] and out H. 213 haue] ame h. 215 not] *om.* W, non h. espye] spie W h. 218 on] upon B D. 221 nor] ney B h D. 222 a] *om.* W. 223 hym] hin H. 225] that he woulde rise againe B W h D.

I will to Cayphas, by my fay,
the sooth openly for to say.
fare well, Sirs, and haue good day!
for I will goe before.

PRIMUS MILES. (30)

We two lenge here, it is no boote;
for needs to Sir pilate we moote,
and tell him, both Cropp and Roote,
so soothly as we wist!

for and *the* Iews knewe, as well as we,
that he were rysen through his posty,
then should the last[ë] errer be
worse then was the first. (Tunc adeunt Pilatum.)

SECUNDUS MILES. (31)

Herken, Sir Pilate, the sooth to sayne,
Iesu, that was on fryday slayne,
through his might is risen agayne,
this is the third day.

Ther came no power him to fett,
but such a slepe on vs he sett,
that none of vs might him lett
to ryse and goe his way.

PILATUS. (32)

Now by *the* othe I haue to Cesar sworne,
all you Doggs sonnes beforn to morne
shall dye! therfore think no scorne
yf it be on you long.

yf that you haue prevely
sould him to his company,
then are you worthy for to dye,
right in your owne wronge.

230 by my fay] by and by B W. 234 two] to B W h D. it] *om.* W D. is] were W h. 236 both] *om.* W. 238 *the*] they D. knewe] knowe h, wist H. 240 errer] errande W. 241 was] *om.* W h. *Stage-direction*] *in the margin in* H. tunc] *om.* B. 247 on vs he] he on vs B h D, he on me W. 249 way] wayes W h. 250 Cesar] sir Caesar B D. othe] othe *that* H D. 251 all] A W. beforn to morne] *om.* B W h D (W *putting into one line:* a you dogges sonnes *and* shall dye therfore). 252 think no scorne] *om.* B W h D. 253 yf] are B. be on you long] one you belonge h.

TERTIUS MILES. (33)

Now by the order *that* I bear of knight, 258
he rose vp in *the* morning-light
by vertu of his ow[e]n might,
I knowe it well afyne, 261

He rose vp, as I say now, 262
and lefte vs lying, I wott near how!
all be-mased in a sowne,
as we had bene sticked swyne. 265

PILATUS. (34)

fye Theif! fye Traytor! 266
fye on thee! thy Thrift is full bare.
fye feind! fye feyture!
Hye hence! fast, I redd, that thou fare. 269

PRIMUS MILES. (35)

That tyme that he his way tooke, 270
durst I neither speak nor looke,
but for fear I lay and quooke,
and lay in a Sownd Dreame. 273

He sett his foote vpon my Backe, 274
that every lith began to cracke;
I would not byde such another Shacke
for all Ierusalem. 277

PILATUS. (36)

fye harlott! fye hownd! 278
fye on thee, thou taynted Dogge!
why lay thou still in that stownd
and lett that Lozenger go on thee, rogge? 281

Sir Cayphas, and Sir Annas, 282
what say you to this trespas?
I pray you, Sirs, in this case
advyse me of some readd. 285

259 light] bright B. 261 knowe] knew H h. well afyne] vereye well W. 264 bemased] me mased B W h H. in] and in D. sowne] swoone D. 267 Thrift] truste B W h D. 269 that] *om.* W. 273 a] *om.* B W h D. Sownd] sowne B. 275 lith] joynt B. 276 byde] abyde B W h D. 279 taynted] taynted taken B D. 280 why] what B W h D. 281 go] so H, go so fir one the rogge B, go so D. 282 Annas] Amnas H. 283 trespas] deed ? *because of the rhyme.*

CAYPHAS. (37)

Now good Sir, I you praye,
herkyns to me what I say—
For much avayle vs it may—
and doe after my Spell!

Pray them now, sir, perdye,
as they loven well thee,
here as the standen all thre,
to keep well our counsell.

ANNAS. (38)

Sir Bushopp, I say to you verament,
vnto your Counsell I fully assent;
this foolishe prophett, that we all to-rent,
through his witchcraft is stolen away.

Therfore lett vs call our Counsell togeather,
and lett vs conclude to the whole matter,
or ells *our* laws are done for ever hereafter.

PILATUS. (39)

Now in good fayth full wo is me,
and so I trow bene all ye,
that he is risen thus prevely
and is from vs escaped.

Now I pray you, Sirs, as you loue me,
Keepe this in close and privitye,
vntill our Counsell, and tyll we
haue hard how he is scaped.

(Tunc tradet eis pecunia*m* et discedunt et venient mulieres plorantes ac Iesu*m* querentes.)

MARIA MAGDALENA. (40)

Alas! now lorne is my lykinge,
for woe I wander and handes wringe;
my hart in sorrow and sighinge
is sadly sett and sore.

287 I say] I you saie W h D, I can say B. 295 fully] fullie me B. 296 foolishe] foolihe H. 300 for ever hereafter] *possibly to be altered into* for aye, *because of the rhyme.* hereafter] *om.* D. 308 he] it H. scaped] shaped H. et] ac B W h. 311 and] and in W.

That I most loved of all thinge,
Alas! is now full low lyinge.
why am I, lord, so longe lyvinge
to loose thy luxom lore?

MARIA IACOBI. (41)

Alas! wayle away! is went
my help, my heale from me is hent;
my Christ, my comforte that me kent
is Clongen now in Clay.

Mighty god omnipotent,
thou geue them hard Iudgment
that my Soveraine hath so shent!
for so I may well say.

MARIA SOLOME. (42)

Alas! now marred is all my might;
my lord, throw whom my hart was light,
shamfully slayne here in my sight;
my sorrow is aye vnsought.

Sith I may haue no other right
of these Devills that haue my lord so dight,
to Balme his Body, that is so bright,
Boyst here haue I brought.

MARIA MAGDALENA. (43)

Suster, which of vs echone
shall remove this great Stonne
that lyeth my sweet Lord vppon?
for move it I ne may.

MARIA IACOBI.

Sister, maystrye is it none,
it semes to me as he were gone,
for on the Sepulcre sitteth one,
and the Stonne away.

316 luxom] luxonne D. 319 comforte] Counsell H. 320 clongen] lodged B. 325 all] *om.* D. 326 my hart] that I B W h D. 329 may] *om.* B W. 333 echone] everye one W, every eichone B h, everychon D. 337 is it] it is h. 338 it] he H.

MARIA SOLOME. (44)

Two Children ther I see sittinge,
all of whyte is ther Clothinge,
And the Stonne besyde lyinge;
goe we neare and see! (Tunc ibunt et in Sepulcrum circumspicient.)

ANGELUS PRIMUS. (45)

What seeke ye, women, what seeke ye here,
with weping and with vnlyking cheare?
Iesus, that to you was deare,
is Risen, leeve you me!

ANGELUS SECUNDUS.

Be not afrayd of vs in feere!
for he is gone, withoutten were,
as he before can you leere,
forth into Galely.

ANGELUS PRIMUS. (46)

This is *the* place, be ye apayd,
that Iesu, our lord, was in layd;
but he is risen as he sayd,
and heathen went away.

ANGELUS SECUNDUS.

Hye you, for ought that may befall,
and tell his Disciples all,
and Peter also tell you shall,
ther fynd him that you may.

MARIA MAGDALENA. (47)

A! hye we fast for any thinge,
and tell Peter this Tydinge;
a Blessedfull word we may him bringe,
sooth if that it weere.

341 ther] here W h, ther *put after* I see B D. 342 Clothinge] Clothnge H. *Stage-direction*] tunc ibunt et asspitiunt in sepulcrum B W h D. *Heading*] primus angellus W h. 345 *Second* what seeke ye] *om.* B W h D. 346 *Second* with] *om.* D. *Heading*] Secundus Angellus W h. 349 of vs] *before* in feere H. 350 gone] wente W h D. withoutten were] as we did see h. *Heading*] primus Angellus W h. 353 place] place therfore B W h D. apayd] payde W h. ye] *om.* D. *Heading*] Secundus Angellus B W h. 359 tell] saye B W h D. 361 A] Ah D.

MARIA IACOBI.

Yea, walke thou, Suster, by one way,
and we another shall assay,
tyll we haue mett with him to day,
my deerworth lord, so deere.

(Tunc discedunt et paulisper circu*m*ambulabunt, et tunc obvient Discipulis, Petro et Iohanni.)

MARIA MAGDA*LENA*. (48)

Ah! Peter and Ihon! Alas! Alas!
ther is befallen a wondrous case;
some man my lord stollen hase,
and putt him I wott not where.

PETRUS.

what! is he removed out of the place
in the which he Buryed was?

MARIA MAGDA*LENA*.

Yea, sickerly, all my solace
is gone and is not there.

IOH*ANNES* EVANGE*LISTA*. (49)

Peter, goe we thidder anone,
ru*n*ning as fast as we may gone,
and looke who hath removed *the* stonne,
and whether he be away.

PETRUS.

Abyde, Brother, sweet Iohn,
lest we meet with any fone!
but now I see non other wonne,
to runne I will assay.

(Tunc simul concurrunt sed Ioh*annes* precuret citius petro, et non intrat sepulchru*m*.)

IOHANNES. (50)

A! peter, Brother, in good fay
my lord Iesu is away!

368 deerworth] worthy W h. discedunt] discedent W h D. petro] petrus W. Iohanni] Iohanni et dicat maria magd*alena* W. 372 wott not] not, *which would ease the line very much*, B. 375 sickerly] sicker B W. Evangelista] Evangelist D. 378 may gone] can W. 379 and] to B W D. tunc] tucunc ambo h D. concurrunt] co*n*currerint H, concurrent W. precuret] precucurrerit H B, precurreret D. citius] *om.* H. non intrat sepulchru*m*] prior veniet ad Sepulcru*m* H. intrat] intrant B W.

but his Sudary, sooth to say,
lyinge here I fynde
By it selfe, as thou see may,
farr from all other Clothes it lay;
now maryes wordes are sooth veray,
as we may haue in mynde.

PETRUS. (51)

Yea, but, as god keep me from woe,
into the Sepulcre I will goe,
to looke whether it be very so,
as Marye to vs can say. (Tunc introibit in Sepulcrum.)
A! lord, Blessed be thou ever and oo,
for as thou towld me and other moe,
I fynd thou hast overcomen our foe,
and rysen art, in good fay.

PETRUS. (52) (Tunc Petrus Lamentando dicat:)

A! lord, how shall I doe for shame,
that haue deserved so much blame,
to forsake thy swete name,
to meet with thee by any way?
I, that in penance and great anye
my sweet lord forsooke Thrye!
save endles hope of his mercy,
ther to trust I may.

(53)

for ne it were his great Grace,
and sorrow in hart that in me was,
worse I were then was Iudas,
my lord so to forsake.

IOHANNES EVANGELISTA.

Peter, comfort thee in this case!
for, sicker, my lord Iesus accepted hase

387 sudary] shouldarye W h. 394 sepulcre] sepulture h. 395 whether] yf B W. 399 overcomen] overcomnen H. petrus] petrus et W. dicat] dicit B. *Heading*] *om.* W h. 401 lord] lore W. 403 swete] holye W. 409 for ne it] for it ne B. 410 in hart] of harte W. that] as h. 411 was Iudas] Iudas was W. Evan*gelista*] *om.* B W h D. 413 this] thes H. 414 sicker] suerlie W h. accepted] *om.* D. my lord] *an omission of these two words would make the verse run smoothly.*

great repentance for thy trespas,
my lord in hart will take.

(54)

Goe we, seeke Iesu anone in hye!
one way thou and another way I.

PETRUS.

Yea, well I hope, through his might,
my penance shall him please.

(Tunc abeunt hic *per* aliam via*m*, ille *per* altera*m*.—molieres venient.)

MARIA MAGDALENA.

Hence will I never, sickerly,
till I be comforted of my anye,
and know wher he is redely,
here will I sitt and weepe.

ANGELUS PRIMUS. (55)

Woman, why wepest thou so aye?

MARIA MAG*DALENA*.

Sonne, for my lord is taken away,
and I wott nere, the sooth to say,
who hath done this thinge.

Alas! why were I not dead to day,
Clought and Clongen vnder Clay!
to se my lord that here lay
once at my lykinge?

(Tunc veniet Iesus Alba indutus Baculu*mque* crucis manib*us* portans et Maria magdalena venienti sit obvia*m* dicens.)

418 and] *om.* W h D. abeunt] vadunt H. molieres venient] *om.* H. 421 Hence] Heathen D. primus] *om.* H. *Heading*] primus angellus W h. 425] B *ends here, but has space for* 4—6 *lines left blank after* aye, *has no* finis, *and the opposite page* (1352) *is also quite blank.* 427 nere] not where W h. 428 this] that W h D. *After* 432] D *has* Finis. W *has:*

finis Deo gracias *per* me Georgi bellin } 1592

Come lorde Iesu Come quicklye } 1592

432 *to the end*] *om.* W B. *Instead of the Latin stage-direction* h *has:* then cometh Iesus with a robe about hym, and a crosse staffe in his hande, and mary magdelena appeared vnto hym in the dawninge of the day, and Iesus shall say to her.

IHES*US*. (56)

Why wepest thou, woman? tell me why!
whom seek[e]st thou so tenderly?

MARIA MAGD*ALENA*.

My lord, Sir, was buryed hereby,
and now he is away;

If thou hast done me this anye,
tell me, leife sir, hastely,
anone this Ilk day.

IHES*US*. (57)

Woman, is not thy name Marye?

MARIA MAGDA*LENA*.

A lord! I aske the mercy!

IHES*US*.

Mary, touche not my Body!
for yet I haue not beene

With my father Almighty;
But to my Brethren goe thou in hye,
and of this thing thou certify
that thou hast soothly seen.

(58)

Say to them all that I will gone
to my father, that I came from,
and ther father he is alsoe;
hye! looke that thou ne dwell!

MARIA MAGDA*LENA*.

A! bee thou blessed ever and oe!
now wayved is all my woe.
this is ioy to them *and* other moe;
anone I will goe tell.

(It maria magda*lena* ad mariam Iacobi et ad mariam Solome.)

433 wepest] reamest h. 434 whom] and whom h. seekst thou] thou seekest h. 437 hast] haue h. me] hym h. 441 the] *om.* h. *Heading*] maria magdelena, *and* H, *too has, though crossed out,* Maria Magd. 444 with] at h. 448 to] *om.* h. gone] go *is required by the rhyme as well as* froo. 450 is alsoe] and I all one H. 452] A blessed be thou ever and oye h. *Stage-direction*] here marye magdelen goeth to mary Iacobi and to mary Salome sayinge h.

MARIA MAGDALENA. (59)

Ah women, wayle now wonnen is:
my lord Iesu is Rysen, iwys;
with him I spake a little or this,
and saw him with myne eye.

My Bale is torned into Blisse,
mirth in mynd ther may none mysse,
for he bade warne that was his,
to heven that he would flee.

MARIA IACOBI. (60)

A! Sister, goe we search and see
whether these wordes sooth[e] bee;
no mirth were halfe so much to me,
to see him in this place.

MARIA SALOME.

A! Sister, I besech thee,
with full will wynde we;
for fayne, me thinkes, me list to fly
to see his fayre face.

(Tunc ibunt mulieres et veniet obviam illis Iesus dicens:)

IHESUS. (61)

All hayle, women! all hayle!

MARIA IACOBI.

A! lord, we leeven, without fayle,
that thou art Rysen vs to heale,
and wayved vs from woe.

MARIA SOLOME.

A! welcome be thou, my lord sweet!
lett vs kisse thy blessed feete,
and handle thy woundes that be so weet,
or that we hence goe.

459 eye] eyes h. 462 he] ha, *but corrected into* hee *in another ink* H. 463 flee] stea h. 469 will] mynd H. 471 fayre] freely h. *Stage-direction*] then shall the women goe and Iesus shall meete them sayinge h. *After* 472] then marye Iacoby makeinge curtesye sayth h. 474 heale] wayle h. 477 blessed] sweete h.

IHESUS. (62)

Be not afrayd, women, of me, 480
but to my Brethren now wend yee,
and bydd them goe to Galelye,
ther meet with me they mon. 483

MARIA IACOBI.

Anon, lord, done it shall be. 484
well is them, this sight to see;
for mankynd, lord, is bought by thee
and through thy gret Passion. 487

(Tunc ibunt ad Petru*m* et ait maria Solome.)

MARIA SOLOME. (63)

Peter, Tydinges good and new! 488
we haue seene my lord Iesu
on lyfe, clean in hyde and hew,
and handled haue his feete. 491

PETRUS.

Yea, well is yee that haue bene trew, 492
for I forsware that I him knew,
therfore shame makes me eschew,
with my lord for to meet. 495

(64)

But yet I hope to se his face, 496
though I haue done so great Trespas;
my sorrow of hart know he hase,
and to yt will take heede. 499

Thither as he buryed was, 500
I will hye me, to runne apace,
of my swet lord to Aske Grace
for my fowle misdeed. (Tunc veniet Iesus obvians Petro.) 503

IHESUS. (65)

Peter, knows thou not me? 504

486] forbought be mankynde lorde by thee h. 487 and] *om.* h. *Heading*] Then they shall goe to peter and mary Salome saith h. 493 forsware] forsoke h. 500 thither] theire h. 502 of] and of h. to] *om.* H. 503 for] of H. *Stage-direction*] here Iesus cometh in with A crosse staffe in his hand h.

PETRUS.

A! lord, mercy I aske thee
with full hart, knelinge on my knee;
forgeue me my Trespase. 507

My faynt flesh and my fraylty 508
made me, lord, falce to be,
but forgeuenes with hart free
thou graunt me, through thy Grace! 511

IESUS. (66)

Peter, so I thee beheight, 512
thou should forsake me that night
but of this deed thou haue in sight,
when thou hast Soverainty; 515

Thinke on thyne ow[e]n deed to day, 516
that flesh is frayle and fallinge aye,
and mercifull be thou allway,
as now I am to thee. 519

(67)

Therfore I suffered thee to fall, 520
that to thy Subiects, hereafter, all
that to thee shall cry and call,
thou may haue minning. 523

Sithen thy self so fallen hase, 524
the more inclyne to graunt Grace!
Goe forth—forgeuen is thy Trespase—
and haue here my Blessinge! 527

finis paginæ Decimæ Octavæ.

508 and] *om.* h. 518 mercifull be thou] merciable thou be h. 523 minning] meaninge h. 524 so] *om.* H. 525] more] mere? H. paginæ Decimæ octavæ] deo gracias 1600 h.

Pagina Decima Nona de Christo duob*us* Discipulis ad castellu*m* Emavs evntib*us* apparente : et aliis Discipulis.

LUCAS. (1)

Alas ! now weale is went away,
myne owne my maister ever I may,
that is now Clongen vnder Clay,
that makes my hart in care.

Sorrow and Sighinge, the sooth to say,
makes me half dead, that is no nay ;
when I think on him, night and day,
for dole I drowp and dare.

CLEAPAS. (2)

Ye, much mirth was in me,
my swete Soverayne whyl I might se,
and his lyking lore with lee,
which now so low is layd.

Brother, now are Day[ĕ]s three
sith he was neiled vpon the Tree ;
lord, whether he rysen bee,
as he before hath sayde ?

LUCAS. (3)

Leife Brother Clephas,
to know that were [a] coynt[ë] case ;
sith he throw hart wounded was,
how should he lyve agayne ?

CLEOPAS.

If that he godhead in him hase,
and commen to buy mans trespase,
he may ryse through his owne Grace,
and his death do vs gayne.

Latin heading] *preceded by* The Saddlers playe *in* W h D, *followed by the same title in* B. discipulis] discipulis et dicat lucas W. 2 myne owne] *probably* mone *is meant* (Zupitza). 3 Clongen] logged B. 6 half dead] both B D. mone W h. 7 night] both night D. 8 drowp] droppe W h. *Heading*] Cleophas D. 10 Soverayne] Severayne H. whyl] when B W h D. might] die (*for* did ?) B. 12 which] and B W h D. 13 are] is B W h D. 14 vpon the Tree] on roode tree W, one the roode tree h. 15 lord] bord (?) D. 16 hath] hade W h. 18 that] this B W h. coynt] cvninge W h. 21 he] *om.* D. 22 mans] ma*n*kynds H. 24 do] to B W h D.

LUCAS. (4)

A mysty thinge it is to me
to haue beleef it should so be,
how he should ryse in dayes thre;
such wonders neuer was wyst.

CLEOPAS.

Sooth thou sayest, now well I se;
leeve may I not, by my luteeye!
but god may of his maiesty
doe what soeuer hym lyst. (Tunc veniet Ih*esus* in habitu peregrinæ et ait:)

IH*ESUS*. (5)

Good men, if your will were,
tell me in good manere
of your talkinge; that, in feare,
and of your woe witt I would.

CLEOPAS.

A! Sir, it seeme to vs here,
a Pilgrem thou art, as can appeare;
Tydings and Tales all intyre
thou may hear what is towld

(6)

In Ierusalem that other day,
thou that walkest many a way,
may thou not hear what men do say,
about ther as thou yeed?

IH*ESUS*.

What are those? tell me, I thee pray.

LUCAS.

Of Iesus of Nazareth, in good fay,
a prophett to ech mans pay,
and wyse in word and deed.

25 mysty] migstie (*for* mightie?) B. 28 neuer was] was neu*er* B. 29 now] full W h. 30 may] *om.* H. luteye] lewtie B W h. my] any D. 32 what soeuer] whateu*er* B. hym] he H. veniet] venit B W h. peregrinæ] peregrino D. periogrem W. ait] dicat Iesu W h, dicat eis B D. 35 talkinge] calling B. that] thar? (Zupitza). 37 seeme] seemes B W. 38 can] doth W h. 39 Tydings] good tyting*es* B, tydinge D. intyre] in teere D. 42 thou that] that thou W. 43 do] *om.* W. 45 tell me] *before* what B. 48 and] in H. 50 cursten] cursen B D, cursed W h.

(7)

To god and man wyse was he,
but Bishopps—cursten mott they be!—
damned him and nailed him on a Tree,
that wronge neuer yet wrought.

CLEOPHAS.

Witterly before wend we
that Israell he should haue made free;
and out of payne, through his posty,
the People he should haue brought!

LUCAS. (8)

Yea, Sir, now this is the third day,
sith they made this affray;
and some women, ther as he lay,
were yerly in the morne;

And feared vs foule, in fay:
they tould vs he was stolln away,
and Angells, as they can say,
the Sepulcre sitting beforne.

CLEOPAS. (9)

Yea, Sir, these wemen, that hard I,
sayd he was Risen redely;
and some men of our company
thither anon can goe;

And fownd it so as it towld of yore,
and they sayd so, neither lesse nor more,
and yet our hartes are full sore,
lest it be not so.

IHESUS. (10)

A! fooles and feeble, in good fay,
latt to beleev vnto gods law!
the prophetts before can thus say;
leeve you on this soothly,

52] that wroughte yet never wronge W h. 54 he] *om.* W. haue] a h. 57 this] *om.* B W h D. 60 yerly] Erlye W h, *om.* B. 64 Sepulcre] sepulture h. these] ther B. 69 towld of yore] so lesse and more B W h. as it towld of yore] lesse and more D. 70] *om.* B W h. 74 law] *the synonymous* lay *is required by the rhyme.* 75 thus] this B W h. say] sawe B W h.

That it needs be, all way, 77
Christ to suffer death, the sooth to say,
and to ioy that lasteth aye,
bring man through his mercy. 80

(11)

And first at Moses to beginne, 81
what he sayeth I shall you minne,
that God was a Greave within,
that burned aye as hym thought. 84

The Greave payred nothing therby: 85
what was that but mayd Mary,
that bare Iesu Sinlesly,
that man hath now forbought? 88

(12)

Also Esay sayd this, 89
as a woman co*m*forts, Iwis,
her Child that hath done amis,
to amend, leeve you me; 92

So god would man reconciled hear, 93
through his mercy, in good maner,
and in Ierusalem, if better weere,
forbought they should be. 96

(Que*m*admod*um* mater consolatur filios suos ita et ego consolabor vos et in Ierusalem consolabimini. Esayas Capitulo sexagesimo sexto.)

CLEOPAS. (13) Is. lxvi, 13.

A! lord geue thee good Grace, 97
for greatly comforted me thou hase.
goe with vs to this place,
a Castle is hereby. 100

IHESUS.

Now, good men, soothly for to say, 101
I haue to goe a great way,
therfore at this tyme I ne may,
but I thank you hartely. 104

83 within] with hym W h. 84 hym] he H. 87 Sinlesly] sincerlye W h. 95 if] in B W D. Capitulo sexagesimo sexto] *om.* h. sexto] sexto et dicat W sexto et dicat capitulo 66 B. 101 for] *om.* D.

LUCAS. (14)

Sir, you shall, in all maner, 105
dwell with vs at our Supper,
for now night aprocheth nere;
tary heer for any thinge! 108

CLEOPHAS.

Now God forbydd that we wear 109
so vncourteous to you here;
for save my louely lord of leer,
thy lore is most lykinge. (Tunc *omnies* ad Castell*um* evnt.) 112

LUCAS. (15)

Sitt down, Sir, here, I you pray, 113
and take a morsell, if you may,
for you haue walked a great way
sith to day at morne. 116

IH*ESUS*.

Graunt mercy, good men, in good fay; 117
to blesse this Bread, sooth to say,
I will anone in good aray,
rightly you beforne. (Tunc frangit pan*em* et ait.) 120

(16)

Eates on, men, and doe gladly, 121
in the name of good Almighty!
for this bread blessed haue I,
that I geue you to day. (tunc Iesus evanescet.) 124

LUCAS.

Graunt mercy, Sir, sickerly! 125
now I read you be right merry!
what! wher is he that sate vs by?
alas! he is away. 128

CLEOPAS. (17)

Alas! Alas! Alas! Alas! 129
this was Iesus in this place.

112 lore] lorde W h D. *Stage-direction*] *in* H *in the margin:* Tunc ibit Iesus cu*m* illis ad castillu*m* B W D h. 113 Sir here] here sire B W h. 114 if] and W. 115 great] longe W. 116 morne] noone B W h D. 117 men] me W. 120 rightly] righte by W. *Stage-direction*] *in* H *in the margin.* frangit] franget W. ait] dicat B h D, dicat Iesus W. *Stage-direction*] *in* H *in the margin.* evanescet] evanesit B H D. 125 Sir] *om.* W h. 126 I read] rede I B W h D.

by breaking of bread I knew his face,
but nothing ther before.

LUCAS.

A burning hart in vs he masse;
for whyle that he with vs here was,
to know him we might haue no grace,
for all his luxom lore.

CLEOPAS. (18)

Goe we, Brother, and that anone,
and tell our Brethren, everychone,
how our maister is from vs gone;
yea, sothly we may say.

LUCAS.

yea, well may we make our mone,
that sate with him in great wonne,
and we no knowledg had him vpon
till he was passed away.

(Tunc Ibunt ad Cateros Discipulos in alio loco *con*gregatos.)

CLEOPHAS. (19)

A! rest well, Brethren, one and all!
wonderously is vs befall:
our lord and we were in a hall,
and him yet knew not we!

ANDREAS.

Yea, leeue thou well this, Cleophas,
that he is risen that dead was,
and to Peter appered hase
this day apert[e]ly.

LUCAS. (20)

With vs he was a longe fytt,
and opened his holy writt,
and yet our wytt[ë]s were so knytt
that him we might not know.

131 of] *om.* h, the W D. 133 masse] made B W h D. 134 that] *om.* B W h, hee D. here] *before* with W h. was] stayde h. 135 might] migh H. 136 luxom] luxon D. 141 well may we] we maye B W h D. 143 had him] hym hade W. Cateros] alios B W h D. *con*gregatos] congregatos dicat Cleophas W. 145 well] *om.* B. 147 lord] master h. in-a] in on W h. 153 vs] *om.* H. 154 opened] vndid B W h D.

CLEOPAS.

Now sicker away was all my witt, 157
tyll the Bred was broken, ech Bytt,
and anone when he brake yt,
he vanished in a thrawe. 160

PETRUS. (21)

Now we be, Brethren, all in feere; 161
I redd we hyde vs somwher here,
that Iewes meet vs not, in no manere,
for malice, leeue you me. 164

ANDREAS.

Lenge we here in this place; 165
P*er*adventure god will shew vs grace,
To see *our* lord in little space,
and comforted for to bee. 168

(Tunc o*mn*ies eunt infra Castellu*m*, et veniet Iesus stans in medio Discipulo*rum*, ac postea dicat.)

IH*ESUS*. (22)

Peace amongst you, Brethren fayre! 169
yea, dread you not, in no maner;
I am Iesus, with out were,
that dyed on rood Tree. 172

PETRUS.

A! what is he that comes here 173
to this fellowship all in feere?
as he to me can now appeare,
a ghost me think I see. 176

IH*ESUS*. (23)

Brethren, why are you so frayd for nought, 177
and noyed in hart for feble thought?
I am he that haue you forbought,
and dyed for mans good. 180

My feet, my handes you may see, 181
and know the sooth allso may yee,

Heading] *om.* W h. 157 away was] a was was W. 160 thrawe] Thrall B H D. 161 be] *om.* W h D. all] *om.* W h. eunt] erunt H. Castellu*m*] castru*m* B W h D. dicat] dicat Iesus W. petrus] petter W h. 175 can now] he can H. now] *before* can W h D. 177 so] *om.* B. 178 noyed] moved h. 179 haue] hath B W h D. 182 sooth] truth W h.

soothly that I am he
that dead was vpon a tree. 184

(24)

Handle me, both all and one, 185
and leeve this well, everichone,
that ghost hath neither flesh ne bone,
as you see now on me. 188

ANDREAS.

A! lord, much ioy is vs vppon, 189
but what he is wott I ne can.

IH*ESUS*.

Now sith you leeve I am no man,
more signes you shall see. 192

(25)

haue you any meat hear? 193

PETRUS.

Yea my lord, leefe *and* dear,
rosted fishe *and* hony, in feere,
therof we haue good wonne. 196

IH*ESUS*.

Eate we then, in good manere: 197
thus you now know, without were,
that ghost to eate hath no power,
as you shall see anon. (Tunc comedet Ih*esus* et dabit Discipulis.) 200

(26)

Brethren, I towld you before, 201
when I was with you, not gayne an houre,
that needly both less and more
must fulfilled bee. 204

In Moses law, as written were; 205
all other prophesyes as then were,

184 tree] *most probably* rood *should be read.* 186 leeve] beleeve W h. well] *om.* h, *before* this B W D. 187 ne] nor W. 192 signes] signe H h. 198 now] *after* thus B W h D. *Stage-direction*] *in the margin in* H. comedet] comedent W, comedit B h D. Discipulis] discipulis suis Iesus B W h D, Iesus *as heading in* D. 202 an] one h. 203 both] *om.* W. 205 law] lawes B. 206 prophesyes] prophettes B W h D. then] nowe B W h D.

is fulfilled, in good manere
of that was sayd of me. 208

(27)

for this was written in prophesye, 209
that I must suffer death needly,
and the third day with victory
ryse in good aray; 212

And prech Remission of Sinne 213
vnto all men that his name doth mynne.
therfore all you *that* be herein,
think on what I say! 216

(Iter*um* evanescet Ihe*sus* et Discipuli versus Bethaniam ibunt et Thomæ obviantes dicat petrus.)

PETRUS. (28)

A! Thomas, Tydinges, good *and* new! 217
we haue seene the lord Iesu.

THOMAS.

Shall I never leeve *that* this is trew,
by god omnipotent! 220

But I see in his handes two 221
holes that neiles can in goe,
and putt my finger eek also
ther as the neiles went. 224

ANDREAS. (29)

Thomas, goe we all in feere, 225
for dread of Enemys better were,
then Iewes should haue vs in their dangere,
and all our fraternitye. 228

THOMAS.

Wher euer you goe, Brethren deere, 229
I will goe with you, in good manere,

207 is] is now B. 209 in] by W h. 212 in] with W h. 213 Sinne] synnes B W h D. 214 men] *om.* W. doth] *om.* h. mynne] mynes h. Iterum] Tunc B W h D. evanescet] evanesit B W h D. versus Bethaniam] bethanie B W h D. ibunt] *before* Discipuli B W h D. obviantes] *before* Thomæ B W h D. Thomae] Thomas D. dicat petrus] *om.* W, dicat postea B. 219 that] *om.* h. 221 his handes] hand H 222 that] the B W h D. 224 went] were B. 227 their] *om.* B. vs] *om* D. 229 Wher] whether h. Brethren deere] goe farre or nere W.

but this talk you tell me here,
I leeve not, till I see.

PETRUS. (30)

Now, Thomas, be thou not away,
and in happ se him thou may,
and feele him also, in good fay,
as we haue done before.

THOMAS.

Wher ever you be, I will be aye,
but make me loeve this thing veray,
you payne you not, therfor, I pray,
to speak of that no more.

(Tunc Ibunt *omnies* ad mansione*m* et recu*m*bent et subito apparebit Ih*esus* dicens :)

IH*ESUS*. (31)

Peace, my Brethren, bothe one and all!
come hither, Thomas! to thee I call:
shew forth, for ought that may befall,
thy hand, and putt in here;

And see my handes and my feet,
and putt in thy hand, thou ne leet!
my woundes are yet fresh and weet
as they first were.

(32)

And be thou no more so dreadinge,
but ever truly beleevinge! (Tunc immittet in latus et vulnera manu*m*.)

THOMAS.

My God! My Lord! My Christ! My Kinge!
now leeve I without weninge.

IESUS.

Yea, Thomas, now thou seest in me,
thou leevest now that I am hee;

234 happ] hope B W. 238 loeve] leeve B W. 239 you payne] *and* pine B. I pray] I you praye B W h D. omnes] omnes iter*um* B W h d. dicens] *om.* W. 241 bothe] *om.* W. 246 hand] hand*es* B. thou] *and* B. 248 they] the D. 249 so] *before* no H. 250 ever truly] eu*er* more true B. *Stage-direction*] *in* H *in the margin.* immittet] emittit B W h D. manu*m*] *after* emittit B W h D. 253] yee now seeth you Thomas in me B. now] *after* seest W h D. *Latin passage*] *om.* B W h D, *in* H *in the margin.*

but Blessed must they all bee
that leeve and neuer see.

(Beati *qui* non viderunt et crediderunt, Ihon.) St. Iohn. xx, 29.

(33)

That I am that same body
that borne was of meek Marie,
and on a Crosse your soules dyd bye
vppon good fryday.
Who so to this will consent,
that I am god omnipotent,
as well as they that be present,
my Darlinges shalbe aye.

(34)

Who so to this will not consent,
ever to *the* day of Iudgment
in hell fyre they shall be brent,
and euer in sorrow and teene.
Whosoeuer of my father hath any mynd,
or of my mother in any kynde,
in heaven Bliss they shall it fynd,
with out any woe.

(35)

Christ geue you grace to take the way
vnto that ioy that lasteth aye!
for thers no night but ever day;
for all you thither shall goe.

Finis Paginæ Decimæ Nonæ.
Iulii 29 Anno D*omi*ni 1607.

257 that same] the same B. 263 be] did B. 264 aye] ever B W. shalbe aye] aye shall bene *would satisfy the rhyme.* 267 brent] brene (brende ?) B. 269 of] on D. any] *om.* B. 274 that ioy] the joye W h. 275 thers] their is B W D. 276 goe] com B. paginæ Decimæ nonæ] deo gracias W h, *om.* D. Iulii 29 Anno D*omi*ni 1607] *per* me Georgi bellin 1592 W, *om.* B D.

Pagina Vicesima de Ascentione salvatoris Iesu Christi. The Taylers.

IESUS. (1)

Pax vobis! ego su*m*, nolite timere!

My Brethren that sit in company,
with peace I greet you hartfully:
I am he that standes you by, St. Luke xxiv, 36.
ne dreed[ë] you nothing!

Well I know and witterly
that you be in greate Extasy,
whether I be Rysen verely,
that makes you sore in longing.

(2)

Ther is no need to be anoyed so,
neither through thought to be in woe;
your handes putt[ë] you now froe
and feele my wondes weet;

And leeues this, both all *and* one,
that ghost hath neither flesh ne bone,
as you may feele me vpon,
on handes and on feet.

Spiritus carne*m* et ossa non habet sicut me videtis habere Lucæ 24.

PETRUS. (3)

A! what is this *that* standes vs bye? St. Luke xxiv, 39.
a ghost me him semeth witterly;
me thinks lightned much am I
this spirit for to see.

ANDREAS.

Peter, I tell thee prively,
I dread me yet full greatly,

Pagina] Incipit pagina W h D, hic incipit pagina B. salvatoris Iesu Christi] domi*ni* B W h D, *continuing* et primo dicat Iesus, *followed by in* D pax vobis: Ego sum: nolite timere. · The Taylers] The Tayleres playe B W h D *before the Latin in all the four MSS.* Iesus] *om.* B. ego sum] *om.* B. timere] timere et dicat Iesus W h. 1 sit] sytten D. 2 hartfully] hartelye W h. 5 witterly] wittely H. 6 greate] an H. 9 Ther] you W, you*r* D, you haue h. 10 through] for B. 11 now] *before* you D. you] *om.* W h. 12 weet] wyde B W h D. 13 leeues] beleeve W h. both] *om.* W. 14 ne] nor B W h. 16 and] or W h. Spiritus] Spiritus quidam B W h D. non habet] not hete B. sicut] sic B W h D. habere] *om.* H. Lucæ 24] *om.* B W h D, W h *continuing:* dicat petrus. 18 me him] mee thinke he D. 20 spirit] spryte D.

that Iesu should do such maystry,
and whether that this be hee.

IHON. (4)

Brethren, good is it to thinke ever more,
what wordes he sayd the day before
he dyed on Rood, gone is not yore,
and we be stidfast aye.

IACOBUS MAIER.

A! Iohon, that makes vs in were,
that alway when he will apeare,
and when vs best list to haue him here,
anon he is away.

IHESUS. (5)

I see well, Brethren, sooth to say,
for any signe I shew[ë] may,
you be not stidfast in the fay,
but flechinge I you fynd.

more signes therfore ye shall see:
haue you ought may eaten bee?

SYMON.

Yea, lord, meat inough for thee,
or ells we wear vnkynd.

IHESUS. (6)

Now eate we then for Charity,
my leife Brethren, fayr and free,
for all things shall fulfilled bee
written in Moses law.

Prophetts in Psalmes sayd of me
that Death behoued me on the Roode tree,
and ryse within dayes three,
to ioy mankynd to draw,

25 Brethren] Brother H. ever more] on ever more H. is it] it is B W h D. 28 we be] bee we D. stidfast] wisted faste W h. 31 best list] liste beste B W h D. 34 signe] signe that W D. 36 flechinge] flyttinge B W h D. 39 meat] heres B, heare is W, here is meate h, here meate D. 40 or] and D. 42 leife] leeve D. 45 sayd] sayden D. 46 Death behoued me] death I behoued B D, death I behoveth h, death I behould W. 47 within] in W.

(7)

And preach to folke this world within, 49
Penance, Remission of ther synne;
In Ierusalem I should beginne,
as I haue done for loue. 52

Therfore beleevs Stidfastly, 53
and comes with me to Bethany!
in Ierusalem you shall all lye,
to abyde the grace aboue. 56

(Tunc comedet Iesus cu*m* Discipulis suis et postea dicat:)

PHILIPPUS. (8)

Lord, from vs do not concele; 57
what tyme thou art in thy wayle,
shalt thou restore Israell
agayn her Realm that day? 60

IESUS.

Brother, that is not to thee 61
to know my fathers privity;
that towcheth his owne posty,
wyt that thou ne[uer] may. 64

(9)

But take you shall, through my behest, 65
vertue of the holy ghost,
that send shall be to help you most,
in world wher you shall wend. 68

My witnes all you shalbe 69
in Ierusalem and Iudye,
Samaria also, and ech contray
vnto *the* worldes ende. 72

(10)

Goe in all the world, through my grace, 73
preach my word in eche place:

49 this] the h. 50 synne] sines B. 53 Therfore] Therfore Brethren H. 54 comes] come yee B W h D. 55 all] *om.* W h. comedet] comedit W. et postea dicat] *om.* H. 57 not] nought D. do] thou B W h D. 58 what] that W h. tyme] tyme that B W h D. 63 his] to his B W h D. 64 thou] yee B W h D. 65 behest] *the rhyme requires* behost. 68 in] in the B. shall] maye W h. wynne D. 72 vnto] to B W h D. 73 Goe] goe ye B W h D. in] *om.* D. through] and through W h D.

all that stidfast beleef hase
and fully, saved shall be.

And who so leeues not in your lore,
the wordes that you preach them before,
damned shall be for euermore,
that payne they may not flee.

(11)

By this thing they shall well know,
who so leves stidfastly on you,
such sygnes apertly they shall show,
wher so ever the tyde to goe.

In my name well shall they,
Devills powers to doe away;
new Tongs shall haue to preach *the* fay,
and other misteries moe.

(12)

And though the poyson eate or drink,
it shall nye them no thinge;
sick men with ther handlinge
shall healed redely bee;

Such grace shall be in their doinge.
now to my father I am goinge;
you shall haue here my Blessinge,
for to heaven I must stye.

(Tunc abducet discipulos in Bethaniam, et *cum* *per*venerit ad loc*um* Ihe*sus*, stans in loco vbi ascendit, dicat: "Data est mihi o*mnis* potestas in Cælo et in Terra.")

IHESUS. (13)

My swet Brethren, leife and deer,
to me is graunted full power,

75 all] *and* B. 76 saved shall be] save shall yee h, saue shall D. 77 leeues] beleeveth B W h D. 78 that] *om.* B W h D. them] then H. 79 damned] dampned D. for] *om.* D. 80 they may not] shall they not h, maye not them B, shall not them W, may them not D. 81 they] you B W h, ye D. 82 on] in B W h D. 83 apertly] southlye B W h D. 86 powers] power B. doe] put B W h D. 87 shall haue to preach the faye] to preach haue shall they B. shall] yee shall D. 88] and Edders to maister also B W h D. 91 handlinge] helpinge H. 93 in] *om.* W h. 95 here] Brethren B W h D. 96 stye] hie B, stee D. abducet] adducet B h D, adducit W. in] suos in B. locum] locom ascendens dicat B W h D. ascendit] ascenderit H. dicat] dicat Iesus B W h D. Terra] terra dicat W.

in heauen and earth, farr and neere,
for my godhead is most.

To teach all men now goe yee,
that in world will followed be,
in the name of my father and me,
and of the holy ghost.

(Tunc Iesus Ascendet et in ascendendo cantabit Ih*esus* vt sequit*ur* :)

IESUS.

Ascendo ad Patr*em* me*um* et Patr*em* vestr*um*, De*um* me*um* et Deum vestr*um*. Alleluia ! Alleluya !

(Et Cantico finito, stabit Ih*esus* in medio quasi supra Nubes.)

ANGELUS PRIMUS.

Quis est iste qui venit de Edom, tinctis vestibus de Bosra ?

ANGELUS SECUNDUS.

Iste formosus in Stola sua, gradiens in multitudine fortitudinis suæ ?

IESUS.

Ego qui loquor Iusticia*m* et p*ro*pugnator sum ad salvandu*m*.

ANGELUS TERTIUS.

Et vestimenta tua sicut Calcantiu*m* in Torculari.

IHESUS.

Torculor Calcavi solus, et de gentib*us* no*n* est vir mecu*m*.

ANGELUS PRIMUS. (14)

Who is this that commeth within,
the blisse of heauen that neuer shall blyn ?
blody out of *the* world of synne
and harrowed hell hath he.

102 followed be] folowe me W, fullfilled bee D. ascendet] ascendit B W. in ascendendo] ascendo H, in ascendo W. cantabit] cantat B, cantet W h, *adding:* god almighti alone, B *adding in its margin:* god singeth aboue (alone ?). cantabit] cantet D. *Iesus* ut sequit*ur*] *om.* D, *substituting* God singeth alonne. *One* Alleluia] *om.* B W h D. *Stage-direction*] *om.* h. Cum autem Impleverit Iesus canticu*m*, stet in medio quasi supra nvbens, et dicat maior angelus minori angelo B W D. (nubens] nubes D.) Angelus primus] primus angelus cantet W h, primus angelus cantat B D. *Heading*] minor angelus respondentem cantet W h (cantat h), minor angelus respondens cantat B D. *Heading*] Iesus cantat solus B W h D (cantet h.) p*ro*pugnator] *pro*pinquator D. *Heading*] Corus cantat B W h D (cantet h.) *Heading*] Iesus cantat solus B W h D (cantet h.) *Heading*] primus angellus in lingua materna dicat W h, primus angellus in materna lingua dicat B D. (dicat] *after* angelus D.) 107 blody] bluddelye W h, bodie B.

ANGELUS SECUNDUS.

Comely he is in his clothinge,
and with full power goeinge;
a number of Payntes with him leadinge;
he semes great of posty.

(Tunc Ihesus stans paulisper in loco eodem dicat.)

IESUS. (15)

I that speake righteousnes,
and haue brought man out of distres;
for Byar I am called *and* was
of all mankynd through grace.

My people that were from me Rafte,
through Synne and through the Devills crafte,
to heauen I bringe, and never one lefte,
all that in Hell was.

ANGELUS TERTIUS. (16)

Why is thy Clothing now so redd?
thy body blody *and* also heade?
thy Clothes also all that bene lead,
lyke to Pressors of wyne?

IHESUS.

for the Devill and his power,
that mankynd brought in great Dangere,
through death on Crosse and bloud so clear,
I haue made them all myne.

(17)

These bloudy dropps that you may see,
all they freshe shall resarved be,
till I come in my maiesty
to Deme the last day.

Heading] Secundus Angellus B W h D. 111 a] *om.* H. *Stage-direction*] Iesus autem pausans eodem loco dicat B W h D, W *adding* Iesus. 113 speake] spake W h D. righteousnes] right wisenesse D. 114 man] men B. 115 I am called] called I am B W D, I am and called h. 119 and never one] good one never H, good never one D. 120 all] of all B. was] were B W h D. *Heading*] Tercius angellus B W h D. 121 now] *om.* B W h. 122 heade] rede B. 123 all] *om.* B W h. 127 on] and H. clear] deere h. 129 bloudy dropps] droppes so bloodye W h. may] nowe B W h D. 130 they] the D. freshe] *om.* H. 132 Deme] dome H.

This bloud shall witnes bear to me, 133
I dyed for man on the Rood tree,
and rose with in day[e]s three;
such loue I loued them aye. 136

(18)

These Dropps now, with good intent, 137
to my father I will present,
that good men that on earth be lent
shall know apert[e]ly, 140

How graciously that I them bought, 141
and for good workes that they wrought,
euerlasting blisse that they sought,
to prove the good worthy; 144

(19)

And that the wicked men, echone, 145
may know and se, all *and* one,
how worthely they forgone
that Blis that lasteth aye. 148

for thes Causes, leeue you me, 149
the Dropps I shedd on rood tree,
all fresh shall resarved be,
ever till *the* last day. 152

(Tunc Ascendet et in ascen*den*do cantant Angeli Canticu*m* subsequ*entem*:)

Exaltare, do*min*e, in virtute tua, cantabimûs,
et psallemus virtutes tuas. Alleluya.

(Tunc descendent Angeli et cantabunt, "Viri Galilei quid aspicitis in Cœlu*m*?")

ANGELUS QUART*US*. (20)

You men that be of Galelye, 153
wher vpon now wonder ye?

133 bloud shall] bloode I shedde B W h D. 134 I] and B W D. the] *om.* W D. rood] bloddie B. 135 rose] rose againe B W h D. 136 them] thee B W h D. 141 that] *om.* h. 142 they] I B W h, I have D. 144 prove] preeve D. 145 men] maie W h D, *in* B *crossed out*. 146 may] *om.* W h D. *Second* and] *om.* B W h D. 147 forgone] forgiue D. 148 aye] ever W h. *Before* 149] B *repeats* 138. *The two stage-directions with the Latin song*] **om.** W h. cantant] cantent D. subsequentem] subscriptum Cantent B D. (cantent] *as heading in* D. Exaltare] Exaltarem*us* D. psallemus] psalmos B. Alleluya] *om.* B D. cantabunt] cantent B D. *Heading*] Quartus Angellus B W h D. **154** wher-vpon] ther vpon W h. wonder] marvayll W.

wayting him that through posty
is now[ë] gone you froe?

ANGELUS PRIMUS.

Iesu Christ, leeue you me,
that stayed to heauen, as you might se,
right so come agayn shall he,
as you saw him goe.

PETRUS. (21)

Loe! Brethren, what these Angells sayen!
that Iesu, which through his great mayne
to heauen is gone, will come agayne
right as he forth[ë] went.

ANDREAS.

Many sith so height he
to send his ghost with hart so free;
and in Ierusalem we should be,
till it were to vs sent.

SYMON. (22)

Brethren, I redd vs in good fay,
that we thither take the way;
and with Deuotion, night and day,
lenge in our prayer.

PHILIPPUS.

For now we know by signes veray
that he is gods sonne, sooth to say;
therfore it is good we goe and pray,
as he commanded here.

IOHANNES. (23)

For now must we leeue it no leasinge;
for bothe by sight and handlinge,

Heading] primus angellus B W h D. 158 stayed] steed W h D, went B. might] *om.* B W h D. 160 saw] seene B W h D. 161 Loe] *om.* B. 162 which] that B W h D. 165 Many sith] manye seithen W, manye sethen D, Many days sith H. 166 with] ech B. so] *om.* D. 167 should be] shalbe B W h D. 173 now we knowe] knowe we mone B W h D. signes] signe B W h D. 175 goe and] goe to B W h D. 177 for now must] now mone B W h D.

speaking, eatinge and drinking,
he proued his Deitie. 180

IACOBUS MAIOR.

Yea, also by his vpstayinge 181
he seemes fully heauen Kinge.
who hath ther in full leevinge,
saved lyfe and soule is he. 184

PETRUS. (24)

Goe we, Brethren, with one assent, 185
and fulfill his Commandement;
but looke *that* none through dreed be blent,
but leevs all stidfastly. 188

Pray we all, with full intent, 189
that he to vs his ghost will sent.
Iesu, that from vs is went,
saue all this Company! Amen. 192

1607 Iulij 30.
Finis Paginæ Vicesimæ.

Pagina Vicesima Prima de Electione Mathie et de Emissione Sp*irit*us sancti, De Symbolo Apostolor*um*. The Fishmongers.

PETRUS (ad condiscipulos). (1)

My deer Brethren, every one, 1
you know well, both all and one,
how our lord is from vs gone
to Bliss that lasteth aye. 4

179 drinking] handlinge W. 180 proued] proves B W h D. 182 heauen] heavens B, heavenlye W h. 184 lyfe] in lyfe H, *but* "in" *in a later hand.* soule] soules h. 190 his] he h. 191 from vs is] nowe is from vs B W h. is] nowe ys D. Amen] *om.* W h. 1607 Iulij 30] *om.* B W h D. paginæ vicesimæ] *om.* D, de Scissorib*us* B, deo gracias W h, W *adding:* per me Georgi bellin 1592, Come lorde Iesus, come quicklye 1592. Pagina] Incipit pagina B W h D, De symbolo Apostolor*um*] qualiter ap*ost*oli fecerunt sembolu*m* ap*ost*olicum viz. "credo in deum patrem etc." et primo inter ap*ost*olos incipiat B W h D. Fishmongers] fishemongers playe B W h D. *before the Latin.* condiscipulos] discipulos B, *om.* H. 1 every] every eich B W h. 2 both] *om.* W. 4 aye] ever W.

Comfort now we haue none, 5
saue his Behest to leeve vppon;
therfore lyve we in this wonne,
that neuer one wend away. 8

(2)

Lenge we stiff in our prayer, 9
for well I wott, withouten were,
he will send vs a Councelere,
his ghost as he beheight. 12

Therfore lenge we all right here, 13
this faythfull fellowship in fear,
till our lord, as he can vs leere,
send vs of heauen light. 16

(3)

(Tum Petrus exurgens, in medio fratrum ibit et dicat:)

My dear Brethren, fayre and free, 17
Holy Scripture—leeve you me—
fully must fullfilled bee,
that David sayd before. 20

All of the holy ghost had he, 21
touching Iudas, wytten ye,
that sould our maister for money,
and now is clean forlore. 24

(4)

Among vs numbred that wretch was, 25
to preach the fayth in eche place,
and now his hyre fully he hase,
for hanged him self hath he. 28

His body bursten for his trespasse, 29
his sowle damned without grace;
therfore, as the psalter mynd mase,
fullfilled now must be: 32

(Fiat habitatio eius deserta, et non sit qui habitet in ea, Episcopatum eius accipiat alter.)

5 we] maye we B W D, we maye h. 6 leeve] truste B W h D. 7 lyve] leeve h D. wonne] one B. 9 Lenge] longe B. 13 all] *om.* B W h D. petrus exurgens] exurgens Petrus D. exurgens] expurgens W. ibit] *om.* B W h D. dicat] dicat petrus B W. 21 all] Also W h. 22 wytten] witt H, wrytten D. 26 the fayth] *before* "to preach" B W h D. 29 bursten] hanged B. 30 his] *om.* W h D. without] as a man bout W h, as a man without D. deserta] in deserto B. ea] eo D. accipiat] accipiet H. alter] alter dicat petro W.

(5)

Therfor men, that now be here, 33
and fellows that aye with vs were,
while Iesu Christ, our mayster deere,
in earth lyving was, 36

That you, that see his power, 37
his Miracles many, in good manere,
dyinge, Rysinge, booth in feer,
may best now bear witnes. 40

(6)

Mathias, I redd, here be one, 41
and Ioseph, that aye with vs hathe gone,
for whom we cast two lotts anone,
and Buske vs all to pray; 44

whether of them it is gods will 45
the same office to fulfill. (Tunc omnes vna voce respondea*n*t.)

OMNES.

We assent vs all ther-tyll,
for that is the best way. (Tunc Genua flectent.) 48

PETRUS. (7)

Thou lord that knowest all thinge, 49
eche hart and will of man lyvinge,
shew vs here by some tokeninge
whom that we shall take; 52

And whether of thes is thy lykinge, 53
in Iudas stidd that be standinge,
thy name to preach to owld and yonge,
and whether that thou wilt make. 56

34 aye] ever W. 35 while] with B W h D. 37 see] seene D. 38 good] *om.* W h. 39 dyinge] diunge H. 41 here] he B. 42 that aye] *after* with vs h, that Ever *after* with vs W. 46 the same] this W, this same B h D. *Stage-direction*] *after* 56 H, *but in the margin* "This must come in place of Tunc colliget." respondeant] respondent *after* Tunc B W h D. vna voce] *om.* h, apostoli una voce B, all speake togeither W D. *Heading*] *om.* W h D. 47 all] *om.* D. assent] assenten D. vs] *om.* W h. 48 that] this B W h D. *Stage-direction*] *in the margin in* H, Tunc omnes ap*osto*li genu flectent et dicat petrus B W h (B *substituting* ap*osto*li *by* populi). 49 thinge] thing*es* B. 56 make] take W, choose h.

(8)

(Tunc colliget Petrus sortes et Deus immittet sortem. Et sors cadet super Mathiam.)

This lott is fallen, Brethren free,
on Mathias, all men may see;
to vs therfore I take thee,
and Apostle the make.

MATHIAS.

Yea, honored be god in Trinity!
though I vnworthy therto be,
and to you that hath chosen me;
dye will I for his sake.

ANDREAS. (9)

Now Peter, Brother, goe we and pray;
for evermore I myn may
my Soverayne, how I hard him say,
here in your company,

IACOBUS MAIOR.

He would not leave vs, by no way,
fatherles Children, in good fay,
but ritch vs soone in better aray
with his ghost graciously.

IOHANNES EVANGELISTA. (10)

Yea, Brethren, also verament
to vs he sayd, in good intent,
in earth here while he was present,
and with vs could lend.

THOMAS.

But if so were that he ne went,
his ghost to vs should not be sent;
and if he yode wher we were lent,
yt he would [to] vs send.

Stage-direction] *after* 48 *in* H. colliget petrus sortes] petrus mittet sortem B W h D. et Deus immittet sortem] *om.* B W h D. mathiam] mathiam et dicat petrus B W h D. 58 Mathias] Mathewe D. 60 and] and an H. 63 that] *before* to W h. and] that D. that hath] have D. 65 Now] no B. 66 I] *om.* W h. myn] mynde h. 71 vs] is H. 74 in] to B W h. 77 he] *om.* W h. 79 we were] he W h.

IACOBUS MINOR. (11)

Yea, sweet and lykeinge was his lore,
and well ye wot that ther were not yore,
but a little while before,
or he to heauen steight.

PHILIPPUS.

He badd we should not goe away
from Ierusalem to no Contray,
but ther abyde—sooth to say—
his hest[ë] from an height.

BARTOLOMEUS. (12)

Also he sayd to vs echone,
that his forgoer, St. Iohn,
with water Baptized many one
whyle that he was here.

MATHEUS.

But we shall Baptise, without Boste,
fully with the holy ghost,
through helpe of him that is most,
soone after, withoutten weere.

Iohannes quidem Baptizauit aqua, vos autem Baptizabimini Sp*iritu* sancto, non post multos hos dies. Acts i, 5.

SYMON ZELOTES. (13)

We mynd theron, lesse and more;
yet some that standen him before,
asked him whether he showld restore
that tyme all Israell.

IUDAS TADDEVS.

And he answered anone right,
that tyme know you ne might,
that in his fathers will was pight,
for that he must conceale.

82 wot] wytten D. that ther] what they B. were not yore] wore B W D. ther were] *underlined in* H. 84 steight] stead W h, steede D. 85 badd] bydde W h. we] me I, W h. 88 height] highe B W h D. Iohannes] quia Ioh*annes* B, Tunc Iohannes W h D. quidem] *after* Baptizauit B. Baptizabimini] baptazamini W, baptazimini D. hos] hodies h. zelotes] *om.* B W h D. 99 him] *om.* B W h D. 100 all] also h. Iudas] *om.* D. Iude W h (*after* Thaddeus), Taddevs] *om.* W. Chaddeus B. 102 might] night H.

Non est vestrum nosse Tempora vel momenta quæ pater posuit in sua potestate. Acts i, 7.

MATHIAS. (14)

Yea, Brethren, that tyme, he vs behight,
the holy ghost should in vs light,
That we might tell to eche wight
his deedes all, by deene;

In Ierusalem and Iudye,
wher in world so ever walke we,
and Samaria, that men should see,
as after may be seene.

Accipietis virtutem supervenientis spiritus sancti in vos, et eritis mihi Testes in Ierusalem et in omni Iudea, Samaria et vsque ad vltimum Terræ. Acts i, 8.

PETRUS. (15)

Knele we down vpon *our* knee,
and to that lord now pray we;
sone I hope, that he will see
To his Disciples all.

ANDREAS.

Yea, in his lyfe so taught he:
aske and haue with hart free,
righteous Boone shall graunted be,
when men will on him call.

(Tunc omnes Apostoli, genu flectentes, cantent: "veni Creator spiritus, mentes tuorum visita, Imple superna gratia, que tu creasti, pectora.")

IACOBUS MAIOR. (16)

Come holy ghost, come Creator!
visitt our hartes in this stowre;
thou art mans Conquerour,
and graunt vs, lord, thy grace!

quæ] qui W h. 110 walke] walked H. Accipietis] accipiet B. omni] *om.* B W D. terræ] terre dicat petrus W. 115 *and* 116 *written as one line in* H. 119 righteous] right wise D. Boone] dome W. omnes Apostoli] apostoli omnes W h. genu flectentes] genibus flectentibus H. cantent] cantabunt H, cantet h. spiritus] spiritus postea Iacobus maior W h. (postea] posta W), spiritus et postea dicatt D B, *all the four MSS. omitting the rest of the quotation.* 122 our] or D. hartes] thoughtes B W h D. this] thie B. 123 art] *om.* B.

IOHANNES.

Thou, that art called Counceler, 125
and sent from heauen as Saviour,
well of lyfe, Leach of Langour,
that prayn here in this place. 128

THOMAS. (17)

Yea, that in fyfty dayes would conceile, 129
grace of thy ghost abowt to deale,
as thou promist for mans heale,
appear now, since I pray. 132

IACOBUS MINOR.

Light[en] our witt[e]s with thy wayle, 133
putt lyfe in our thought[e]s leale,
fulsome thy frendes that be frayle,
with vertues lasting aye. 136

PHILIPPUS. (18)

Vanish our enemyes farr away ! 137
and graunt vs peace, lord, to our pay ;
for while thou art our leader aye,
we may eschew anoy. 140

BARTHOLOMEUS.

Through thy might know we may 141
the father of heaven, in good fay ;
and thou, his sonne—sooth to say—
thou art in Company. 144

MATHEUS. (19)

Worshipped be thou, ever and oe, 145
the father and the sonne also !
lett thy ghost now from thee goe,
and fayth that we may fynde. 148

126 sent] send W H D. 127 Leach of] lyght in B. lenghte or W D, length or h. 128 here] he B. 129 Yea] Hee D. fyfty dayes] seven month B, seven monthes W D. 134 leale] wholle B. 135 fulsome] full soone B, lixom W h. 136 aye] ever W. 137—140] *follow after* 152 *in* H *and* 141—144 *are given to* Philippus. 139 while] why H. Bartholomeus] philippus H, *which has the same heading before* 137—140 *after* 152. 142 of] in H. in] full in D H. 143 thou] ye B W h D. sooth] all soth B D, in soth W h. 145—148] *are given to* Bartholomeus *and* 149—152 *to* matheus *in* H, *while* W *omits* 149—152. 145 Worshipped] Worshipp H. ever and] *and* euer B. 146 and] *om.* H.

SIMON.

That we aske with hart throe, 149
to fulsome vs agaynst our foe,
graunt thy men here, one and moe,
to haue thee ever in mynde. 152

IHESUS. (20)

Glorious father, fayr and free, 153
you know well of your Deitie
that I haue done your will. 155
The Apostles that you haue chosen to me, 156
with grace, wisdome, and p*ro*phesye,
that you will them fulfill. 158

(Tunc omnes Apostoli contemplabunt vel orabunt, quovsq*ue* Spiritus sanctus missus fuerit.)

DEUS PATER. (21)

My sonne, beloued, lyfe and deer, 159
your faythfull asking ever here,
that you aske is not a reere;
I know your clean intent. 162
with will full liberall and cleare, 163
my ghost to them shall appeare,
to make them wyser then they wear;
that is my full assent. 166

(22)

My ghost to earth shall goe downe 167
with Seven giftes of renowne,
ther to haue by Deuotion,
confirme them to be sadd; 170
That they may be ever ready bowne, 171
in heauen bliss to wear the Crown,

Simon] Simounde D. 150 fulsome] full soone B. 151 one and] both one and D, and be B. moe] loe B. 152 to] that B D. *Heading*] Litell god B D, God the sonne W, Deus h (B D *adding in their margins* Christ must speak in heauen. 154 your] *om.* W. Deitie] dutie B h D. 155 *and* 156—159] W *om.* 156 The] They D. 157 p*ro*phesye] prosperitye H D, posteritie B. 158] *om.* B. contemplabunt] contemplantes B W h D. orabunt] orantes B W h D. fuerit] fuit B W h D. *Heading*] Deus dicat B W h D. 160 faythfull] healthfull W h D. 161 a reere] to arere B D, to deare W h. 162 I] to W h. 168 giftes] geistes W. 169 ther] their B W h. by] my W. 172 heauen] heuens B.

ever to raygne in possession,
ther to be mery and gladd. 174

(23)

My Patriarches and Prophetts here, 175
that through their fayth to me wear deere,
Angells and Archangells clere,
all in my Blisse woninge; 178

yee wot well, withoutten were, 179
how I haue mendid, in good maner,
man that was lorne through Lucifer,
and through his owne lykinge. 182

(24)

My sonne I send downe from my Sea 183
into a Virgin, fayr and free,
and mankynd tooke, as lyked me
on man to haue mercy. 186

That Righteousnes might saved be, 187
seinge man had lost his liberty,
I made man in one degree,
his bale behoued to bye. 190

(25)

Now man fully haue I bought, 191
and out of Bale to Bliss brought;
his kynd also, as me good thought,
is mixt with in my godhead. 194

This man, *that* I haue made of nought, 195
that Sathanas through synne had sought,
by this way I haue so wrought,
none good in hell be leade. 198

(26)

But while I was in that degree, 199
in earth abyding as man should be,

176 their] your W h D. 183 send] sente h. 185 mankynd] manhood B W h D. 187 righteousnes] rightious B W. 188 seinge] synce D. 190 behoued] behoveth W h. to bye] for to be H, to lye B. 193 thought] taughte W. 194 mixt] might h. 195 This] thus W h D. I] *om.* D. haue] thus B D; *om.* W h. 196 had] *om.* H. 200 abyding] woninge B W h D.

chosen I haue a good menye,
on which I must haue mynd.

Now they haue made their mone to me
and prayed especially, as I see,
whom I must suffyce with hart free,
or ells I were vnkynd.

(27)

Through out *the* world they shall gone,
my deeds to preach to many one,
yet stidfastnes in them is none
to suffer for me anye.

ffleching yet they be, echone,
But whe*n* my ghost is them vpon,
then shall they after be stiffe as stonne,
my deedes to certify.

(28)

Dread of death, ne no distres,
Shall let them of stidfastnes;
such loue in them *and* such goodnes
My spirit shall ever inspyre;

That to speak and [to] expresse
all languages that evar yet was,
they shall haue conninge more and lesse,
through force of heauenly fyre.

(29)

Also they shall haue full power
to Baptize men in water cleare,
that beleuen, in good manere,
to haue full mynd on me.

And on all such, withouten were,
the holy ghost at their prayer
shall light on them, that they may leere
in fayth stidfast to bee.

204 especially] speciallye B W h D. 205 whom] w*hi*ch B W h D. 208 to] *om.* D. many one] manye a one W. 211 ffleching] fleitting B W h. 213 be] be as W h. 215—218] *om.* W. 224 water] watter watter W. 229 may] might h.

(30)

Now will I send, anone in hye,
to my Brethren in company,
my ghost to gladd them graciously,
for that is ther willinge.

In lyknes of fyre freely,
that they may strengthed be therby,
my workes to preach more stidfastly,
and therby haue more conninge.

(Tunc Deus emittit Sp*irit*um sanctum in spetie ignis et in mittendo cantent Duo Angeli "Accipite sp*irit*um sanctu*m*, q*uorum* remiseritis peccata, remittant*ur* eius," etc. et cantendo p*ro*citient ignem sup*er* ap*osto*los.)

Angelus pr*imus*. (31)

Rest well, all that bene here!
my lord you greets and his ghost deare;
he bydds you dreed no bost ne bere
of Iew[e]s, farre nor neere.

But looke you goe anon in hye,
into all *the* world by and by,
and also preach the fayth mekely,
and his word so deere.

Angelus secun*dus*. (32)

And through this ghost that I you bringe,
you shall haue vnderstandinge
of every leed speakinge,
what so ever they say.

And this world, that is flechinge,
you shall despice over all thinge,
and heauen at your endinge
you shall haue to your pay.

233 gladd] gadd D. 236 strengthed] streitned B W h D. 238 haue] be h, *om.* D. emittit] immittet H, emittet D. sanctum] *om.* W. *Stage-direction*] h *has instead of the Latin:* heare the holy ghoste descendes vpon the xii apostles and then the angells speake followinge. cantent] cantat B. Angeli] angeli antiphonu*m* W D. remiseritis] *the stage-direction ends here in* H. remittantur eius] remittentur eis D. ap*osto*los] ap*osto*los finito p*er* ? B, ap*osto*los finitoque angelus in coelo dicat D. *Heading*] angelus B D, primus angelus W h (B W *adding* in celo dicat). 240 deare] here h. 241 ne] nor W h D. 242 farre] far (?) H. nor] ner W, ne D. neere] nye h. 246 word] worckes B W h. deere] dreade B W. *Heading*] the second angell B D, Secundus Angellus W h. 247 I] *om.* W. 249 leed] lande W h, londes B, lond D. 251 flechinge] flittinge B W h. 252 over] euer D. 254 to] at W h.

PETRUS. (33)

A! mercy, lord, full of might!
booth I feele and se in sight
the holy ghost is on vs light;
of fyre this house full is.

ANDREAS.

Now haue we that was vs beheight,
for all of loue my hart is pight,
and wyser then is any wight
me think I am, iwis.

IACOB*US* MAIOR. (34)

Yea, lord, blessed must thou be!
for booth I feel and eke I see
the holy ghost is light on me,
thus quitt I am my meede.

IOH*ANNES* EVANGEL*ISTA*.

ffor such loue, by my lewtye,
this fyre hath sett in my hart free,
that death to dye for my maister, truly,
I haue no maner of dread.

THOMAS. (35)

And I thank thee, both god and man,
for since this fyre light me vpon,
of all languages well I can,
and speak them at my will.

IACOBUS MINOR.

I that before was but a fone
am waxen as wyse as Solomon;
ther is no science but I can ther on,
and cuninge to fulfill.

PHILIPPUS. (36)

And I that neuer could speak thinge,
save Hebrue that I learned yonge,

258 of] for D. full is] is full W. 259 was vs] vs was B. 265 holy] holyest h. Evangel*ista*] *om.* B W h D. 268 with this fier in my harte can flie B W h D. 269 dye] doe D. truly] free B W h D. 270 of] *om.* B W h. 275 that before] before that W h D. 277 can] am B. 280 that] as D.

now I can speak, at my lykinge,
all languages bothe low and hye. 282

BARTOLOMEUS.

And so stiff I am of belevinge, 283
that I dowbt neither Prince ne kinge,
my maisters miracles for to minge,
and for his loue to dye. 286

MATHEUS. (37)

A! blessed be my maister deere, 287
that so little while can vs leere;
all languages that ever weer,
vpon my Tonge bene light. 290

SYMON *ZELOTES.*

My beleif is now so clear, 291
and loue in hart so Printed here,
to moue my mynd in no maner
ther is no man hath might. 294

TADDEUS. (38)

Yea, sith this fyre came from an highe, 295
I am waxen so wonderous sleigh,
that all languages, farr and neighe,
my Tonge will spek now right. 298

MATHIAS.

Now sith my lord to heauen steight 299
and send his ghost, as he beheight,
to all distresses now am I dighte,
and dye for the loue of god Almight. 302

PETRUS. (39)

Now, Brethren, I redd vs all in feere, 303
make we the Creed in good manere,
Of my lord[e]s dedes deare,
that gladed vs hath to day. 306

282 bothe] *om.* W h. 284 neither] no W h. 287 A] And h. 288 that] *om.* W h D, that in B. little] little a B. zelotes] *om.* B W h D. 292 here] lere D. *Heading*] Iude W h. 295 highe] height H. an] *om.* D. 296 wonderous] woundor W. sleigh] sleight W H. 298 right] a right B h D. 299 steight] steegh B W h D. 300 and] hath B. send] sente h. he] you H *originally, but altered in a later hand.* 301 dighte] drest B D. dreight H. 302 and] and will W, to B h. 305 deare] here H. 306 gladed] gladdeth h.

And I will first beginne here, 307
seinge Christ betoke me his power,
lewd hereafter that we may leere,
to further them in the fay. 310

PETRUS. (40)

Credo in De*um* patre*m* *om*nipotentem Creatore*m* Coeli et Terræ.

I Beleue in God Omnipotent, 311
that made heauen and earth *and* firmament
with stidfast hart and true intent,
and he is my comford. 314

ANDREAS.

Et in Iesu*m* Christu*m* fili*um* eius vnicu*m* Dominu*m* nostru*m*.

And I beleue, wher I am lent, 315
in Iesu, his sonne, from heauen sent,
vereye Christ, that vs hath kent,
and is our Eldars lord. 318

IACOB*US* MAIOR. (41)

Qui conceptus est de Sp*iritu* sancto, nat*us* ex maria Virgine.

And I beleue, without boste, 319
in Iesu Christ, of might moste,
Conceaved through the holy ghost,
and borne was of Mary. 322

IHO*HANNES*.

Passus sub Pontio Pilato, Crucifixus, mortuus, et sepultus.

And I beleue, as I can see, 323
that vnder Pilate suffred he,
scourged and nayled on Rood tree,
and buryed was his fayr body. 326

308 seinge] synce D. 309 lewd] the lawe W, the lewte B, the truth h, the lewd D. 310 to] and h. *Before* 311] H *has already here as Stage-direction* Tunc venient duæ alienigenæ, *which ought to come after* 366. B W h D *have:* Tunc petrus Incipiat. *Heading*] *om.* B D. 312 and] *om.* B. *The heading* Andreas] *after the Latin passage* W, *and so everywhere down to verse* 355. nostrum] nostru*m* et dicat W. 315 wher] more W h. am] be B W h D. 317 vereye] verely H. 318 lord] lore W. virgine] virgine dicit W. 319 And] *om.* D. without] with W h. 320 of] in B W h. might] mightes B h D, mightest W. 321 conceaved] conseveith W. sepultus] sepultus et dicat Iohannes W. 325 on] upon h. 326 his] he h.

THOMAS. (42)

Descendit ad Inferna, tertia die Resurrexit a mortuis.

And I beleue and sooth can tell,
that he ghostly went to Hell;
deliuered his that ther did dwell,
and rose the third[e] day.

IACOBUS MINOR.

Ascendit ad Coelos, sedet ad dexteram Dei patris Omnipotentis.

And I beleue fully this,
that he stayd vp to heauen blis,
and on his fathers right hand is,
to raigne for euer and aye.

PHILIPPUS. (43)

Inde venturus est Iudicare vivos et mortuos.

And I beleue with hart stidfast,
that he will come at the last
to iudge mankynd, as he hath cast,
both the quick and the dead.

BARTOLOMEUS. Credo in Spiritum Sanctum.

And my Beleue shall be most
in vertue of the holy ghost,
and through his help, without bost,
my lyfe I think to lead.

MATHÆUS. (44)

Sanctam Ecclesiam Catholicam, Sanctorum Communionem.

And I Beleue, through gods grace,
Such leefe as Holy Church hase,
that god his body graunted vs was,
to vse in forme of Bread.

SYMON ZELOT. Remissionem Peccatorum.

And I beleue with Devotion,
of Sinnes to haue Remission
through Crist his Blood and passion,
and heauen when I am dead.

mortuis] mortuis dicit Thomas W. 332 stayd] sended B. heauen] heuens B. Inde] vnde W h. est] et W. mortuos] mortuous dicat W. 337 to iudge] and deeme B W h D. Communionem] communionem dicat W. 344 leefe] beleffe B W h D. 345 god his] godes B W h D. zelot] *om.* B W h D. peccatorum] peccatorem B W h. 348 sinnes] synne B W h D. 349 Crist his] Cristes B W h D.

THADDEUS. (45) Carnis Resurrectionem.

And I Beleue, as well we mon, 351
in the general Resurrection
of ech body, when Christ is bowne
to Dome both good and evill. 354

MATHIAS. Et vitam eternam. Amen.

And I Beleue, as well we may, 355
everlasting lyfe after my day
in heauen to haue, ever and aye,
and so overcom the Devill. 358

PETRUS. (46)

Now, Brethren, I read all we 359
goe, echon, to dyvers contray,
and preach to Shyre *and* Citty
The fayth, as Christ vs bade. 362

ANDREAS.

Yea, leif brethren, kisse now we 363
Echon an other, before we dye;
for gods will must fulfilled be,
And *that* is now great need. (Tunc venient duo Alienigenæ.)

PRIMUS ALIENIGENA. (47)

A, fellow, fellow, for gods pitty! 367
are not these men of Galely?
our languages they can as well as we,
as ever eate I Bread. 370

SECUNDUS ALIENIGENA.

Yea, well I wott, by my lewty, 371
that with in thes day[ë]s three
one of them could not speak with me,
for to haue been deade. 374

Heading] Iude W h. 351 well] all B W h D. 352] of christes body eichone was borne h. 354 Dome] deme B W h D. amen] *om.* B W h D. 355 well] all B W h. 357 to] for to B D. 361 Citty] to Citty B W h D. 362 bade] byd h, beede D. 363 brethren] Brother H D. *Stage-direction*] *by a mistake after* 310 *in* H, W *and* B *add:* quorum dicat primus alie*nigena*, h D *only* quorum dicat. venient] venit B. 367 gods] cockes B. 369 languages] language B W D. 371 yea] *om.* B W h D.

PRIMUS ALIENIGENA. (48)

Of all languages that be hereby,
that come to mesopotamye,
Capadocia and Iewry,
the Ianglen, withouten ween;

Of *the* Isle of ponthus and Asye,
frizeland and Pamphilye,
of Egipt right in Lybby,
which is besyde Syrene.

SECUNDUS ALIENIGENA. (49)

Yea, also men of Arabye,
And of Greece, that is therby,
hard them prayse full tenderly
God of his great grace.

And we hard them witterly
prays god fast, bothe thou and I;
follow we them therfore and espye
how goeth this wonderous case.

finis Decimæ primæ pagine.

Pagina Vicesima Secunda de prophetis prophetantib*us* de Die novissimo de Antech*r*isto de Enock et helia. The clothiars or shermen.

EZECHIELL.

Facta est super me manus D*omi*ni et eduxit me Sp*iritu*s D*omi*ni et demisit me in medio Campi, qui erat plenus ossibus, et Circu*m*duxit me per ea in Giro. Hæc in libro Ezechielis Capitulo Tricesimo Septimo.

Stanza 48] *in margin in a later hand* "Richard Morris." H. alienigena] *om.* H. 376 come] came H. 379 ponthus] ponce H (*a mistake for* Patmos ?). 380 pamphilye] pamphami W. 381 of] *om.* B W h D. in] into B W h D. 382 which] that B W h D. 383 Arabye] rabie W. 385 hard] herden D, had hard B, *but the* had *is crossed out.* 386 great] owne W h. 389 them] *om.* W h. espye] spye W. follow we them] ffellowe goe we D. Decimæ primæ pagine] *om.* D B, deo gracias W h, W *adding per* me George bellin 1592, h Finis Geo Bellin 1600. Decimae *by mistake for* vicesimae. *Heading*] The Clotheworkers playe secunda Ezechell B W h, The Clotheworkers Playe D. Antech*r*isto] Antechisto H. Latin] *om.* D. *Heading*] *om.* W h D. Facta] fatea h. manus] manib*us* W. eduxit] aduxet W. demisit] dimisit W. circu*m*duxit] circu*m*dixit W h. hæc] hic W h. libro] *om.* B. Ezechielis] ezechiell B h. capitulo] *om.* B W h D. tric. sept.] *om.* h, 37° D. *Before* 1, *new heading*] Ezechiell B W h.

(1)

Harkens all that louen heale! 1
I am the Prophet Ezechiell;
what I saw I will not conceale,
but as me thought I will tell. 4
God his ghost can with me deale, 5
that ledd me longe with wordes leale,
into a feild wher in Bones fell,
all bare with out flesh or fell. 8

(2)

Then spake that ghost thus vnto me, 9
sayd: mans sonne how lyketh thee?
thinkes thou not well that this might be,
thes Bones might turne and lyve? 12
Then bade he me tell and prophesy, 13
that he would revive them sone in hye,
with flesh and Sinew and Skynn therby,
which sone he can them geue. 16

(3)

After that ghost he them geete, 17
ryse out of their graves he them leet,
and made them stand vpon ther feet,
Speake, Goe and See. 20
This saw I right in my sight, 21
to know that he was god Almight,
that heauen and earth should deal *and* dight,
and neuer shall ended be. 24

EXPOSITOR. (4)

Now that you shall expresly know 25
thes Prophetts wordes vpon a row,
what they do signify I will shew;
that much may doe you good. 28
By them vnderstand may I 29
the day of Dome skilfully,

1 Harkens] herken B W h D. 3 not] *om.* B W h. 5 God his] godes h. 7 in] *om.* W h D. 8 or fell] *om.* D. 9 thus] *om.* B W h D. 10 sayd] and said B D. lyketh] lykest H D. 11 that] *om.* B W h. might] may D. 14 in hye] one hie B. 15 Sinew] synewes D. 18 out] *om.* B D. of] *om.* W h.

when men, through gods posty,
shall ryse in flesh and blood.

(5)

Therfore this Prophett sayd full yare,
he saw a feild of Bones bare,
and soone that ghost with them can fare,
gaue them flesh and lyfe.

Beleus this fully, withouten wene,
that all, which dead *and* rotten bene,
in flesh shall ryse, as shalbe sene,
man, mayde and wyfe.

(6)

They that shall be saued, shall be as bright
as seven tymes the Sonne is light;
the Damned Thester shall be in sight,
ther Dome to vnderfoe.

Both saued and damned after that day
Dye they may not, by no way.
god geue you grace to doe so aye,
that bliss you may come to!

ZACHARIAS. (7)

Zacharias Propheta. levavi oculos meos et vidi, et ecce quatuor Quadrigæ egredientes de medio duoru*m* montiu*m*. Hoec in libro Zachariæ Prophetæ. Cap*itu*lo Sexto.

I, Zachary,—men, leues you me,—
lifte vp myne eyes a sight to see,
and as me thought verely,
fowr Charretts came anon

Out of two hills—leue you me—
Siluer hills they were, as weten we;
great wonder I hadd, in my degree,
whether that they would gone.

35 them] him H. can] *before* with B. 36 gaue] *and* gaue B. 37 Beleus] Beleeue D. 43 Thester] sorte B. 44 vnderfoe] vnderstande W h. 48 come] goe W. *Heading*] *after the Latin in* D. Zacharias propheta] *om.* B W h D. ecce] dice W h. egredientes] agredientes W. duorum] *om.* h, quorum W. hoec] *om.* B W h D. libro Zachariæ prophetæ] *om.* B W h D. in] *om.* D. 51 verely] by my lewtye B W h D. 52] *in a later hand, in the margin of* H: Lord haue mercy on me and grant me thy gra . . . 54 as] at B.

(8)

Redd Horses in one were redely,
an other Black, that went then by;
the third was whyte, I wott not why,
the fourth of Divers hew.

They were stiff drawing lightlye;
then anon Answered I
to that Angell, in my body,
which towld me wordes trew.

(9)

I asked him then what it might be,
and he Answered anon to me:
These Charretts, he sayd, w*hi*ch thou doest se,
four wyndes they be, iwis,

Which shall blow and ready be
before Christ that prince which is of posty;
ther is none so fell their fitt may flee,
nor wyn ther will from this.

EXPOSITOR. (10)

Now for to moralize aright,
which this prophet saw in sight,
I shall founde, through my might,
to you in meke manere;

And declare that soone in height,
more playnly as I haue tight.
listens now with hart[ë]s light
this Lesson for to learne.

(11)

Four Charretts this prophett se, how they
out of two hills tooke ther way;
the hills of Siluer, the sooth to say,
the horses of Divers hewe.

Which hills signify may
Enoch and Helie, in good fay,

57 Redd Horses] *In red ink* H. 60 Divers] *Written in red and black letters alternately* H. hew] hewes W h. 61 lightlye] bigly H, lighty B, biglye D. 66 to] vnto B h D. 70 Christ *after* prince H. which is] high of h. 71 fitt may] feete to D. 75 founde] shewe h. 79 listens] lightens W. 80 learne] *the form* lere *is required by the rhyme*. 81 se] saw se H. they] *om.* W. 84 hewe] hewes W h. 86 Enoch and Helie] *In red ink* H.

that as good siluer shall be aye,
Stidfast men and trew. 88

(12)

Four Charrtts, he saw, as thinkes me, 89
skilfully may likoned be
to Saynts of four maner of degree,
that then shall suffer anye. 92

ffour horses also is certaynty, 93
of dyvers hewes that he can se,
four maner of Saynts in dignity,
liken them well may I. 96

(13)

Martirs, Confessors, ther be two, 97
men mislevinge converted also,
that turned shall be from synne and woe
through Enoch and Helye. 100

Virgins also, both one and moe, 101
here be divers hews two,
that through gods grace shall goe
for him to suffer anye. 104

(14)

Thes Redd horses call I may 105
all maner of martyrs, in good fay,
for redd may well betoken aye
mans blood-shedinge. 108

The whyt, he sayth, token ther way 109
aboue the earth to goe astray,
as such as neither night nor day
dreden death nothinge. 112

(15)

The black horses which went them bye, 113
by them well may signifye
Preachers of gods word truly,
that Confessours shall be. 116

90—94 *om.*] W h. 91 maner] maners D. 93 is] *om.* B, *before* also D. certaynty] *ser*taine B. 98 mislevinge] misbeleevinge D. 102 two] too D. 109 The] They D. token] betokeneth W, tokeneth h. ther way] thereby h. 111 as] are H. *Second* as] that D. 113 which] *om.* h. 114 well] *after* may B W h D.

The Skewed horses, by myne intent,
the which into the Sowth forthwent,
I may well liken Verament
to Iews and Paynims eke.

(16)

yet through fayth with hart fervent,
shall come to good amend[e]ment,
when Enoch and helye haue them kent,
Saluation for to seeke.

DANIELL. (17)

Ego, Daniel, videbam in visione mea nocte, et ecce quatuor venti pugnabant in magno mari, et quatuor Bestiæ grandes ascendebant de mari. hæc in libro Danielis Cap. 7°.

I, Daniell, as I lay on a night,
me thought I saw a wonderous sight:
fowr wynds to geather the can feight
aboue the Sea vpon hye.
ffowr Beastes out of that sea yeede;
to the fourth Beast I tooke good heede,
for that to speak of now is neede;
the other all I will leave.

(18)

That Beast was wonderous stiff *and* stronge,
of Teeth and neiles sharp and longe,
eatinge over all that he could fonge,
the remnant he fortreed.
Vnlyke he was to any lead:
Tenne hornes he had vppon his head,
in the midst one little horne can spread
aboue all other on hye.

(19)

That Horne had mouth to speak and eyes to see,
And spak great word[e]s—leeue you me—

118 forth] *parte* W h. 121 yet] but B W h. fayth] harte W. hart] faith W. 122 come] torne B W h D. 123 haue] shall h. 124 seeke] kepe W. *Heading*] *after the Latin passage* W. nocte] nocke W h. mari] mare W h D. grandes] gradentes D. ascendebant] asendebunt W h. mari] mare B W h D. hæc in libro Danielis] *om.* B W h D. septimo] septimo dicat W. 128 vpon] one, *which best suits the metre* B. 129 sea] they H. yeede] the yeade D. 130 fourth Beast] foure bestes B. 132 all] all now W. 136 fortreed] fortredde D. 137 any] any of H B D. 139 the] *om.* H. 140 on] in D. 141 Horne] *In red ink* H. eyes] hornes W.

but of the Tenne *the* first three
sone wear consumed away. 144

That one horne had so great posty, 145
the remnant meek to him to be,
that heighest was in that degree,
and endured so many a day. 148

(20)

Then was it towld me right ther, 149
that ten hornes tenne Kinges weere,
but them all that one should fear
that sprang vpward so fast. 152

And that he should worke agaynst *tha*t Kinge, 153
that of nought made all thinge,
but little whyle, without leasinge,
that Kinge his might should last. 156

EXPOSITOR. (21)

By this Beast vnderstand I may 157
the world to come next Domes day;
and by that horne, in good fay,
in middst the tenne can springe, 160

Antechrist I may vnderstand, 161
that then great lord shall be in land,
and all the world haue in hand,
three years and a halfe duringe. 164

Tradentur in manu eius vsq*ue* ad tempus et tempora et dimidiu*m* Temporis et vsq*ue* ad vnu*m* Annu*m* duos Annos et dimidiu*m* Anni. Hæc in libro Danielis Cap. septimo.

(22)

Ten hornes Ten Kinges in land shall be, 165
Of which Antechrist shall slay Three,
the other Seven this case shall see
and putt them to his grace. 168

This shall befall witterly, 169
by the vnderstanding that haue I
of Daniells Prophesye,
that here rehearsed was. 172

145 so] such B W h. 150 tenne Kinges weere] *In red ink* H. 151 them] *om.* W h D. 158 the world to come] *In red ink* H. 163 in] in his W h. 164 a] *om.* H D. *Latin passage*] *om.* h. et] ad W. et] *om.* W. vnum] *om.* D. hæc in libro] *om.* B W D. 167 this] that B. 169 shall befall] shalbe full h.

IOHANNES EVANGELISTA. (23)

Dabo duob*us* testibus meis et prophetabunt Diebus mille Ducentis et Sexaginta amicti Saccis. hæc in libro Apocalypsios. Cap. xj°.

I, Ihon, Christes owne Darlinge, 173
as I lay in great longinge
vpon my maisters Barme slepinge,
wonders saw I many one. 176

My ghost was Ravished, with out leasing, 177
to heauen before that highest Kinge;
ther saw I many a wonderous thinge,
one will I tell anon. 180

(24)

Ther hard I God greatly com*m*end 181
two witnesses, which he thought to send
falce faythes for to defend,
that raysed were by his foe. 184

He sayd, they should Prophesye 185
a thowsand dayes, witterly,
tow hundreth and sixti,
in Sackes cladd they should goe. 188

(25)

He called them Chandlers of great light, 189
burning before gods sight;
fyre out of ther mouthes they should feight,
theyr enemyes to destroy. 192

whoso euer them harmed, as sayd he, 193
dead behoued him for to be;
to lett they rayne they had posty
in tyme of their prophesy. 196

(26)

He sayd, they should haue power good, 197
to turne the water into blood,

Heading] *after the Latin passage* W. meis] meus h. amicti] amiciti W, *om.* B. Saccis] *om.* B. hæc in libro] *om.* B W h D. Apocalypsios] apocalipsis D B h, apocalispis W, Cap.] *om.* W. xj°] vndecimo D. 175 Barme] breste B W h D. 176 wonders] wounders sightes h. 180 tell] tell you B W h D. 181 commend] comaunde B. 182 to] for to W h. 186 and 187, a thowsand dayes *and* tow hundreth and sixti] *In red ink* H. 188] H *has in its margin* 1260. cladd] cloth B. 189 chandlers] chandelours D. 191 feight] send B. "leight" ?? (Zupitza). they] *om.* h. 192 to] for to W h D. 193 sayd] saith W h. 194 behoued] behooveth h. him] them h. 195 *First* they] the D.

and overcom their Enemies *that* were wodd
and mayster them through their might.

And when they had done their devour,
A Beast should come of great power
from beneth, withouten were,
against them he should feight;

(27)

And slay them also should he
in middst of the holy Citty,
wher Christ was nayled on a tree,
forsoth as I you tell.

But after three dayes and halfe one,
they shall ryse, speak, and gone,
and into heauen betaken anon,
in ioy euermore to dwell.

EXPOSITOR. (28)

Now, lordinges, what these thinges may be,
I pray you harkyns all to me;
and expresly in certaynty,
as I haue might and grace,

I shall expound this ilke thinge,
which Sainct Iohn saw thus sleeping,
through helpe of Iesu, heauen Kinge,
anone right in this place.

(29)

Thes two witnesses wytterly,
he sayd they should come and prophesy;
the one is Enoch the other hely,
shall haue great might and mayne;

That when Antechrist comes in hye,
godds people for to destroy,
that he deceyveth falcely,
they shall convert agayn.

200 through their might] throwly B, through their power W. their might] *om.* h D. 201 devour] vower W h. 206 of] *om.* h. 210 shall] should h. 214 harkyns] harcken B W h D. 215 and] as H D. 217 I] and I W h. ilke] same W. 219 heauen] heavenlye W h. 221 witnesses] witnes B D. 223 the one] that one D. Enoch *and* hely] *In red ink* H. 227 deceyveth] deceaived W h. falcely] full falsely W h.

(30)

Many signes they shall show,
which the people shall well know,
and in their token truly trow
and leeve it stidfastly.

And all that tyme, leeve you me,
Antechrist will slay through his posty,
but very martys they shall be
and come to heauen on hye.

(31)

The beast, that Ihon spake of heare,
is Antechrist, without[en] were,
which shall haue the Devills power,
and with thes good men meete.

And at the last, witterly,
he shall slay Enoch and Hely
in Hierusalem, as read I,
even in midds of the Street.

(32)

Now that you shall know and seene,
what men Enoch and Hely beene,
I will you tell, withouten wene,
whyle that I haue tyme.

They are two good men—leue you me—
to Paradice through gods posty
were ravished both, and ther shall be
ever till the day do come.

(33)

The one was taken, for he was good,
longe before Noe his flood,
and ther he lyves in flesh and blood,
as fully leeven we.

The other was taken, withouten were,
after that many a hundreth yeare,

233 tyme] torne B W h D. 237 of] one B. 243 Hierusalem] *In red ink* H. 244 midds] myddest D. 245 and] *om.* h. 247] *om.* W. 248 tyme] *the rhyme requires* tome. 252 do] shall W h. 254 Noe his] Noyes W h. 256 we] yea W.

and ther togeather they bene in feer,
vntill that tyme shall be.

Signa Quindecim magna quæ *secundum* opiniones *Doctorum* extremum precedent Iudicium ab antiquis *Hebreorum* Codicibus selecta a Doctore huius pagine *recitanda*.

(34)

Now xv Signes, whiles I haue space,
I shall declare, by gods grace,
of which Saynt Iherom mention mase
to fall before the day of Dome.
The which were written vpon a Rowe,
he found in bookes of hebrew;
now will I tell in word[ë]s few,
a Whyl if you will dwell.

(35)

The first day, as I written fynd,
The Sea shall ryse against kynd,
and as a wall agaynst the wynd,
aboue all hills on hye,
fforty Cubyttes, as read we.
the secon*de* day so low shall be
that scarcly a man the Sea shall se,
stand he neuer so nye.

(36)

The Third day after, as read I,
great fishes aboue the Sea shall lye,
yelle and rore so hideously,
that onely god shall heare.
The fourth day next after then,
Sea *and* water all shall Brenne
agaynst kynd, *that* mon may ken,
Tinder as though it wear.

After 260 H W D *and* B *have in their margins:* Signa 15. precedent] procedunt W h D. pagine] pagina B W h. recitanda] recitando W, reticenda D. *Heading*] 15 Signa h. 263 Saynt Iherom] *In red ink* H. 264 fall] come B. 265 vpon] on B W h D. 266 bookes] boke B W h D. 268 dwell] wone?? *which only partly would correct the rhyme. Most of the following* 15 *stanzas are numbered in the margin in* D. 269 first day] *In red ink* H, *and so* "second" &c. *throughout.* 270 against] against it B. 273 we] I H. 274 seconde] secon H. 275 scarcly] skarse h. a man the Sea] the sea a man h. 276] *om.* B. 282 brenne] burne B D. 284 Tinder] the Ende W h.

(37)

The fift day, as read we,
all maner Herbs, and also Tree,
of bloody dew all full shall be,
and man and beast all Dased.

ffoules shall gather them, as I fynd,
to feilds echone in ther kynd,
of meat and drink shall haue no mynd,
but stand all madd and mased.

(38)

The Sixt day, in *the* world over all,
Builded things to ground shall fall:
Church, Citty, Howse, and wall,
And men in Greeves dare.

Leat and fyre also, Verament,
from the sonne to the firmament
Vp and downe shall stryke and glent,
and all night so foule fare.

(39)

The Seventh day, both rocke and Stonne
shall break in sonder and feight as fone;
the sownd therof shall hear no man
but onely god Amight.

The Eight day, earth-quake shall be,
that men and Beast—leue you me—
to stand or goe shall fayle posty,
but fall to ground all right.

(40)

The Ninth day, as our bookes sayen,
hills shall fall and wax all playne;
Stonne turne to Sand through gods mayne,
so streat men shall be stadd.

285 day] day day H. 286 Herbs] of herbes D. 288] *om.* B W h. man and beast] manye a beaste D, *but in a different hand.* 291 of meat] to eate W. 292] *om.* B W. 294 ground] earth B. 296 Greeves] graves D. 297 Leat] late B, Layte D. 302 in sonder] asunder D. 303 therof] where of W h. 306 Beast] beast*es* B. leue] beleeve W h. 308 right] night H. 312 stadd] skadde? W.

The Tenth day, men that hydd hath be, 313
out of their Caves they shall flee;
to speak togeather haue no posty,
but goe as they were madd. 316

(41)

The Eleventh day, from morow to even, 317
all Buryalls in the world open shall beene,
that dead may Ryse, withouten wene,
aboue the earth standinge. 320

The Twelft day, Starrs shall fall in hye, 321
and fyre shoot from them hydeously;
all maner of Beastes shall rore *and* crye,
and neither eate nor drinke. 324

(42)

The Thirdtenth day, shall dye all men, 325
and ryse agayne anon right then.
The fourtenth day, all shall brenne,
both[e] earth and eek heaven. 328

The Fiftenth day, made shall be 329
new earth, new heaven, through gods posty;
which heauen god graunt vs in to be,
for his names seven. 332

Conclusio. (43)

Now haue I touuld you, in good fay, 333
the tokens to come before Domes day:
God geue you grace to do so aye,
that then you worthy be, 336

To come to the Blisse that lasteth aye, 337
as much as here we and our play,
of Antechrists sygnes you shall assay:
he comes sone, you shall see. 340

Finis Paginæ vicæsimæ Secundæ.

317 Eleventh] leventh W, elevon D. 318 open shall beene] shall be open D. 321 Twelft] Twelffe D. 322 and] of B W h. 323 Beastes] Bastes H. 325 thirdtenth] thirteene D. 326 agayne anon] anon agayne D. 327 fourtenth] foureteene D. 329 fiftenth] fyfteene D. 332 seven] sake h. Conclusio] *om.* B W h D. 333—337] *twice in* B; *but once crossed out, in which stanza the scribe had written* you then worthie *in verse* 336. 336 then you] you them W h D, you B. 338 here we] we heare W h. Finis] Amen, finis D. paginæ vicæsimæ secundæ] *om.* B D, deo gracias, *per* me georgi bellin 159 W, 1600 h.

Pagina Vicesima Tertia de Adue*n*tu Antechristi. The Diars.

ANTECHRISTUS. (1)

De celso Throno Poli, pollens clarior Sole, 1
age, vobis monstrare descendi, vos Iudicare;
Reges, et Principes, sunt Subditi sub me viue*n*tes;
Sitis Sapientes vos, semp*er* in me credentes, 4

Et faciam flentes gaudere atque dolentes; 5
Sic omnes Gentes gaudebunt in me sperantes.
Descendi Presens Rex, pius et Perlustrator,
Princeps eternus vocor, Christus, vester saluator. 8

(2)

All leeds in land now be light, 9
that will be ruled throughout *the* right;
your Sauiour now in your sight
here may you safely see. 12

Messias, Christ, and most of might, 13
that in the law was you beheight,
all mankynd ioy to dight,
is comen, for I am he. 16

(3)

Of me was spoken in prophesy 17
of Moses, David and Esay;
I am he they call Messy,
forebyar of Israell. 20

Thes that leuen in me stidfastly, 21
I shall them saue from anye,
and such ioy, right as haue I,
with them I think to deale. 24

Dicitur enim de me, Ezechiel Cap. 36° "Tollam vos de gentib*us*, ot congregabo vos de vniuersis terris, et reducam vos in terram vestra*m*."

The Diars] *om.* B, The dyars playe W h D *before the Latin heading. Heading*] Antechriste D. 2 vobis] vos B W h D. descendi] descen D. 3 viue*n*tes] vementes W h. 5 dolentes] delentes H. 15 ioy] to Ioye B W h D. 16 he] H *adds, though in smaller letters:* "to save." 21 Thes] those B W h D. in] on D. 23 such] *om.* B W h D. *Latin quotation*] *om.* h. dicitur enim] *after* me B W, *om.* enim D, *and* dicitur *after* me D. Ezechiel Cap. 36°] Ezechielis tricesimo sexto D. vestra*m*] vestru*m* et dicit W.

(4)

But one hath ligged me here in land, 25
Iesu he height, I vnderstand;
to further falcehood he can fonde,
and fared with fantasy. 28
His wickednes he would not wonde 29
till he was taken and putt in Band,
and slayn through vertue of my sand;
this is sooth, sickerly. 32

(5)

My people of Iews he cowld twyn, 33
that their land come they neuer in;
then on them now must I myn,
and restore them againe. 36
To build this Temple will I not blinne, 37
and as god honored be therin,
and endless wayle I shall them wyn,
all that to me be bayn. 40

De me enim dicitur in Psalmo: "Adorabo ad Templu*m* sanctu*m* enim in timore tuo."

(6)

One thing me glades, be you bould, 41
as Daniell the prophett afore me towld;
all women in world me loue should,
when I were come in land. 44
This prophesy I shall well hould, 45
which is most lykinge to yonge *and* ould;
I think fast manye to houlde,
and ther faymes to fownd. 48

(7)

Also he tould then, leue you me, 49
*tha*t I of giftes should be free,
which prophesy done shall be,
when I my Realm haue nomman; 52

25 me] *om.* B, him H D. 31 sand] sond D. 34 come they] came the D. 35 then] *om.* W. on] of B. 38 and] so B, *om.* W h D. *Latin quotation*] *om.* h, *after* 56 *in* H *with the marginal remark:* This should come in place of "Dabit eis." enim] *om.* B, tuu*m* W D. 42 afore] before B W h D. 44] and their faireness to founde W h. 45—57] *om.* h. 47 fast manye to houlde] to force many fould H, to fast manye hould D. to] *om.* B. 49 then] them D. 50 giftes] geifte W h. 52 nomman] wonnan B W, wonnen D h.

And that I should graunt men posty,
Ryved Riches, land, and fee;
it shall be done, that you shall se,
when I am hither common.

Dabit eis potestatem et multis terra*m* dividet gratuito.
Danielis Decimo tertio.

(8)

What say you, kinges, that here be lent?
are not my wordes at your assent?
that I am Christ omnipotent,
leeue you not this, echone?

PRIMUS REX.

We leuen, lord, with out lett,
that Christ is not common yet;
if thou be he, thou shalt be sett
in Temple as god alone.

SECUNDUS REX. (9)

Yf thou be Christ, called Messy,
that from our bale shall vs bye,
doe before vs maistery,
a Signe that we maye see.

TERTIUS REX.

Then will I leue that it is so,
if thou do wonders or thou goe;
so that thou saue vs of our woe,
then honored shalt thou be.

QUARTUS REX. (10)

fowle haue we leued many a year,
and of our weninge bene in were;
and thou be Christ now comnen here,
then may thou stint all stryfe.

ANTECHRISTUS.

That I am Christ and Christ will be,
by very signes sone shall you see,
for dead men through my posty
shall ryse from death to lyfe.

53 men posty] mercye W h. 54 ryved] *om.* B. tertio] tercia et dicitt W. 64 alone] above W. 68 maye] *om.* H. 73 we] *om.* H. 75 now] *om.* D. 78 sone] *om.* W h.

(11)

Now will I turne, all throughe my might,
Trees down, the Rootes vpright;—
that is marvayle to your sight!—
and fruit growing vppon.

So shall the grow and multiply
through my might and my maystry;
I put you out of heresy,
to leue me vppon.

(12)

And bodyes that bene dead and slayne,
if I may rayse them vp agayne,
then honours me with might and mayne;
then shall no man you greeve.

forsooth then after will I dye,
and Ryse agayne through my posty;
If I may doe this marvelously,
I redd you on me leeve.

(13)

Men buryed in grave, as you may see,
what maistry is now hope ye,
to rayse them vp through my posty,
and all through myne accord!

whether I in my godhead be,
by very signe you shall se.
Ryse vp, Dead men, *and* honours me,
and know me for your lord! (Tunc Resurgent mortui de Sepulcris.)

PRIMUS MORTUUS. (14)

A! lord, to thee I aske mercye!
I was dead, but now lyve I;
now wott I well and witterly
that Christ is hether commen.

SECUNDUS MORTUUS.

Him honour we and all men,
devoutly kneling on our knen.

84 and] with W, that h. 85 the] they D. 86 might] night H. 87 out of] into th*at* ?, B. 91 with] with with W. 95 may] *om.* H. 97 as] *om.* D. 100 myne] my owne B W D. 102 signe] signes W h. *Stage-direction*] *in* H *in the margin.* 105 to] of B.

worshipped be thou ther, amen!
Christ, that our name is nu*m*men.

ANTECHRISTUS. (15)

That I shall fulfill holy writt,
you shall wot and know well it,
for I am wall of wayl and witt,
and lord of every land.

And as the Prophet Sophony
speakes of me full witterly,
I shall rehearce here redely,
that Clark*es* shall vnderstand:

Expecta me in die Resurrectionis meæ in futurum quia Iudiciu*m*, vt congregem Gentes et colligam regna. Sophon. 3.

(16)

Now will I dye, that you shall see,
and ryse agayne through my posty;
I will in grave that you putt me,
and worship me alone;

For in this Temple a tombe is made,
therin my body shall be layde;
then will I ryse, as I haue sayd.
take tent to me, echone!

(17)

And after my Resurrection,
then will I sitt in great renoune,
and my ghost send to you downe.
I dye, I dye, now am I dead.

P*RI*MUS REX. (18)

Now sith this worthy lord is dead,
and his grace is with vs lead,
to take his body it is my redd,
and bury it in a grave.

111 worshipped] worship H D. 112 that] *om.* W h D. name] nane D. nu*m*men] named B, comen W h D. 115 of] *om.* W h. 118 full] righte W. 119 here] *om.* W h. 120 clarkes] Carkes H. resurrectionis] resurgens W. regna] ragula h. 3] *om.* W h. 128 tent] teene W h. 130 renoune] renoume H. *Between* 131 *and* 132] B W h D *insert* in forme of fier full soone. 132] *In red ink* H.

SECUNDUS REX.

forsooth, and so to vs he sayde,
in a Tombe he would be layd;
now goe we forth all in a brayd,
from disease he may vs saue. (tunc eunt ad Antechristum.)

TERTIUS REX. (19)

Take we the body of this sweet,
and lay it low vnder the greet!
now, lord, comfort vs, we thee beseke,
and send vs of thy grace!

QUARTUS REX.

And if he ryse sone through his might,
from death to lyfe, as he beheight,
him will I honour, day and night,
as God in every place. (Tunc recedent de Tumulo vsque ad terram.)

PRIMUS REX. (20)

Now wott I well that he is dead,
for now in graue we haue him layd.
if he ryse as he hath sayd,
he is of full great might.

SECUNDUS REX.

I can not leeve him vpon,
but if he ryse him selfe alone,
as he hath sayd to many one,
and shew him here in sight.

TERTIUS REX. (21)

Till that my Sauiour be risen agayne,
in fayth my hart may not be fayne;
my body eke will not be bayne
till I him se with eye.

QUARTUS REX.

I most mowrne with all my mayne
till Christ be rysen vp agayne,

137 he] *before* to W. 139 forth] further D. 140 disease] destres W. *Stage-direction*] *in* H *in the margin*, tunc transeunt ad Antechristum B W h D. 142 lay] burye W D. 147 day] both daye D. 150 layd] lead D. 155 many] manye a W. 159] *om.* B W h D. 160 eye] ioye h.

and of that miracle make vs fayne.
Ryse vp, lord, that we may see! 164

(Tunc Ante*christus* levat Corpus suu*m* surgens a mortuis.)

ANTECHRIST*US*. (22)

I Ryse! now Reuerence dose to me! 165
god glorified, greatest of degree!
if I be Christ, now leues ye me,
and werch after my wyse. 168

PR*IM*US REX.

A! lorde, welcome must thou be! 169
that thou art god now leeue we;
therfore goe, sitt vp in thy See,
and keepe our Sacrifice. (Tum Sacrificant.) 172

SECU*N*D*US* REX. (23)

for sooth, in Seat thou shalt be sett, 173
and honored with lambe and Geatt,
as moses Law that lasteth yett,
as he hath sayd before. 176

TERTIUS REX.

O! Gracious lord, goe, sitt downe then! 177
and we shall, knelinge on our knen,
worship thee as thyne owne men,
and worch after thy lore. (Tunc Ascendet Antechristus ad Cathedra*m*.)

PR*IM*US REX. (24)

Hether we be commen with good intent, 181
to make our Sacrifice, lord excellent,
with this lambe that I haue here hent,
kneling thee before. 184

SECU*N*D*US* REX.

Thou graunt grace to doe and say 185
that it be plesinge to thee aye,

a mortuis] mortus (sic!) W h. 165 dose] nowe doe W. 166 greatest] created B W h D. 167 me] *om.* H D. 168 werch] werch you H. my] the H. wyse] will W. *Stage-direction*] tunc transeunt ad Ante*christ*um cu*m* sacrificio B D h, *om.* W. 174 lambe and Geatt] lande greate B W h. 176] hath ofte said heretofore B. 178 knelinge on] kneele upon B h, knee upon W. 180 lore] lorde h. ascendet] auscendit D. *Heading*] *om.* B W D. Quartus rex h, *which reading may be the correct one.* 183 I haue here] here is B. 184 thee] here H. *Heading*] *om.* B W h D. 185—189] *om.* h. 186 that] and yf W.

to thy blis that come we may,
and neuer from it be lore!

ANTECHIRSTUS. (25)

I lord, I god, I heighe Iustice,
I Christ, that made the dead to ryse,
here I receaue your Sachrifice,
and blesse you, flesh and fell. (Tunc ab Ante*christo* revert*erunt.*)

You kinges, I tell withouten bost,
I will now send my holy ghost,
to know me lord of might most,
of heauen, earth and Hell.

(Tunc emittet Spiritu*m*, dicens: Dabo vobis Cor novu*m* et Spiritu*m* novu*m* in medio vestri.)

QUARTUS REX. (26)

A! god! a! lord! micle of might,
this holy ghost is in me pight;
me thinks my hart is very light,
sithe it came into me.

PRIMUS REX

Lord, we thee honour, day and night,
for thou shewest vs in sight
right as Moses vs beheight.
honored most thou be!

ANTECHRISTUS. (27)

Yet worthy workes to your will
of prophesy I shall fulfill,
as Daniell prophesyed you vntill,
that landes I should devyse.

That prophesy it shall be done,
and that you shall see right sone;
worshipps me all that you mon,
and doe after the wyse.

188 lore] borne W, flore (slore?) B. 189 *First* I] A W. *Stage-direction*] tunc recedunt Antech*ris*to B, Tunc recedent antichristo W h D. 194 *and* 195] I will now send my hollie ghoste, you king*es* also to you I tell B W h D. (to] *om.* W h). 195 might] mightes D. vestri] vestro B. *Stage-direction*] Heare his ghost decendes h. *Heading*] Seu*er*alis rex B W h D. 207 you] *om.* W h. 208 landes] baundes W. I] *om.* W h. should] shall D. 209—213] *om.* h.

(28)

You kinges, I shall advaunce you all,
and because your Regions be but small,
Cityes, Castles shall you befall,
with Townes and Towrs gay;

And make you lordes of lordshipps fayre,
as well it fall[e]s for my power;
yea, looke you doe as I you bad,
and harkyns what I say.

(29)

I am very god of might,
all thinges I made through my might,
Sonne and Moone, Day and night;
to Blis I may you bringe.

Therfore kinges, noble and gay,
token your people what I say,
that I am Christ, god veray,
and tell them such Tydinge.

(30)

My people of Iews were put me from,
therfore great ruth I haue them on;
whether they will leeve me vpon,
I will full soone assay.

For all that will leeve me vpon,
wordly welth shall them fall on,
and to my blisse they shall come,
and dwell with me for aye.

(31)

And the gyftes that I behight,
you shall haue, as is good right;
hence or I goe out of your sight,
ech one shall haue his Dole.

217—221] *om.* H W h. 217 lordshipes fayrer] lordshipp fayre D. 218 falles] fall D. 219 bad] leere H D. *Collier in "five miracle plays."* 221—241] *om.* h. 223 Sonne and Moone] *In red ink* H. 225—237] *om.* W h. 234 them fall] haue full B. 237 gyftes] geifte W. 239 Thence] hence D. 240 haue] knowe B W D.

To thee I geeue Lumbardy,
and to the Denmark and Hungary,
and take thou Pathmos and Italy,
and Roome it shall be thyne.

SECUNDUS REX. (32)

Graunt mercy, lord, your gyftes to day!
honour we will thee alway;
Never so rich were we, in good fay,
nor none of all our kynne.

ANTECHRISTUS.

Therfore be treu and stidfast aye,
and truly leves on my law,
for I will harken on you to day,
Stidfast if I you fynd.

(Tunc recedet Ante*christus* et venient Enoch et Helias.)

ENOCH. (33)

Almighty god in maiesty,
that made the heauen *and* earth to be,
fyre, water, Stonne and Tree,
and man through thy might;

The poyntes of thy privity
any earthly man to se
is impossible, as thinkes me,
for any wordly wighte.

(34)

Gracious lord that art so good,
that who so long in flesh and blood
hath graunted lyfe and heauenly food,
let neuer our thoughtes be defyled!

But geue vs, lord, might and mayne,
or we of this shrew be slayne,
to convert thy people agayne,
that he hath thus begyled.

241—244] *Names of places in red ink* H. 243 Pathmos] ponthous W h. 244 thyne] thyn whole, ? *because of the rhyme.*—(Zupitza.) 245 gyftes] gifte W. 247] for wee were never so rich in good faye B W h D. (good] *om.* B). 248 kynne] *the form* kynde *is required by the rhyme.* 250 law] *the rhyme requires* lay. 252 stidfast] sidfast H. venient] venit h. 256 thy] his B. 258 *and* 259] *om.* W. 260 for] *om.* W or h. wordly] eirthlye W. 264 thoughtes] though h. 266 be] we be W.

(35)

Sith the worlds beginninge
I haue lyved in great lykeinge,
through help of hye heaven kinge,
in Paradyce without anoye,

Till we hard tokeninge
of this Thefes cominnge,
that now on Earth is rayginnge,
and doth gods folke destroy.

(36)

To paradyce taken I was that Tyde,
this Theefs comminge to abyde,
and Helye, my brether, here me besyde,
was after sent to me.

With this Champion we must Chyde,
that now in werld walketh wyde,
to dispreue his Pompe and pryde
and payre all his Posty.

HELIAS. (37)

O! lord, that madest all thinge,
and long hath lent vs lyvinge,
lett neuer the Devills power springe,
this man hath him within!

God geve you grace, both owld and yonge,
to know deceite in his doinge,
that you may come to that lykinge
of Blisse that neuer shall blynne.

(38)

I warne you, all men, witterly,
this is Enoch, I am Helye,
been commen his errowrs to distroy
that he to you now shewes.

He calls himself Christ and Messye;
He lyes, forsothe, apertlye!

269] since first the worlde begane h. 270 *and* 271] *inverted in* h. 271 heaven] heavenly W h. hye] high and D. 275 on] in W. 276 folke] folkes D. 277 taken I was] I was taken D. 278 Theefs] thef his B D. 279 Helye] *In red ink* H. 287 never] nover H. 289 both] *om.* D. 296 now] *before* to W.

He is the Deuyll, you to anoy,
and for none other him knowes.

TERTIUS REX. (39)

A! men, what speak yeu of Helye
and Enoch? they be both in compny;
of our blood they beene, witterly,
and we be of their kynd.

QUARTUS REX.

we reeden in Bookes of our law,
that they to heauen were I-draw,
and yet bene ther is the co*m*mon saw,
written as men may fynd.

HENOCH. (40)

We be those men, forsoth, I wis,
co*m*men to tell you do amis,
and bring your soules to heauen blis,
if it were any boote.

HELIAS.

This Devills lymme that comen is,
that sayeth heauen and earth is his,
now we be ready—leve you this!—
agaynst him for to moote.

PR*IMUS* REX. (41)

If that we hear witt mon,
by proofes of Disputation,
that you haue skyll and reason,
with you we will abyde.

SECU*N*DUS REX.

And if your skylls may doe him downe,
to dye with you we will be bowne,
in hope of Saluation,
what so euer betyde.

Heading] primus rex W h D. 315 be] *om.* H. 317 mon] anon H. 321 and] *om.* W h. 321—325] *written in* H *after* 332, *but the mistake is corrected in the margin by:* these iiii rowes should come in after "we will abyde," *and a* hic *opposite to* abyde. 324 so] *om.* D. betyde] may betyde D.

ENOCH. (42)

To doe him downe we shall assay, 325
through might of Iesu, borne of a May,
by right and reason as you shall say,
And that you shall well heare. 328

And for that cause hether are we sent 329
by Ih*esus* Christ Omnipotent;
and that you shall not all be shent,
he bought you all full deere. 332

(43)

Be gladd, therfore, and make good Cheare, 333
and doe, I redd, as I you leere,
for we be comen in good manere,
to saue you every one. 336

And dread you not for *that* falce feend, 337
for you shall see him cast behynd,
or we depart and from him wend,
and shame shall him light on! 340

(Et sic transibunt Henoch et Helias ad Antechristu*m*.)

ENOCH. (44)

Say, thou very Devills lym 341
that sitts so grysely and so grim!
from him thou came and shalt to him,
for many a soule thou deceaves. 344

Thou hast deceived men many a day, 345
and made the people to thy pay,
and bewitched them into a wrong way,
wickedly with thy wyles. 348

ANTECHRISTUS. (45)

A! falce features, from me you flee! 349
am not I most in maiesty?
what men dare mayne them thus to me
or make such distaunce? 352

328 you] *om.* h. 329 are we] were wee B D, we be W h. 330 Ih*esus* Christ] *In red ink* H. 334 doe I] I doe B W h D. you] *om.* W h. 340 him light] light him D. *After stage-direction in* D, *heading* Enock. 341 very] wery H. 344 deceaves] *the synonymous* beguyles *would rhyme with* wyles. 346 made] brought B. 351 mayne] name B W h.

HELIAS.

Fye on thee, feature! fye on thee! 353
the Devills owne nurry!
through him thou preachest and hast posty
a whyle, through sufferance. 356

ANTECHRISTUS. (46)

O! you hipocrytes that so cryen! 357
lozells! Lordans! lowdly you lyen!
to spill my law you aspyne,
that spech is good to spare. 360

you that my true faith defyne, 361
and needles my folke denyne,
from hence hastely but you hyne,
to you comes sorrow and care! 364

ENOCH. (47)

Thy Sorrow and care come on thy head! 365
for falcely through thy wicked redd,
the people is putt to paine. 367

I would thy body were from thy head, 368
Twenty myles from it layd,
till I hit brought agayne. 370

ANTECHRISTUS. (48)

Out on the, wyseard, with thy wyles! 371
for falcsely my people thou begyles:
I shall the hastely honge. 373

And that Lurdane that standes the by, 374
he putts my folke to great anye,
with his falce, flattering tonge. 376

(49)

But I shall teach you curtesy, 377
your Sauiour to know anon in hye;
false Theeves, with your heresy,
and if you dare, abyde! 380

Heading] *twice in* W. 358 lowdly] so lovdlye W h. 359 aspine] spine W h. 362 my folke] *twice in* D. 363 but] *om.* h. hyne] hence hyne D. 367 paine] pyne H B D. 369 miles] myle D. layd] lead B W h. 371—377] *om.* h. 371 wyseard] rasarde W, roysard D. 374 the] thy H.

HELIAS. (50)

Yes, forsooth, for all thy pryde, 381
through grace of god Almight
Here we purpose for to abyde; 383

and all the world that is so wyde, 384
shall wonder on thee, on every syde,
sone in all mens sight. 386

ANTECHRISTUS. (51)

Out on you, Theevs, both two! 387
ech man may see you be so,
all by your aray: 389

Muffled in Mantells none such I know; 390
I shall make you lowt full low,
Or I depart you all fro,
to know me lord for aye. 393

ENOCH. (52)

We be no Theues, we thee tell, 394
thou false feind, commen from hell!
with the we purpose for to mell,
my fellow and I in feere, 397

To know thy power and thy might, 398
as we thes kinges haue beheight,
and therto we be ready dight,
that all men now may here. 401

ANTECHRISTUS. (53)

My might is most, I tell to thee; 402
I dyed, I rose through my posty;
that all thes Kinges saw with ther *E*ye,
and every man and wyfe. 405

And miracles and marvayles I did also; 406
I counsell you therfore, bothe two,
to worshipp me and no mo,
and lett vs no more stryve. 409

382 *and* 383] *ought to be inverted in their order as Collier prints them in his* "five miracle plays," *inverted in* D. 392] *the metre is improved by an omission of this line, which is not necessary to make sense.* 398—402] *om.* B. 401 now] *after* maye W h. 409 us] us nowe W h D.

HELIAS. (54)

They were no Miracles, but marvayls thinges 410
that thou shewed to these kinges;
into falsehood thou them bringes
through the feindes craft. 413

And as the flowrs now springes, 414
falleth, fadeth, and hings,
so thy ioy now it raignes,
that shall from thee be rafte. 417

ANTECHRISTUS. (55)

Out on thee, Theefe, that sitts so still! 418
Why wilt thou not one word speak them tyll?
but lett them speak all ther will,
that commen me to reprove! 421

DOCTOR.

O! lord, maister, what shall I say then? 422

ANTECHRISTUS.

I beshrew both thy knenne! 423
art thou now for to kenne?
In fayth, I shall thee greeve. 425

(56)

Of my godhead I made thee wyse, 426
and sett thee ever at mickle price;
now I would feele thy good advyse,
and heare what thou would saye. 429

Thes Loullords they would faine me greeve, 430
and nothing on me they will leeue,
but ever be ready me to repreue,
and all the people of my law. 433

DOCTOR. (57)

O! lord, thou art so mickle of might, 434
me think thou shouldst not chyde nor feight,

411 to] unto W h D. 412] *om.* B W h D. 414 flowrs] flower B W h D. 415 fadeth] faith W h. 416 now] *om.* W h. it] *om.* B. 417 be] *after* shall B W h D. 419 one word] *om.* W h. 420] *om.* D. 421 reprove] *the form* repreve *is required by the rhyme.* 423 knenne] kenne W, cyne h. 424 now] *om.* H. 429 saye] sayne H, sayen D. 430 loullords] lowlers B D, lossilles W h. faine] *om.* H. 431 leeue] beleeve W h. 432 be] are B. 433 law] *the synonymous* lay *is required by the rhyme.* 435 not] *om.* H, ne W h. shouldst] should D.

but cursse them, lord, through thy might,
then shall they fare full ill: 437

For thos whom thou blessest, they shall well speed, 438
and those whom thou Cursedst they are but dead;
this is my Counsell and my redd,
yonder heretykes to spill. 441

ANTECHRISTUS. (58)

The same I purposed—leeve thou me!— 442
all thinge I knew through my posty;
but yet thy witt I thought to see,
what was thyn intent. 445

Hit shall be done full sickerly, 446
the sentence geaven full openly
with my mouth truly,
vpon them shall be hent. 449

(59)

My curse I geue you to amend your meeles, 450
from your head vnto your heeles!
walke ye forth in the twenty Devills way! 452

ENOCH.

Yea, thou shalt neuer come in Cœlis, 453
for falsely with thy wyles
all this people thou begyles,
and puttes them all to paine. 456

ANTECHRIST. (60)

Out on you, Theues! why fare ye thus? 457
Whether had you leiffer haue: payne or blisse?
I may saue you from all amys;
I made the day and eke night, 460

And all thinge that is on earth growinge, 461
flowers fresh that fayre can springe;

438] *om.* W. whom] *om.* h. blessest] blesses D. 439 whom] *om.* B. cursedst] cursest D. 443 thinge] thinges B h D. 445 what] that W. thyn] myne W. 446 sickerly] witterlye W h. 451 unto] to D. 452 devills way] *probably* devills *should stand at the end of the line, rhyming with* meeles—heeles, *and* way *somehow rhyming with* paine *of* 456, *represents only the remnant of a whole 3-accent line.* 453 Cœlis] clisse W h. *In red ink* H. 455] *om.* B W h D. 456] the people are put in pyne D. paine] pyne H B. 458 leiffer] rather W h. 459 saue you] you saue B W h D. 460 eke] Eke the B W h D. 461 thinge] thinges B D, *om.* W. is] are D.

also I made all other thinge,
the Starrs that be so bright. 464

HELIAS. (61)

Thou lyest! Vengeance on thee befall! 465
out on the, wretch! wroth thee I shall;
thou calls thee kinge and lord of all—
a feind is thee within! 468

ANTECHRISTUS. (62)

Thou lyest falsely, I thee tell; 469
thou shalt be damned into hell;
I made the man of flesh and fell,
and all that is lyvinge. 472

for other godds haue you none, 473
therfore worshipp me alone,
the which hath made the water and Stonne,
and all at my lykinge. 476

HENOCH. (63)

Forsoth, thou lyest falsely! 477
thou art a feind, come to anye
gods people that stands vs bye;
in hell I would thou were! 480

HELIAS.

Fye on thee, felone! fye on *th*ee, fye! 481
for all thy witchcraft *and* sorcery,
to moote wi*th* thee I am ready,
that all *th*e people may heare. 484

ANTECHRISTUS. (64)

Out on you, Harlotts! whenc came ye? 485
wher haue you any other god but me?

ENOCH.

Yes! Christ, God in Trinity, 487
thou false feature attaynt!

That sent his sonne from heauen Sea, 489
that for mankynd dyed on rood tree,

463] *om.* W. 467 calls] callest D. 470 shalt] will D. 479 stands] stande D. 480—485] *together with the heading in the margin in* H. 484 the] thee W, this h. 485 came] come B W h D. 489 sent his] gods H.

that shall sone make thee to flee,
thou feature false and faynt! 492

ANTECHRISTUS. (65)

Ribbaldes ruled out of raye, 493
what is the Trinitie for to say?

HELIAS.

Three Persons, as thou leeve may, 495
in one godhead in feere;

father and Sonne, that is no nay, 497
and the holy ghost, stirring aye,
that is on god veray,
bene all three named here. 500

ANTECHRISTUS. (66)

Out on you, Theeves! what say yee? 501
will you haue one god and three? . . .
. . . .
how dare you so say? 504

Madmen, madmen! therfore leeve on me, 505
that am one god, so is not he;
then may you lyve in joy and lee,
all this land I dare lay. 508

ENOCH. (67)

Nay, Tyrande! vnderstand thou this: 509
without beginninge his godhead is,
and also without endinge, iwis;
thus fully leven we. 512

And thou that ingendered was amis, 513
hast beginninge, and now this blis
an end shall haue, no dread ther is,
full foule, as men shall see. 516

ANTECHRISTUS. (68)

Wretches! Goles! you be blent; 517
godds Sonne I am, from him sent;

491 sone] ful soone B W D. make thee] *before* full sone W. 496 feere] free W h. 501 say] sayen D. *After* 502] *a line seems to be omitted, the apparent omission of which is not indicated in any MS.* 505 *One* madmen *om.* h. 515 an] and H D. 516 full] fully B W h. 517 Goles] glowes W, gowles B h, gulles D.

how dare you maintayne your intent
sith he and I be one? 520

Haue I not, sith I came him froe, 521
made the dead to speak and goe?
and to men I send my ghost also,
that leeved me vppon. 524

HELIAS. (69)

Fye on thee, felone! fye on thee, fye! 525
for through his might and his maistry,
by sufferance of god almighty
the people is blent through thee. 528

yf thos men be raysed, witterly, 529
without the Devills fantasy,
here shall be proued apertly,
that all[e] men shall see. 532

ANTECH[R]ISTUS. (70)

A! fooles! I redd you leue me vpon, 533
that miracles haue shewed to many one,
to the people everychon,
to putt them out of doubt. 536

Therfor I redd you hastely 537
converts to me most mighty;
I shall you saue from anoy,
and that I am about. 540

ENOCH. (71)

Now of thy miracles would I see. 541

HELIAS.

Therfore comen hether be we: 542
do what is thy great posty,
and some therof to leere! 544

ANTECHRISTUS.

Sone may you se yf you will abyde, 545
for I will neither feight nor chyde.

522 speak] rise W h. 523 send] sent D. 524 leeved] leeve W. 526 maistry] maiestie D. 528 is] are D. 531 apertly] p*er*fectlye W h. 542 be we] we be W. 544 some] soone h.

of all the world that is so wyde,
ther in is not my peere. 548

ENOCH. (72)

Bringe forth thos men here in our sight, 549
that thou hast raysed agaynst the right,
if thou be so mickle of might,
to make [them] eate and drinke! 552

for very god we will thee know, 553
such a signe if thou wilt show,
and doe the reuerence on a row,
all at thy lykeinge. 556

ANTE*CHRISTUS*. (73)

Wretches! damned all be yee! 557
but nought for that it falleth mee,
as gracious god abydinge be,
yf you will mend your lyfe. 560

You Dead men, ryse, through my posty! 561
come! eate and drinke that men may see,
and proue me worthy of Deitie!
so shall we stint all stryfe. 564

P*RIMUS* MORTUUS. (74)

Lord, thy bidding I will do aye, 565
and for to eate I will assay.

SECU*NDUS* MORTU*US*.

And I also, all that I may, 567
will doe thy biddinge here.

HELIAS.

Haue here Bread, both two, 569
but I must blesse it or I goe,
that the feind, mankynd[e]s foe,
on it haue no power. 572

(75)

This Bread I blesse with my hand, 573
in Iesus name I vnderstand,

560 your] you H. mortuus] mortuis D. 567 I] I will h. 570 or I] or it H, ere it B, or yt D. 574 Iesus name] *In red ink* H.

the which is lord of sea and land,
and king in heaven so hye.

"In nomine patris" that all hath wrought,
"Et filii virginis" that deare vs bought,
"Et spiritus sancti" is all my thought:
One god and Persons three.

PRIMUS MORTUUS. (76)

Alas! put that Bread out of my sight!
to look on it I am not light;
that printe that is vpon hit pight
it putts me to great feare.

SECUNDUS MORTUUS.

To looke on it I am not light,
that Bread to me it is so bright,
and is my foe, both day and night,
and putts me to great deere.

ENOCH. (77)

Now you men that haue done amis,
you see well what his power is.
converts to him, I redd, iwys,
that you on Rood[e] bought.

TERTIUS REX.

A! now we know, apertly,
we haue bene brought in heresy,
With you to death we will for thy,
and neuer efte torne our thought.

QUARTUS REX. (78)

Now, Enoch and Helye, it is no nay,
you haue taynted thy Tyrant this same day.
blessed be Iesu, borne of a may!
on him I leeue vppon.

PRIMUS REX.

Thou feture, ferd with fantasy,
with Sorcery, witchcraft *and* nigromancy,

576 in] of D. so] on D. 577—580] *The Latin words and the last line in red ink* H. 584 it] that h. 587 both] *om.* W. 588 deere] dread B W h. 592 bought] hath bought B W h D. 596 efte] *om.* W, more h. our thought] from thie B. 598 taynted] taunted h. thy] the D. 601 ferd] fere W h.

thou hast vs lead in heresy;
fye on thy workes, echon!

SECUNDUS REX. (79)

Ihesu, for thy mickle grace,
forgeue vs all our trespase,
and bring vs to thy heauenly place,
as thou art god and man.

Now am I wyse made through *th*i might;
blessed be thou, Ih*esu*, day and night!
the grisely grome girts him to feight,
to slay vs here anon.

TERTIUS REX. (80)

Of our lyues let vs not reche,
thoughe we be slayne of such a wretch
for Iesus sake that may vs leech,
our soules to bring to blisse!

QUARTUS REX.

That was well sayd, and so I assent;
to dye, forsoth, is my intent,
for Christes loue Omnipotent,
in cause that is rightwyse.

ANTE*CHRISTUS*. (81)

A! false fayturs, turne ye now?
ye shall be slayne, I make a vow,
and thos Traytors that torned you,
I shall make them vnfayne;

That all other, by very sight,
shall know that I am most of might;
for with this sword now will I feight,
for all you shall be slayne.

(Tunc Ante*christus* Occidet Enochu*m* et Heliam, *omnes* q*ue* Reges cu*m* gladio, postea vero redibit ad Cathedra*m*; et Michael cu*m* gladio in dextra dicat:)

610 thou] *om.* W. 611 the] this D. girts] gretes B W h D. 613 reche] wreache D. 615 leech] teache D. 619 loue] sake h. 627 now will I] I thinke to W. *Stage-direction*] Heare Ante*christus* kylles them h. occidet] occidit W. omnes] et omnes D. reges] conversus B W, reges conversos D. cu*m*] *om.* B. postea] et D. et] cu*m* B W D. dicat] *after* cum *and before* Michaell B W D. dextra] dextera sua B W D.

MICHAELL ARCHANGELUS. (82)

Antechrist, now commen is thy day:
raygne no longer thou ne may.
he that hath ledd thee alway,
to him now must thou goe.

No more men shall be slayn by thee;
my lord will dead that thou be.
he that hath geuen thee this posty,
thy sowle shall vnderfoe.

(83)

In Sinne ingendered first thou was,
In Sinne ledd thy lyfe thou hase;
In Sinne now an ende thou mase,
that marred hast many one.

(84)

Three year and half one, witterly,
thou hast had leave to destroy
gods people wickedly,
through thy foule redd.

Now thou shalt know and wytt in hye,
that more is gods maistry
then eke the Devills *and* thyne, therby,
for now thou shalt be dead.

(85)

Thou hast euer served Sathanas,
and had his power in every place,
therfore now getts thou no grace,
with him thou must [be] gone.

(Tunc Michael occidet Antechristu*m*, et in occidendo clamat: "Helpe, Helpe, Helpe, Helpe!")

629 is] *after* now B W h D. thy] this W h D. 630 longer] longer now B. thou ne] nowe thou D. 632] now him thou mvst goe to B W h D. 636 vnderfoe] vnderfree? B. 637—641 *form the first half of a stanza, which is made complete by* 649—653, *and ought to come after* 648 *and before* 649. 639 now] *after* ende B W D, *probably the right place for it.* 640 many] manye a W. 641 Three year and half one] *In red ink* H. 641—645] *om.* D. 646 maistry] maiestie B W h D. 648 for] *om.* W. 649] *cf. above* 637 v. l. 651 now getts thou] thou gettes nowe D. occidet] occidit W.

ANTECHRISTUS. (86)

Helpe, Sathanas and Lucifer! 653
Belzebub, bould Bachler!
Ragnell, Ragnell! thou art my deere!
now fare I wonder evill! 656

Alas! Alas! wher is my power! 657
Alas! my witt is in a weer;
now body and Soule, both in feer,
and all goeth to the Devill. 660

(Tunc morietur Ante*christus* et venient duo Demones, et dicat Primus Demon, vt sequitur:)

DEMON *PRIMUS*. (87)

Anone, maister, anon, Anon! 661
from hell grownd I hard thee grone;
I thought not to come my self alone,
for worship of thyne estate. 664

with vs to Hell thou shalt gone; 665
for this death we make great mone,
to winne more soules into our wonne,
but now it is to late. 668

DEMON SECUNDUS. (88)

Withe me thou shalt; from me thou come; 669
of me shall come thy last Dome,
for thou hast well deserued. 671

And through my might and my posty 672
thou hast liued in Dignitye,
and many a soule deceyued. 674

DEMON *PRIMUS*. (89)

This Body was gotten, by myne assent, 675
in clean whordom, verament,
of mother womb; or that he went,
I was him with in; 678

And taught him aye, with my entent, 679
Synne by which he shall be shent;

dicat] dicunt B W h D. primus demon] *om.* BW h D. *Heading*] primus Demon B W h D. 665 thou] that thou B. 667 wonne] pon W h. *Heading*] *Secundus* demon D. Demon *primus*] *inverted in* B W h D *everywhere*. 677 *and* 678 *written as one line in* H. 679 aye] ever W. with] *om.* W.

for he dyd my commandement,
his soule shall neuer blynne. 682

DEMON SECU*ND*US. (90)

Now, fellow, in fayth gret mone we may make 683
for this lord of estate that stands in this stydd.
many a fatt morsell we had for his sake,
of soules *tha*t should be saved in hell be the hydd. 686

(Tunc aufertur Corpus Ante*christ*i a Demonibus.)

DEMON P*RIM*US.

His soule with sorrow in hand haue I hent, 687
yea, Penance and payne sone shall he feele;
to Lucifer, that lord, it shall be p*re*sent,
that burne shall as a Brand, his sorrow shall not keele. 690

DEMON SECU*ND*US. (91)

This Procter of Prophesy hath p*ro*cured many one 691
in his lawes for to leeue, and lost for his sake
Their soules bene in sorrow, and his shall be sone,
such maystryes through my might many one do I make. 694

(Postqua*m* Demones loqunti fuerint, Resurgent Eenoch et Helias, ab Ante*christ*o Cœsi, et Auditorib*us* status suos com*mon*strabunt.)

DEMON PR*IM*US. (92)

With Lucifer that lord long shall he lenge; 695
In a Seat aye with Sorrow, with him shall he sytt.

DEMO*N* SECU*ND*US.

yea, by the heeles in Hell shall he henge, 697
In a Dongeon deep, right in hell pitt.

DEMON PR*IM*US. (93)

To hell will I hye, without any fayle, 699
with this presant of price, thither to bringe.

682 shall] shalt H. 683 we] *after* make B. 684 in this] us in h. 686 be] haue bene B D. saved] *om.* B, hang W. hydd] *om.* B. *Stage-direction*] *om.* W, tunc capiant A*nimam* eius, et potius corpus B D, Heare the devills Carry Antichristi a way h. 688—700] *om.* W h. 690 keele] B *and* Collier *in* "five miracle plays," feele H. 692 in] one D. 694 do I] I do D. Postqua*m*] Posteaq*uam* D. fuerint] sunt B D, *and* Collier. resurgent] resurgens D. cœsi] cœsti D. 699—703] *om.* h.

DEMON *SECUNDUS.*

Take thou him by the Topp and I by the Tayle;
a sorrowfull songe, in fayth, shall he singe.

DEMON *PRIMUS.* (94)

A! fellow, a Dole looke that thou now deale
to all this fayr company, hence er thou wend.

DEMON *SECUNDUS.*

Yea, sorrow and Care ever shall they feele;
All sinnfull shall dwell in hell at ther last ende.

ENOCH. (95)

A! lord that all *the* world shall lead,
and Dome bothe the Queck and dead,
that reuerenc thee thou on them read,
and them through right releeve.

I was dead and right here slayne,
but through thy might, lord, and thy mayne,
thou hast me raysed vp agayne;
Thee will I loue and leeve.

HELIAS. (96)

Yea, lord, blessed must thou bee!
My flesh now glorified I see;
witt ne sleight agaynst thee
Conspired may be no way.

All that leeuen in thee stidfastly,
Thou helps, lorde, from all anoy,
for dead I was and now lyve I;
lord, honored be thou aye!

MICHAELL. (97)

Henoch and Helye, come you anone!
my lord will that you with me gone
To Heauen blis, both blood and bone,
euermore ther to bee.

701 Take thou] Thou take D. topp] W *makes one line end here, and the next with* songe. 703—707] *om.* W h. 703 now] *om.* B D. 704 hence] here? B. er] or D. 706 All sinnfull] *om.* B D. shall dwell] shall they dwell B D *after* in hell. 707 world] *om.* B W h D. 708 dome bothe] both deme B W h D. 710 releeve] releeved H. 711 I] And I H. 712 lord] *om.* W. 717 ne] ner W. 718 be] be by W h D. 722 lord] *om.* B W h D. aye] ever W.

You haue bene longe—for you be wyse— 727
dwellinge in earthly Paradize;
but to heauen, wher him selfe is,
now shall you goe with me. 730

(Tunc Michael Archangelus adducet Henochum et Heliam ad Cœlum et Cantabit: "Gaudete Iusti in Domino etc.")

ffinis Vicesimæ Tertiæ Pagine.

Pagina Vicesima Quarta et omnium Postrema de Iudicio Novissimo. The Webstars.

DEUS. (1) Ego Sum Alpha et O, Primus et Novissimus.

I God, greattest of degree, 1
In whom begining none may be,
that I am Peerles of Posty
Apertly shall be Proved. 4

In my godhead are Persons three; 5
may none in fay from other be,
yet Souerayne might that is in me
may Iustlye be moved. 8

(2)

It is full yore sith I beheight 9
to make a reconinge of the right;
now to that Dome I will me dight,
that Dead shall duly dreed. 12

Therfore, my Angells, fayre and bright, 13
looke that you wake eche wordly wight,
that I may see all in my sight,
that I Blood for can bleed. 16

730 goe] *om.* H. *Stage-direction*] tunc ab ducens eos ad celum cantabit angelus: gaudete iusti in *domino* et cc. B W h D. (celum] cælos D. vicesimæ tertiæ pagine] pagine xxiii, deo gracias W h, W *continuing: per* me Georgi bellin 1592, h *adding:* 1600. pagine] paginae *before* vicesimae D.

Before the Latin] The Websters playe W h D. novissimo] extremo B W h D. The webstars] *om.* B W h D. O] *transcribed as* omega B D, oo W. *The first* 24 *verses are numbered in* H. 1 of] in W h. 4 Apertly] nowe apertly B W h D. shall] that shal B h D. 6 be] fley B W h, flee D. 7 might] lord B. 8 Iustlye] mystely H. moved] meeved H B W D 9 yore sith] youre syns D. 11 me] thie B. 12 that] that I W. 14 wake] awake W. 16 for] forth D.

(3)

Shew you my Crosse apertly here, 17
Crown of Thornes, S[p]onge and Spear,
and Neiles, to them that wanted neuer
to come to this anye. 20

And what Weed for them I weare, 21
vpon my Body now I bear;
the most Stoutest this sight shall stear,
that standeth by Street or Stye. 24

ANGELUS *PRIMUS*. (4)

Lord, that madest through thy might 25
heauen and earth, Day and Night,
without distance, we be dight
your bidding for to done; 28

And for to awake ech wordly wight 29
I shall be ready, and that in height;
that they shall show them in thy sight,
thou shalt see, lord, full soone. 32

ANGELUS SECU*N*D*U*S. (5)

Take we our Beames, and fast Blow; 33
all mankynd shall them know,
good accomptes that now can show,
soone it shall be seene. 36

That haue done well in their lyving 37
they shall haue ioy without endinge;
that evill hath done without amendinge,
shall euer haue Sorrow and Teene. 40

(Tunc Angeli Tubas accipient et flabunt; et Omnes mortui de Sepulchris resurgent quoru*m* Primus Papa Saluatus dicat vt seq*uitur*:)

PAPA SALUATUS. (6)

A! lord, mercy now aske we, 41
that dyed for vs on *th*e rood tree;

18 Thornes] thorne B W h D. 19 neuer] nere D. *Heading*] primus Angellus B W h. 32] that shalbe lorde full soone W. thou] that B. *Heading*] Sec*undus* angellus B W h D. 33 Beames] beanes W h. 34 mankynd] manking B. 35 accomptes] accompte B W h D. 37 That] The that h. well] Evill W. 39 hath] have D. amendinge] mendinge B W h D. Sepulchris] Sepulchis H, sepulcor h. resurgent] surgente B W h, surgent D. papa saluatus] *om.* B, papa salvata W. saluatus] *om.* h. dicat] *before* primus D. vt sequitur] *om.* B W h D. 41—81 *are numbered with* 1—10 *in* H, *and so throughout.* 42 the] *om.* W.

it is three hundreth years and three
since I was putt in grave.

Now through thy might and thy posty,
thy Bames blast hath raysed me
in fleshe and Blood, as I now se,
my Iudgment for to haue.

(7)

Whyle that I lived in flesh and Blood,
thy great Godhead, that is so good,
Ne knew I neuer, but ever was wood,
worshipps for to wynne.

The witts, lord, thou sent to me,
I spend to come to great Degree;
the highest offyce vnder thee
in earth thou puttst me in.

(8)

Thou grantedst me, lord, through thy grace,
Peters power and his place;
yet was I blent, Alas! Alas!
I dyd not thyne assent.

But my fleshly will that wicked was,
the which raysed now thou hase,
I-forthered, lord, before thy face,
shall take his iudg[e]ment.

(9)

When I in earth was at my will,
this world me blent, bothe lowd and still,
but thy Commandement to fulfill
I was full negligent.

But purgyd it is with paynes ill,
in Purgatory that sore can grill;
yet thy grace I hope to come till,
after my great Torment.

46 Bames] beanes W h. 47 in] I D. 54 spend] spente W. 57—61] *om.* h. 57 grantedst] grantest D. 61—65] *om.* h. 66 me] be H. bothe] *om.* B W h. 68 was] way H. full] ever H. 69—73] *om.* h.

(10)

And yet, lord, I must dreed thee 73
for my great sinnes, when I thee se,
for thou art most in maiesty;
for mercy now I call. 76

The paynes *tha*t I haue long in bee, 77
as hard as hell—saue hope of Lee!—
agayne to goe neuer suffer me
for ought that may befall! 80

IMPERATOR SALUATUS. (11)

A! lord and Soveraine Saviour, 81
that lyvinge putt me to honoure,
and made me kinge and Emperour,
highest of kythe and kynne; 84

My flesh, that fallen was as *the* flower, 85
thou hast restored in this Stower,
and with paynes of great Langour
clensed me of my sinne. 88

(12)

In Purgatory my soule hath bene 89
a Thousand yeare in woe and teene;
now is no sinne vpon me seene,
for purged I am of pyne. 92

Thoo that I to sinne were Bayne and bowne, 93
and coveted Riches and renowne,
yet, at the last, Contricion
hath made me one of thyne. 96

(13)

As hard paynes, I dare well say, 97
in Purgatory are night and day,
as are in hell, save by on way:
that one shall haue an ende. 100

76 for] of H D. 78 saue] as W h. of] as W h. 90 yeare] yeaires B W h. 91 sinne] woe W h. 93 that] *om.* B W h. 97 paynes] payne D. 98 are] *om.* W. 100 one] onste B W, once h.

(14)

Worshipped be thou, high Iustice,
that me hast made in flesh to ryse;
now wott I well those *that* haue bene wyse
shall come into thy welth.

Graunt me, lord, amo[n]gst moe,
that purged am of synne and woe,
on thy right hand that I may goe
to that everlastinge healthe.

REX SALUATUS. (15)

A! lord of lordes, and kinge of kinges,
and Informer of all thinges,
thy power, lord, spreads and Springes,
as soothly here is seen.

After Bale Boot thou bringes,
and after Teene tyde Tydinges,
to all that ever thy name minges,
and Buxvm to thee bene.

(16)

Whyle I was lord of land and leed,
in Purple and in riche weed,
me thought to thee I had no need,
so wronge the world me wyled.

Thoughe thou for me thy Blood can sheed,
yet in my hart more can I heed,
my flesh to forther and to feed;
but the soule was ever beguyled.

(17)

My foule body, through Sinne blent,
that rotten was and all to-rent,
through thy might, lord Omnipotent,
raysed and whole it is.

101 worshipped] worshipp H. high] righte W h. 104 into] vnto B D. 105 graunt] And graunt h. 108 healthe] wealth h. 109 lordes] lorde h. 112 here] ther W h. 113 After] And H. 114 tyde] *om.* B. 115 that] *om.* H. name] names D. minges] mynes B W h D. 120 me] in W. 121 sheed] bleed H W. 126 all to] also B W.

My soule that is [in] Bale Brent, 129
to my body thou hast now sent,

to take before thee Iudgment
of that I haue done amis. 132

(18)

But, lord, though I were sinful aye, 133
Contrition yet at my last day,
And Almes dedes that I dyd aye,
hath holpen me from hell. 136

But well I wott that ilke way 137
that Abraham went, weind I may,
for I am purged to thy pay,
with thee euermore to dwell. 140

REGINA SALUATA. (19)

Pearles Prince of most Posty, 141
that after Langour sendeth Lee,
that now in body hast raysed me,
from fyre to rest and roe; 144

My flesh that as flower can flee, 145
and Powder was, through thy pitty
togeather hath brought, as I now se,
the soule the body too. 148

(20)

Whyle I in earthe riche can goe, 149
in softe Sendal and Silk alsoe,
velvet also that wrought me woe,
and all such other weedes, 152

All that might excyte Lechery, 153
Pearles and precious Perrye,
agaynst thy biddinge vsed I,
and other wicked dedes. 156

129 Bale] balleus W h, bales B, in bales D. 133 though] al though W. 135 I] *om.* W h. 138 weind] wende W h. 140 with] to W h. saluata] salvator W h. 141 of most] most of h. 142 sendeth] lendeth B W h D. 145 flee] flye D. 146 powder] power W h. thy] *om.* H. 147 I now] nowe I W h. 148 the body] and bodye D. 150 Sendal] sandalles B W h D. 153—157] *between* 164 *and* 165 *in* B W h D. 154 pearles] perrelles D.

(21)

Neither prayed I, ne fast; 157
save Almes deeds, if any past,
and great Repentance at the last
hath gotten me to thy grace; 160

That saved I hope fully to be, 161
for purged synnes that were in me,
thy last Dome may I not flye,
to come before thy face. 164

(22)

After Purgatory paynes, 165
from me thy lordship thou ne laynes;
to flee thy Dome me ne gaynes,
thoughe I were neuer so great. 168

Sith I haue suffred woe and Teene, 169
In Purgatory long to beene,
let neuer my sinne be on me seene,
but, lord, thou it forgett! (Tunc venient Damnati.) 172

PAPA DAMNATUS. (23)

Alas! Alas! Alas! Alas! 173
now am I worse then ever I was;
my Body the soule agayne hase,
that longe hath bene in hell. 176

To geather they be, now is no grace, 177
defyled they be before thy face,
and after my death here in this place,
in payne ever to dwell. 180

(24)

Now Bootles is to aske mercy; 181
for lyvinge, highest in earth was I,
and Conning, chosen in Clergie,
but Coueteousnes did me care. 184

162 synnes] signes H. 166 lordship] lorde shipes W. ne laynes] me lames ? B. 167 flee] warne B W h D. 170 to] too D. venient] venit h. Damnati] damnata W. *Stage-direction*] *in the margin in* H. 174 am] as B. 175 agayne] *before* the soul h D. 178 defyled they] fyled to B W h D. 180 ever] Evermore W, *om.* B. 183 chosen] closen B D. 184 but] and B W.

Also Siluer and Simonye 185
made me Pope vnworthy;
that burnes me now full bitterly,
for of Blis I am full bare. 188

(25)

Alas! why spend I wrong my witt, 189
in Coveteousnes my hart to knytt?
hard and whott now feele I it:
Hell hould[e]s me right here. 192

My Body burnës, every bytt; 193
of sorow must I neuer be shutt;
me to saue from hell pitt
now helpeth no prayer. 196

(26)

Of all the Soules in Christianty 197
that damned were whyle I had degree,
now geue Accoumpt behoueth me,
through my laches forlorne. 200

Also damned now must I be, 201
Accoumpt befalls or ells to flee;
make me Deafe, I coniure thee!
as I had neuer bene borne. 204

IMPERATOR DAMNATUS. (27)

Alas! now Stered I am in this stower! 205
alas! now fallen is my flower!
Alas! for sinne now no Succower;
no siluer may me save. 208

Alas! that ever I was Emperour! 209
alas! that euer I had Towne or Tower!
Alas! I Buy hard now my honour:
Hell paynes for it I haue. 212

187 bitterly] witterlye W h D, worthelie B. 189 Alas] also B W h D. spend] spente h. 192 houlds] howles h. 193 bytt] white B. 196 no] to W. 200 laches] lawes B W h D. 201 now] *om.* B W h. Damnatus] dampnata W. 207 no] cease B W h D. 209 ever I] I ever H D. 210 euer I] I ever D. 211] Alas hardlye I bye myne hon*our* W h, alas hard doe I buy my honour B D. (do I buy] bye I D.

(28)

Alas ! in world why was I ware ?
alas ! that euer my mother me bare !
Alas ! ther is no gayne Chare,
skape maye I not this chance.

Alas ! doe evill who is that dare ?
to threap no more now no care,
for to payne we ordayned are
euer, without deliuerance.

(29)

Now is manslaughter vpon me seene,
now Couetuousnes makes my cares keene ;
now wrong worchinge, withouten weene,
that I in world haue wrought.

Now Trayterous turnes do me teene,
and false Domes, all by dene ;
In Glotony I haue in beene,
that shall now deer be bought.

(30)

Now know I what I dyd by wronge,
and eke my lither liuing longe ;
falshod to hell makes me to fonge,
in fyre ever foule to fare.

Misgotten money I mixed amonge,
now is me yelded to hell thonge.
why were I not dead as is the donge ?
for dole I droupe and dare.

REX DAMNATUS. (31)

Alas, vnlyking is my lott !
my weal is gone, of woe I wott ;

214 my] *om.* D. 215 gayne] Ioye W, eyme h, yeane B D. Chare] cheare W h, chaier B. 216 skape maye I] scake I may H. 217 is] *om.* B. 218 now no] vs ney B W D, me ney h. 219 we ordayned] ordeyned we h. 222 now] nowe towe W h. 226 dene] deme B H. 227 in beene] been in H W h. 229 by] with B W h D. 231 fonge] songe W. 233 misgotten] misbegotten B, my misbegotten W h. I] ever I B W h D. mixed] mixen W. 234 me yelded] in yelled W. thonge] yonge B W h D. 235 dead] as dead h. is the] *om.* h. 236 dole] deale h.

my synne is seene, I was a Sott;
of Sorrow now may I singe.

To hell payne that is so hott,
for my misdede now wend I mott.
Alas! that I had bene sheep or goat
when I was crowned kinge!

(32)

When I was in my maiesty,
Soverayne of Shyre and Citty,
never dyd I good in no degree,
through me was any grace.

Of poore had I neuer pitty,
sore ne sicke would I never se;
now haue I Langour, and they haue lee;
Alas! Alas! Alas!

(33)

Wronge I ever wrought to eche wight,
for Penyes poore in payne I pight;
Religion I reaved agaynst the right;
that keenly now I know.

Lechery I held but light,
In Couetuousnes my hart was clight;
one good deede in gods sight
now haue I not to show.

REGINA DAMNATA. (34)

Alas! Alas! now am I lorne!
Alas! with teene I am to-torne!
Alas! *that* euer I was woman borne,
this bytter bale to byde!

I made my mone, both even and morne,
for fear to come Iesu beforne,
that Crowned for me was with thorne
and thrust into the Syde.

239 synne] sight B. a Sott] in sette B W h D. 240 now] *om.* B W D. 243 Alas] aslas B. 246 and] and of B W D. 253 I ever] Ever I W h D, *om.* B. 254 penyes] pouchinge W. 256 keenly] kneelye D. 257 but] it B W h D. 259 gods] god his D. Damnata] Damnatus h. 262 I am to] nowe am I B W h D. 263 euer] *om.* B W h D. woman] of woman B D. 264 byde] a byde W h. 265 both] *om.* B W. 267 for me was] was for me B.

(35)

Alas! that I was woman wrought! 269
alas! why made god me of nought,
and with his precious Blood me bought,
to worch agay[n]st his will? 272

Of Lechery I neuer roght, 273
but ever to that sinne I sought,
and of that filth in deed *and* thought
yet hadd I never my fill. 276

(36)

fye on Pearles! fye on pryde! 277
fye on gowne! fye on gnyde!
fye on hewe! fye on hyde!
these harrowen me to hell. 280

Against this chaunce I may not chyde. 281
this bitter Bale I must abyde;
yea, woe and teene I suffer this tyde,
no lyvinge tonge may tell. 284

(37)

I that so seemly was in sight, 285
wher is my Blee that was so bright?
wher is Barone, wher is knight,
for me to aledge the law? 288

wher in world is any wight, 289
that for my fayrnes now will feight?
or from this deathe I am to dight,
that dare me heathen draw? 292

IUSTICIARIUS DAMNATUS. (38)

Alas! of Sorrow now is my Saw! 293
Alas! for hell I am in awe;
my flesh as flowr, that all to-flaw,
now tydes a fearly fitt. 296

270 made god me] god made me B W h D. 271 precious Blood] *In red ink* H. 273 roght] wroughte W. 275 and] that W D. filth] synne W. 276 my] *om.* B, that D. 280 these] those B. harrowen] arrow B. 283 yea] with W h. 284 may] can B. 286 was] is h D. 287 is] is the W h (*both times*). 288 aledge] leadge W h. 293 of] *om.* B. 295 flowr] flowers W h.

Alas! that ever I learned law!
for suffer I must many a hard Thraw,
for the Devill [now] will me draw
right even to hell pitt.

(39)

Alas! whyle that I liued in lond,
wronge to worch I would not wond,
but false causes tooke in hond,
and much[e] woe did als.

When I sought Siluer or rich sound,
of Barone, Burges or a Bonde,
his moot to further I would found,
were it neuer so false.

(40)

Now is the Devill ready, I see,
his moote to further agaynst me;
before the Iudge of such posty,
that me will not avayle.

Hart and Thought both knoweth he;
thoughe I would lye, no boote will be.
Alas! this hard[e] fitt to flee
rufully I must fayle.

(41)

All my lyfe ever was I bowne
to trouble poore in Tower and Towne;
payr holy Churches possession,
and sharply them to shend;

To ryve and robb Religion,
that was all my Devotion;
therfore me Tydes Damnation
and payne withouten ende.

298 hard] *om.* h. 299 will] *om.* B W. 300 to] into D. hell] his B W h D. 301 lond] land H. 302 wronge] wrought D. 303 false] falsely D. tooke] toke to be hard B. hond] hand H. 304 als] Elles B W D, else h. 305 rich] riches W h. sound] founde B W. 306 a] of B W h D. bonde] bound D. 307 moot] matter W h. I] ever I B W h D. 308 so] to B. 309 I] *om.* H. 310 moote] matter W h. 311 before] for B W h D. Iudge] Iudge is W h. 314 will] to W h. 317 ever was I] I was Ever W, ever I was h D. 319 Churches] church B D.

MARCATOR DAMNATUS. (42)

Alas! Alas! now woe is me!
my foule Body, that rotten hath be,
and Soule togeather now I se;
All stinketh full of sinne.

Alas! marchandyze marreth me,
and purchasing of land and fee,
in hell payne euermore to be,
and Bale that neuer shall blynne.

(43)

Alas! in world fervent was I
to purchase landes falsely;
Poore men I dyd such anye,
made them their land to sell.

But when I dyed, witterly,
all that hadd my Enemye;
bouth Body and Soule damned therby
ever to the payne of hell.

(44)

Yet might not falce purchace suffyze,
but ofte I dealed with Marchandyze,
for ther me thought winninge would ryze;
I vsed it many a year.

Ofte I sett vppon falce Assyze,
rayvinge poore with layinge myze,
falcly by god and Saynts hyse
a Thowsand sythes I swear.

(45)

Occour I vsed willfully,
Wanne I neuer so much therby,
to holy Church neuer Teithed I,
for me thought that was lorne.

325 woe is] woes W h. 329 marreth] make B W h, maketh D. 330 of] after W h. fee] see W. 335 poore] to pore B. such] much B. 336 made] *and* made B. land] landes B W h D. 338 hadd] I hade B W h D. 339 bouth] and H. 341—349] *om.* h. 346 rayvinge] rauening B. myze] mise B W. 347 and] and by W. Saynts] sante W, saynte D. 348 sythes] tymes W, othes B. swear] swore B W, sware D. 349 *and* 350 *substituted by* 353 *and* 354 *in* h. 351 Teithed] tryed W h. 352] alas that euer I was borne h.

Why made thou me of nought, lord, why? 353
to worch in world so wickedly,
and now Burne in *the* devilles Belly.
Alas! that ever I was borne! 356

(Finitis Lamentationibus mortuor*um*, descendet Iesus quasi in nube, si fieri. poterit; Quia *secundum* Docto*rum* Opiniones in Aere prope terra*m* iudicabit filius Dei. Stabunt Angeli cu*m* Cruce, Corona Spinea, lancea, aliisq*ue* Instrum*entis*, o*mnia* demo*n*strantes.

IHESUS. (46)

You good and evill, that here be lent, 357
here you come to Iudgment:
if you wist wherto it would apent,
and in what manere! 360

Butt all myne, as I haue ment, 361
Prophetts, Patriarches here present,
must know my Dome with good entent,
therfore I am now here. 364

(47)

But you shall heare and see expresse, 365
I doe to you all Righteousnes;
lovesome Deedes, more and lesse,
I will rehearce now heere. 368

Of earth throughe me made man thow was, 369
and putt in place of great cleannes,
from which thou fast through wikkednes
away thou waved were. 372

(48)

When thou had done this Trespace, 373
yet wayted I which way best was,
thee to recouer in this Case
into my Co*m*panye. 376

353 lord] *before* of nought W D. 354 wickedly] wrechedly W. 355 devilles] Devill H. 356] Alas] alas alas W. descendet] descende D. Docto*rum*] doctori W h, doctoris D. Aere] quere W h. Spinea] spinæ W, spina h. aliisq*ue* instrum*entis*] et instrumentis aliis B W h D. omnia] ipsa B W h D. demonstrantes] demonstrant D, monstra h, demonstra dicat Iesus W. 357 lent] blente W h. 358 come] bene comen W h. to] to your B W D. 363 with] in h. 365 heare] *om.* H. and] *after* see H. 366 righteousnes] rightwysenes D. 367 lovesome] luxome W h. more] bouth more B h. 372 away] wa, *all the rest destroyed in* W. 373 thou] then h D. 376 into] to W.

How might I doe thee more grace 377
then that selfe kynd, that thou hase,
take here now, as in this place
appeareth apertely? 380

(49)

After dyed on *the* rood tree, 381
and my blood Shedd, as thou may se,
to prive the Devyll of his posty,
and winne that was away. 384
The which Blood, behoulds ye, 385
fresh houlden till now I would should be,
for certayne poyntes that lyked me,
of which I will now say. 388

(50)

One cause was this certaynly, 389
that to my father Almighty
at my Ascention offer might I
this Blood, praying a Boone: 392
That he of you should haue mercy, 393
and more gracious bee therby,
when you had sinned horribly,
not takinge vengeance to soone. 396

(51)

Also I would, without[en] were, 397
this Blood should now be shewed here,
that the Iews dyd in this manere,
might know apert[e]ly, 400
How vnkyndly they them bare. 401
behould on me, and you may leere
whether I be god in full power,
or ells man onely. 404

(52)

Also my blood now shewed is, 405
that good therby may haue blisse,

378 that] *om.* W. 379 as] is W h, *om.* D. this] *om.* H. 380 appeareth] as appeareth W, as peareth h. 383 prive] depryve H. 386 fresh] fleshe D. till now I would should be] that I shall see W h. 387 lyked] liketh W h. 389 this] this now B. 391 I] *om.* h. 396 takinge] taken B. 399 this] that B W. 401 vnkyndly] vnkinde B D. bare] bere B.

that avoyded wickednes, iwys,
and euer good workes wrought.

And evill also, that dyd amys,
must haue great sorrow in sight of this,
that lost that ioy that was his,
that him on Rood bought.

(53)

Yet for all this great torment
that I suffred here whyl I was lent,
the more I spared in your intent,
I am not as I feele;

for my body is all to-rent
with Othes false, alway fervent;
Mo lymme on me but it is hent
from head right to the heele.

(54)

Now that you shall apertly se,
fresh Blood bleed, man, for thee,
good to ioy and full great Lee,
the evill to Damnation;

Behould now all men on me,
and se my Blood fresh out flee,
that I bledd on rode tree
for your Saluation. (Tunc emittet Sanguine*m* de Latere suo.)

(55)

How durst you euer doe amysse,
when you vnbethoughte you of this?
that I bledd to bringe you to blis,
and suffered such woe?

Ne you must not whyte, iwys,
though I doe now as right is;
therfore eche man reccon his,
for righteousnes must goe.

407 avoyded] awayved H. 412 rood] rood tree B W h D. 413 great] *om.* W. 414 *First* I] *om.* B W h D. 415 I] *om.* H B D. 418 alway] alwayes B D. 419 on] of B W. hent] rente W, lent D, lent *or* bent B h. 422 man] *om.* B W h. 424 the] *om.* W h. 425 men] men looke D. suo] eius B W h D, *continued by* et dicit *in* W, *by* et dicat *in* h. 430 vnbethoughte] vnthough H, vnthought B D. 432 such] moche W h. 435 man] one W.

PAPA SALUATUS. (56)

A, lord, though I liued in sinne,
in Purgatory I haue bene in;
suffer my Bale for to blyn,
and bringe me to thy blisse.

IMPERATOR SALUATUS.

Yea, lord, and therin haue I be
more then three hundreth years and three;
now I am clean, forsake not me,
although I did amis.

REX SALUATUS. (57)

Lord, receiue me to thy grace,
that payne hath suffred in this place;
although I foule and wicked was,
washen it is away.

REGINA SALUATA.

And I, lord, to thee cry and call,
thyne owne Christen and thy thrall,
that of my sinnes am purged all;
of thy ioy I thee pray.

IHESUS. (58)

Come hither to me, my Darlings dere,
that blessed in world allway were;
take my Realme all in feere,
that for you ordayned is.

ffor while I was on earth here,
you gaue me meat in good maner,
therfor in heauen blis clear
you shall ever leng iwis.

(59)

In great Thirst you gaue me drinke;
when I was naked also Clothing,
and when me neded harboringe
you harbored me in Could.

440 thy] this B W h D. saluatus] salvator W. 441 I] *after* and B W h D. therin] *after* haue B D. 446 this] that W h. 450 Christen] Chisten H B. 451 am] are W h. 454 allway] allwayes B W h D. 457 on] in W h. 460 leng] long B. 461 Thirst] Thrist B

And other Deedes to my lykinge 465
you did on earth ther lyvinge;
therfore you shall be quitt that thinge
in heauen an hundreth fould. 468

PAPA SALUATUS. (60)

Lord, on this I can not myn, 469
earth when I was dwelling in,
thee in mischeif or any vnwyn
to shew thee such a will. 472

IMPERATOR SALUATUS.

No, sickerly I can haue no mynd 473
that euer to thee I was so kynd,
for their might I neuer thee fynd,
such kyndnes to fullfill. 476

IHESUS. (61)

Yes, forsooth, my frend[e]s deare, 477
Such as poore and naked were
you Cladd and fedd them both in feere,
and harbored them also. 480

Such as were also in great danger 481
in hard Prison in earth here,
you visited them in meek manere,
all men in such[e] woe. 484

(62)

Therfor, as I you ere tould, 485
you shall be quitt an hundreth fould;
in my Blisse—be you bould—
euermore you shall be, 488

Ther neither honger is ne could, 489
but all things as your selues would;
euerlasting ioy to yonge and owld
that in earth pleased me. 492

467 that] this h. saluat*us*] salvata W. 469 I can] can I B W D. I can not] can not I h. 471 mischeif] miserye h. 472 thee] *om.* B W h D. 473 can] coulde W. 474 kynd] vnkinde B. 475 might I neuer thee] I might thee never B W h D. 482 in earth] one Eirthe W. 483 meek] like B. 485 you ere] ere you B. 491 and owld] an, *as all the rest is destroyed* W.

(63)

Therfore, my Angells, goe you anone, 493
and Twyn my chosen, everychon,
from feble that haue bene my fone,
and bringe them into Blis. 496

On my right hand they shall be sett, 497
for so full yore I them beheight,
when they did, withouten lett,
my biddinge not amys. 500

ANGELUS *PRIMUS*. (64)

Lord, we shall neuer blyn 501
tyll we have brought them blisse within;
those Soules that bene withouten Sinne,
full sone, as you shall see. 504

ANGELUS SECU*N*DUS.

And I know them well afyne, 505
which bodyes, lord, that bene thyne;
they shall haue ioy without pyne,
that neuer shall ended be. 508

(Tunc Angeli cantabunt euntes ac venientes "Lætamini in D*omi*no" vel "Saluator mu*n*di D*omi*ne": tunc *om*n*e*s Salvati eos sequentur, Postea venient Demones, q*uorum* p*rimus* dicat:)

DEMON *PRIMUS*. (65)

A, Righteous Iudge, and moste of might, 509
that ther art sett to Dome the right,
mercy thou was, now is gright
to saue these men from pyne. 512

Doe as thou hast yore behight; 513
thes that be synfull in thy sight,
to reckon their deedes I am dight,
to proue these men for myne. 516

493 you] *om.* W. 495 feble] them B W h D. 496 into] vnto D. *Heading*] primus angellus B W h D. *Heading*] Sec*u*nd*us* Angellus B W h D. 505 afyne] and fyne W h. 506 bene] haue bene B. cantabunt] Ibunt ac cantibunt B W h D. (cantibunt] cantabunt D. vel] *om.* B W h D. Domine] *om.* W h. tunc] ac B W h D. omnes] eos W. omnes salvati] salvati omnes W. eos] *om.* W. venient] veniu*n*t D. *primus* dicat] dicat primus B D, dicat primus demon W h (demones) W. *Heading*] primus Demon B W h. 510 Dome] deeme h D, judge B. 514 thes] thoes B W h D. 516 proue] proves W.

(66)

Iudge this Pope myne in this place,
that worthy is for his trespase,
and oughte to be thyne throughe grace,
through synne is commen my hyne.

A Chiristan man I wott he was,
knew good from evill in ech case,
But my Commandement done he hase,
and ever forsaken thyne.

(67)

Through m*er*cy he should be thyne,
but myne through wretchednes and synne;
thyne through Passion that thou was in,
and myne through Tentation.

To me obedient he was aye,
and thy Commandement*es* putt away;
thou Righteous iudge therfore I pray,
Deem him to my Pryson.

(68)

This Emperour also, that standeth by,
I howld him myne full witterly,
that held him ever in heresy,
and leeved not on thy lore.

Therfore I tell thee verament,
myne he is without iudgment;
thou saydst when thou on earth went,
that leved not, Damned were. Qui non credit iam Iudicatus est.

(69)

This Kinge and Quene would neuer know
Poor men, them Almes [for] to show;
therfor putt them all from yow,
that stand before thy face.

519 oughte] made H. 520 is] *om.* h. my hyne] myne B W h D. 521 A] *om.* W, *as the margin of the page is destroyed.* I wott he was] he was I wotte W. 522 knew] ew W, *for the same reason.* 523 But] *om.* W, *as the margin of the page is destroyed.* 524 and] *om.* W. 525 Through] *om. all but the* h W. 526 wretchednes] wickednes B W h D. 527 that thou was in] *om. except the first* th. W. that] *om.* D. 530 commandementes] commandemente W h D. 536 leeved] lyved B. lore] *a form* leere *would correspond to* were *of* 540. 539 saydst] sayd D. 540 that] all that H. not] *om.* B. iam] *om.* h. 543 yow] thoo W.

And I shall lead them till a low, 545
ther fyre shall burne though no man blow;
I haue tyed them on a row;
the shall neuer passe that place. 548

DEMON SECU*N*DUS. (70)

Nay, I will Spute with him this, 549
that sitteth as highe Iustice;
and if I se he be righteous,
soone I shall assay. 552

And eyther he shall forsooth, iwis, 553
forsake that of him written is,
or these men that haue done amys,
Deme them vs to day. 556

(71)

These words, God, thou sayd expresse, 557
as Mathew therof beareth witnes,
that right as mans deed was,
yelden he should bee. 560

And least thou forgett, good man, 561
I shall mynne the vpon,
for speak Latyne well I can,
and that thou shalt sone see: Matt. xvi. 27. 564

Filius hominis venturus est in gloria patris sui cu*m* Angelis suis,
et tunc reddet vnicuiq*uam* secundum Opus suu*m*.

(72)

Therfor Righteous if thou be, 565
these men are myne, as mott I thee;
for one good deede here before thee
haue they not to Show. 568

Yf ther be any, say on, lett se; 569
if ther be none, deme them to me,

545 a] *om.* W. 546 ther] wher B W. 547 tyed them on] them tyed vpon B W h D. *Heading*] Secu*n*dus demon B W h D. 551 righteous] *the form* rightwise *would rhyme.* 553 eyther] other B W h D. 554 that] *om.* W. 556 vs] to vs W, as B. 558 beareth] beare W. 559 deed] deedes B W h D. 560 yelden] helden B W h. gloria] *only* g *in* W, *as the page is injured.* patris] *twice in* D. et tunc] *only* e *in* W. suum] *om.* h. Opus suum] *om.* W. 565 be] *om.* W. 566 I thee] *om.* W. 569 yf ther] *only* er *in* W, *as the page is damaged.* lett] lettes h. 570 if] *om.* W.

or els thou art as false as we,
all men shall well know. 572

DEMON *PRIMUS*. (73)

Yea, this thou sayd, verament, 573
that when thou came to iudgment,
thy Angells from thee should be sent,
to part the evill from the good, 576

Ant putt them into great Torment, 577
wher Reeminge, Grininge were fervent,
which wordes to Clarks here present
I will rehearce, by the roode! Math. xiii. 49, 50. 580

Sic erit in Consummatione Seculi; exibunt Angeli et separabunt malos de medio iustorum, et mittent eos in Caminum Ignis, vbi erit Fletus, et Stridor Dentium.

(74)

Therfore deliuer thes men hence, 581
and, as broke I my Penne,
I shall make them to grynne
and ruthfully to Reeme. 584

And in as whot a Chimney 585
as is ordayned for me,
baked all shall they be,
in Bitter Bale to brenne. 588

(75)

This Popelard Pope here present, 589
with Couetuousnes aye was fully bent;
This Emperour also, verament,
to all synne did inclyne. 592

This kinge also all righteous men shent, 593
damned them throughe false iudgment,

571 *First* as] *om.* W. 572 men] men it B. *Heading*] primus demon B W h. 576 part] put B W h D. from the] for H. 578 wher] ther B h, ther is W. grininge] out grennynge D, greminge W h. were fervent] very fervent B D, veramente W h. 580 by the roode] nowe heare W h, *om.* D. seculi] seculis W. separabunt] sperabunt W h D. iustorum] Iustus W. erit] erat H. 581 deliuer] delyver mee D. thes] thse H. hence] heine B W, home h, *om.* D. 582 Penne] panne B W h D. 584 reeme] crye W. 585—589] *om.* W. 587 baked] Bathed H h D. all shall they be] the all shalbe h D, all they shalbe B. 588 to] and B h D. brenne] brune B. 590 aye was] was Ever W, was aye B h D. 591 This] this I B. 593—597] *om.* W. 593 all] *om.* h.

and dyed so without amendment;
therfore I hould him myne. 596

(76)

This Quene, whyle she was lyvinge here, 597
spared neuer synne in no manere,
and all that might, by Mahound so dere,
excite her Lecherye, 600
She vsed mans hart to sturr, 601
and therto fully ordayned her;
therfore she hath lost her lurr,
heauen blis, right as dyd I. 604

IHESUS. (77)

Lo, you men that wicked haue bene, 605
what Sathan sayeth you heare and seene;
righteous Dome may you not fleene,
for grace is putt away. 608
when tyme of grace was enduringe, 609
to seeke it you had no lykinge;
therfore must I for any thinge
doe righteousnes to day. 612

(78)

And though my sweet mother dere 613
and all the Saint*es* *th*at ever were,
prayed for you right now here,
all it were [now] to late. 616
No grace may goe through ther prayer, 617
then Righteousnes had no power;
therfore goe to *the* fyre in feere,
ther gaynes none other grace. 620

(79)

When I was hungry and thirsty booth, 621
and naked was, you would not me cloothe,

602 therto] *after* ordayned B. 603 her] a H. lurr] lure D. 604 heauen] hevens B. 605 Lo] *om.* W, *as the page is damaged.* 606 what] *om.* W. 607 righteous] . . . ous W. fleene] flye H. 608 for grace] . . . ace W. 609 when tyme] . . . me W. 610 to seeke it] *om.* W, *for the above reason.* 611 therfore] *om.* W. I] *om.* W. 612 doe righteousnes] . . . nes W. to] this B. 612 *is the last verse in* W (p. 168 v.), *about two leaves being lost.* 613 though] thou H. 617 goe] growe D. 620 none] noe D.

also sicke and in great woe,
you would not visytt me;

Nor yet in Prison to me come,
Nor of your meate geue me some,
nor me to *you*er harbour noome,
never yet in will were yee.

PAPA DAMNATUS. (80)

When waste thou naked or harbourles,
hungry, thirsty, or in sicknes?
eyther in any Prison was?
we saw thee neuer a could!

IMPERATOR DAMNATUS.

Had we thee hongrye or thirsty seene,
Naked, sicke, or in Prison bene,
harbourles or in any teene,
haue harboured thee we would.

IHESUS. (81)

Nay, when ye saw the least of myne
that on earth suffered pyne,
with your Riches you would not them Ryne,
nay fulfill my desyre.

And sithe you would nothing enclyne
for to helpe my poore hyne,
to me your loue it was not fyne,
therfore goe to the fyre.

DEMON PRIMUS. (82)

A, Sir Iudge this goeth aright,
By Mahound much of might!
you be myne, eche wight,
ever to lyue in woe.

A dolefull deathe to you is dight;
for such hyre I you behight
when you served me, day and night,
to be rewarded so.

623 in] *om.* H. 626 geue] to geue h D. 632 saw] see B. 635 any] any other H. 639 them] *om.* D. ryne] then relieue B. 642 hyne] lyne h. *Heading*] primus Demon h D.

(83)

Goe we forth to hell in hye;
With out ende ther shall you lye;
for you haue lost, right as dyd I,
the Blisse that lasteth euer.

Iudged you be to my Belly,
ther endlesse Sorrow is and nye;
one thinge I tell you truly:
Deliuerd bene you never.

Demon secundus. (84)

Nay, maister, forgett not these Theues two,
for by Mahound! they shall not goe;
ther dedes, lord, amonge moe
sone I can them spye.

This Iustice, lord, was euer thy foe,
but falsehod to further he was euer throe;
therfore dome him to sorrow and woe,
for he is full well worthy.

(85)

This Marchant also that standeth here,
he is myne, withouten were;
as ofte tyme he him forsweare
as seedes be in my secke.

And Occour also vsed he,
that my Powch is so hevy,
I swere by Mahound so free,
it wel ny breakes my necke.

(Tunc Demones exportabunt eos et venient Eva*n*gelistæ.)

Matheus. (86)

I, Mathew, of this bear witnesse,
for in my Gospell I wrett expresse,
this, that my lord of his goodnes
hath rehearced here.

655 right as] as right h. 658 nye] anoy H. *Heading*] Secundus Demon h. 664 sone] some B. can] came B. 666 but] *om.* h. 667 dome] deeme h D. 669 standeth] staneth H. here] by here h. 671 tyme] tymes D. 673 Occour] Occurre D. Eva*n*gelistæ] Evangele h, quatuor Evangelistae D.

*

And by me all were warned before,
to saue ther Soules for euermore,
that now through lyvinge they bene lore,
and damned to fyre in fere.

MARCUS. (87

I, Marke, now apertly say,
that warned they were by many a way,
ther lyvinge how they should aray,
heauen blisse to recouer;

So that excuse them they ne may,
that they beene worthy, in good fay,
to suffer the Dome geven to day
and Damned to be for ever.

LUCAS. (88)

And I Luke, on earth lyvinge,
my lords words in every thinge
I wrott and taught through my Conninge,
that all men know[e] might.

And therfore I say forsoth, iwis:
Excusation none ther is;
against my talkinge they dyd amisse;
this Dome it goeth aright.

IOHANNES. (89)

And I, John, the Evangelist,
bear witnes of thinges that I wist,
to which they might full well haue trust,
and not haue done amisse.

And all that ever my lord sayde here,
I wrott it all in my manere;
therfore excuse you, withouten were,
I may not well, I wisse.

Laus maxima omnipotenti!

682 for] *om.* D. 683 lyvinge] lykeinge B h D. 685 Marke] Marcus B. 686 a] *om.* h. 688 recouer] *the form* rekever *is required by the rhyme.* 689 they ne] non h. 692 and] *om.* h. for] *om.* D. 693 Luke] Lucas B. 694 words] workes B h D. 698 none ther] ther non B. 699 against] truste h. 700 aright] righte h. 703 to] *om.* h. 705 sayde] sayeth B H D. 706 all] *om.* B h D Laus maxima omnipotenti] *om.* B h, Deo gratias D.

Deo gratias.

Finis Vicesimæ Quartæ Paginæ.

Anno Do*m*ini 1607, Augusti Quarto, Anno Regni Regis Iacobi Quinto; per Iacobu*m* Miller.

Instead of the close of H *from* Deo gratias *to* Miller] h *reads* Finis deo gracias

Come lorde Iesus } 1600
Come quickly

To hym this booke belonges
I wishe contynuall health,
in daily vertues for to flow,
with floudes of godly wealth.

praye ever (*in the margin besides the last 4 verses*). B *and* D *close:*

This is the last of all the xxiiiier pageant*es* or playes played by the xxiiiier craft*es* men of the Cittie of Chester, written in the yere of *our* Lord god 1604, And in the second yere of the reigne of King Iames, by the grace of god, of England, ffraunce and Ireland, defender of the faith, and of the realme of Scotland the xxxviith, per me gulielmu*m* Bedford.

xxiiijer] xxiiij[tie] D. or playes] and playes D. 1604] 1591 D. second] xxxiiij[th] D. King James] our sovereigne Ladye queene Elizabeth, whom god preserve for euer, Amen. Finis D. by the grace of god, &c.] *om.* D.

Underneath Finis D *has*, By me Edward Gregorie, scholler, at Bunburye, the yeare of our lord god 1591.

GLOSSARY

afright = afraid, 16, 884
agryse = ? ? 18, 133
algates = by all means, in any case, anyhow
als = in the same way, also, 16, 88
anker = anchorite, hermit
anow = enough, enow, 13, 261
aspiue = to espy, to watch, to look for an opportunity, to lie in search of, 23, 358
attaynt = convinced, convicted, 23, 488 and 597
ayesell = vinegar, 17, 123

baine, bane = bowne
bale-brent = burnt in torture
bames = beames, 24, 47
barme = lap, 22, 175
barnteame = offspring, descendants, 16, 443 and 486
baron = bairn, child, son, 11, 99
basenetes = helmets, 10, 319
baynable = obedient? 6, 321
beames = trumpets? 24, 33
beede = to offer, 16, 339
beere = behaviour, ill-behaviour, tumult, 3, 109; 6, 402; 14, 90; 16, 62; 21, 241
beheight = promised, 15, 146
Belamy = friend, said to a stranger
Beleave = with your leave, 8, 362
betaken = to hand over, to surrender, to endow with; to commit, 21, 308
bewsprytt = bowsprit, 3, 93
bibble = to drink, to gobble, 7, 154
bisse = precious stuff, fine linen, 5, 62; 10, 2
blam ner = a precious stuff, 10, 2
blinne = to end, to cease, 16, 472; 18, 81
bloting = ? ? 7, 414
bode = message, order, command
bosiart = ? term of abuse, 7, 287
bourding = jesting, mocking
bowne = bound, going to, 10, 194; ready, obedient
boyst = box; especially a balm-box? 18, 332
boyster = boaster, braggart, 17, 183
brayd = moment, start, whiff, 23, 139
breeres = briars, thorns
buske = to prepare, get ready
bydene = at once; together
bylle = to blow, to make sound? 7, 163
bytt = bite, 16, 106

can = know, understand, 21, 273
carpe = to dispute, jangle, 16, 90
carsell = ? 6, 225
cater = designation of a side, of a die, or of a cast at dice, 16, 514
chaffer = ware, merchandise, property, 14, 362
cheare = face, mien
ches = chose, 16, 641, var. lect.
chist = chest, ark, 3, 206
cleave = stick, be faithful, belong to a party, 13, 67
cloe = to beat, to thrash, 10, 437
Clongen, *pp.* of clingen = to wither, to fade away,
clowte = rag, clout, swaddling clothes, 10, 209
conioyne, congeon = fellow, villain, 10, 145
conning = king, sovereign, 24, 183
corde = to fit, to suit
corsett = a garment, 16, 497
coynt = clever, 2, 224; quaint, 19, 18
coyntoice, countise = contrivance, plot, cunning, cleverness, acquaintance, 2, 192
coysell = ? 6, 225
crach = crib, manger, 6, 131

dare = tremble, 22, 296; 24, 236
dased = bewildered, astonished, 22, 282
deadlie, deadly = mortal, 2, 92
deadlish = mortal, 12, 27
deare, dere = to injure, to damage, 10, 271
deere = injury, inconvenience, 23, 587
deghter = daughter, 13, 486
deuyne = to prophesy, to suspect, 23, 362
dice = to cast dice for, to gamble, 16, 492
dight = to get ready; to prepare, to manage,
dilfully = sorrowfully, 16, 673
dinnge = dying, death, 21, 39
discreeve = dishonour? 6, 141
Dosaberd, Disabeard = a smart fellow, a choice man (Wright), then ironically a term of abuse, 12, 94
dowbt = to fear
downe = hill, down, 10, 51; in the expression: "ouer dale or downe"
drury = affection, love, 7, 598
dye = Dee
dyversory = diversorium, inn, public-house, harbour, 6, 532

eame = uncle, 16, 487
eft = again, bask, afterwards, 2, 610; 15, 252
eluish = foolish, 8, 314
ere = ever, 14, 71
erstely = first, Banes, 67
este = favour, predilection, preference, 2, 376

fantasy = witchcraft, 23, 600
fayne = glad
fearly = dangerous, dreadful, 17, 92
feature, fayture = deceiver, humbug, 18, 268
ferd = hadst to do, occupiedst thyself, 23, 600
fere = mate, husband, 12, 227
fett = to fetch
fidder = feather, 7, 51
finde = to procure the means to get somewhere, 6, 107
followed = baptized, 20, 102
fonge = to catch, 22, 135
foode = foster-child, 16, 630
fopee = ? 23, 47, v. l.
for bought = bought, delivered, 19, 179
forther = to further, to advance, to grant advantages to, 24, 63
for-treed = to trample down, to crush beneath one's feet, 22, 136
fownd = to endeavour, to struggle for
frankish = frantic? 3, 100
frapped = beat, knocked about? 13, 292
fray = to ask, 10, 408
freake = warrior, man, fellow
freey = liberal, munificent, 23, 50
fulsome = to help, to assist, to support, 21, 135 and 150
fytt = a blow, 16, 67 and 398

gaine = convenient; inclined to do, gracious
gambon = gammon, 7, 139
gange = to go, 7, 623
geates = goats, 3, 163
giff = if, 16, 179
glent = to move swiftly, to slide away
glore = to sing: glorum, glarum etc.
gole = ? term of abuse, 7, 273; 13, 432
golians = ? ? 7, 258
graynes = groins, chine, back-bone, 16, 326
greet = grit, little stones, 7, 75
grennes = grins, 7, 273
gright = terror, consternation, 24, 511
gright = forfeited, 2, 391; 2, 396 and 419
grill = to vex, to anger, to irritate, to torture, 3, 46; 4, 341; 5, 226
growsing = grousing, food? 7, 146
groyne = snout of a pig, 7, 122
gurd = to strike, to beat, 16, 68 and 393
guyde = gorgeous, costly clothing, 24, 278

hackstock = chopping-block, 3, 46
han = have, 16, 268 and 369; 19, 132
hartfullie = heartily, thoroughly, soundly,
heathing = ? heather, briars, thorns? 16, 333
heighte = promised, 5, 116
hell-thonge = fetter of hell, hell-prison
hend = to hand round, 7, 138
hend = swift, nimble, quick, skilful, obedient, 3, 271; 16, 382
hent = to take, 16, 415
here = to praise, 16, 791, varia lectio
hest = order, command, 5, 158

het = promise
hett = commanded, bad, 17, 237
heye = hay
hill = to cover, 2, 503 and 231
hillinge = coverture, apron, 2, 273
hoste = hest, 5, 158, v. lect.
hunter = harlot, 10, 313
hyndermost = last, quite behind, 7, 595
hyne = slave, thrall, 24, 520

i-ment = meant, decreed upon the intention, 6, 74
in-feare = together, likewise
informer = formator, creator, 24, 110
intier = entire, 11, 126
intisement = enticement

janglinge = chiding, quarrelling, murmuring
janock = oat-cake, 7, 120 (according to Wright)
jawce = ? ? 7, 215
Jesaine, Jasane = lying-in, confinement, 9, 246

Kempes = champions, 10, 229
Kent = shown, instructed, 7, 356
Kever = to recover, 7, 482; to gain, to earn, 2, 8
Kynd = nature, 21, 193

layd = dirty, ugly, 15, 153
layne, leane = to conceal, deny, 4, 311; 24, 166
leach = physician
lead = layd = wrong? 9, 77; 15, 153 v. lect.; ugly, 20, 123
lead = man, human being, 22, 137
leale = loyal, honest, upright
leare = to teach, to show, 5, 86; 16, 328; 21, 229; to learn, 22, 80
leasinge = lie, falsehood, lying, 22, 177
leat = lightning? 22, 297
ledden = language, song
lee = protection, salvation, 16, 621; 24, 28
leech = to cure, to heal, 13, 332
leed = people, nation, 21, 249; 24, 117
leere = face; beauty? 14, 33; beautiful, nice? 18, 9
leese = to loosen, to weary, to cease? 7, 163
leeve = believe, think
lemed = beamed, shone, 7, 389
lend = to land, to arrive, to stay, to dwell
lenge = to dwell, to remain, to linger, to stay, 17, 14
lent = landed, arrived, 8, 111
lesse, leas = lie, falsehood, 17, 49
let = to leave off
lewed = laymen, laity; unlearned, unexperienced, 21, 309
liccoris = eager for dainties, 2, 198
light = alighted, come down, descended
lither = lecherous, immoral, wicked, reprobate, 10, 115
liveray = means of sustenance, food, 7, 165
loos = fame, power, influence, charm, 5, 116
lordan, lurdane = clumsy lown, cad, 23, 358
lorne = lost, 5, 100
losingere = flatterer, term of abuse, 10, 254
low = flame, glare, 10, 438
lowe = hill
lowt = loude = sound, noise, 7, 172
lowte = to stoop, to bow, to subject one's self, 5, 47; 6, 154
luxom, lixsom = pleasant, handsome, 19, 136
lyckes = leeks, 7, 114
lyne = lie, tell falsehoods, 23, 351
lyveras = ? ? 7, 214

madd = to rave, to be crazy, to be mad, 16, 634
malison = curse, 2, 678
manner = manor, comfortable building, 6, 410
mase = makes, makest, 16, 205; 16, 354
mased = amazed, 22, 292
maundye = last supper of Jesu, 4, 128
Mawmentrye = idols, 5, 2; 5, 248
maye = maid, virgin, girl, 6, 126
maystry = miracle, feat of witchcraft, 20, 23
meanye, mesnie = household, servants, followers, congregation
mell, melen = to speak, to talk, to have intercourse
menske = courteous behaviour, kindness, grace, bounty, 9, 203
messel = leprous, a leper, 14, 18
mete = measure, dimension

middle-yorde = earth, 4, 269
minge = to remember; to mention
mirrette = merit, 17, 60, var. lect.
moote = to relate, tell, 9, 255
mot = must, shall
mould = earth, 6, 197
muting = whispering, muttering
myn = to think, 2, 170; to remember, to remember kindly, 15, 93, lect. var.; 21, 66

nawger = auger, 6, 409
needly = needs, by all means, 14, 322
nere = never, 12, 7; 18, 427
nicke = to deny, 16, 37
nome = taken, 16, 419
nurry = foster-child, illegitimate child, 4, 155
nyce, nice = foolish, stupid, 2, 53
nye (= noye) = anoy

oo = always, for ever, aye, perpetually
or = ere, before, 3, 103
ordayne = to order, to procure, to take care for some one's comfort, 13, 250

panch cloute = ? ? 7, 128
paye = satisfaction, pleasure
paye = to injure, to impair
peny = tribute? 6, 97
penyble = trying, painful
perye, pyrrye = precious stones, jewelry, 6, 588; 10, 410
piercer = instrument of a carpenter, piercer, gimlet, 6, 409
pight = fastened; dependent; filled? 21, 260
pintle = penis, 10, 363
popelard = hypocrite, canter; a term of abuse, 5, 273; 16, 547; 17, 149
postee, posty = power, might, 14, 13
poydrace = ? ? 16, 530

quicken = to get alive, to revive,
quintly = curiously, quaintly, 13, 259 and 290

rade = quick, quickly, 2, 106
reave = to rob, to snatch, take away, to deprive, 13, 252; 17, 132 and 160
reem = to cry, to weep, 13, 431; 18, 433, var. lect.
rekever = to recover, 24, 688
rewkes = ? ? 10, 193
ribbotes = ? a term of abuse, 10, 159 and 309
ritch = to make rich, to endow, 21, 71
rocked = ? ? 10, 31
rogge = ? a term of abuse, 18, 281
roght = cared for, 24, 273
rowe = rest, quiet, 7, 401
rowndfull = ? a heap of coins? 16, 510
rwes = rues, gives pain, 16, 387
ryne = to touch, to approach, 214, 639
ryved = ryf? = plenteous, abundant, 23, 54

sad = serious, undeviable,
sand = messenger, chargee, 23, 37
seinge = since, 21, 308
semblant = face, mien, 2, 57
sere, seer = so ever, 14, 281
seuen year = a kind of protest, to indicate a long space of time, or to assert a fact very strongly, 16, 762 and 782
shad = ? ? 7, 280
shaye, straye = ? milky way? 4, 164
shooe = she, 2, 185
shrewen = to curse, to beshrew
shroes = shrews, villains, 5, 106
sibbe = family, kindred, 7, 566
sicke = to sigh
sigaldry = sorcery, 16, 167
Sir = sire, father, 13, 158
skewed = piebald? 22, 117
skill = reason, right
sleelie = slily, 2, 409
slich = slitch, limns, 3, 73
slye = contrivance, sleight, 12, 144
sorte = swarthy, dark, 22, 43, var. lect.
spowld = saliva, spittle, 16, 349
stanold = term of abuse, 16, 187 and 320
stayed, styed, steed = steight, 20, 158; 21, 84; 21, 332
sted, styd = place
stear = to move, to touch, to seize with pity, 24, 23
steight = arose, ascended
stene = to stone, 12, 229 and 284, lect. var.
stowre = time, hour, 21, 122
strang = strange, extraordinary
stray = straw? 17, 227
stream = to strain, torture, 16, 568
strynde = breed, kind, 452
swedling swayne = baby in swathing clothes, 8, 392

sween = trance, ecstacy, 5, 96
swem = grief, sorrow, 16, 442; a pity, 16, 482 and 523
swyre = neck, 14, 389

tabret = clothes, gown, 13, 304
tach = blemish, fault, stain, blot, 7, 296
talch = tallow ? 7, 36
talent = inclination, wish, purpose, 10, 278
tane = taken, 16, 271 and 371
tarboyle = jar with tar ? 7, 185
tarboyst = tar-box ? 7, 78 and 185
tayle = ? ? 7, 410
teene = to ruin, to torment
teene = affliction, vexation
temporaltye = worldly power and splendour, 9, 68
tend = attend, listen, 23, 128
thee = to thrive, prosper, fare
thester = dark, 22, 43
thesterness = darkness
this = thus, in such a way
thole = to suffer, to undergo, to abide, 2, 659; 19, 31
thrall = servitude, trouble, 13, 50
thraw, throw = moment, time, 19, 160; "on a thraw" = in a whiff, very soon, 7, 31
threpe = to maintain a point of controversion, 12, 143
thro = ready, zealous, eager
throe = through, 16, 794
thry = three times, thrice, 12, 144
tildes = tents, 7, 6
to-dight = in a woful plight, 16, 673
to-flaw = flew asunder, away like dust vanished, 24, 295
tome = leisure, 16, 368, var. lect.
trusse = to pack up, to get ready
tug = to mumph, to eat
tupp = rain, 6, 282
twayne = two, 2, 89
twene = two, 3, 126, var. lect.
twyn = to separate, to pass, get away, 16, 507
tyde = good, pleasant, 24, 114
tyde = to happen; to undergo, to suffer, 24, 296
tyke = dog, cur, 7, 276
tyte = quickly, 16, 449
tytefull = with a full udder ? 7, 11

underfoe = to receive
unwoth = ? ? 16, 774, lect. var.

vprist = resurrection, 18, 149

waryson = guerison, reward
weare = to defend, 2, 101
wemlesse = stainless, pure, chaste, 12, 28
wemmonslie = womanly ? 6, 157
were = doubt, 12, 192; 16, 77; 18, 350
wher = whether, 16, 790
whott = hot, 24, 191
wonne = wan, wretched with pain and suffering, 16, 555
wonne = to linger, hesitate, 16, 786
wonne = one, 18, 383
would = wold, forest, 7, 175
wraw = angry, fierce, 3, 209
wydewher = far about, in many places, 16, 5
wynn = joy, pleasure
wyseard = wizard, fellow practising witchcraft, 23, 371

yare = of yore, 22, 33
yeald = to requite, reward
yeede = went, 22, 129
yelden = requited, rewarded, 24, 234 and 560
yode = went, 13, 307
yoo = ewe, 7, 30
youle = to howl, to cry, 13, 431

10149568R00140

Printed in Great Britain
by Amazon.co.uk, Ltd.,
Marston Gate.